Iowa

26321   Anf 977.7'63

Scot, barbara J.

Prairie Reunion

DATE DUE

977.7
Scot, Barbara J., 1942-
Prairie reunion / Barbara J.
Scot.

DEMCO

Prairie Reunion

Also by Barbara J. Scot

THE VIOLET SHYNESS

OF THEIR EYES:

NOTES FROM NEPAL

PRAIRIE

REUNION

Barbara J. Scot

Farrar, Straus and Giroux

NEW YORK

Library of Congress Cataloging-in-Publication Data
Scot, Barbara J.
Prairie reunion / Barbara J. Scot.
p.   cm.
1. Scot, Barbara J. 2. Scotch Grove (Iowa)—Biography.
3. Scott Family.   I. Title.
F629.S39S36 1995   977.7'63—dc20 [B]   95-13111 CIP

The author gratefully acknowledges permission to reprint from the following
sources: Complete Poems, 1904–1962, E. E. Cummings, reprinted by
permission of the Liveright Publishing Corporation. Iowa Sketches, by
John Newton Hughes, reprinted by permission of the Hughes family. The Violet
Shyness of Their Eyes: Notes from Nepal, copyright © 1993 Barbara J. Scot
(Calyx Books, 1993), reprinted by permission of the publisher. Lyrics from
"Devoted to You," written by Boudleaux Bryant, copyright © 1958 Acuff-Rose
Music, Inc., House of Bryant Publications in the U.S., used by permission; all
rights reserved. Excerpts from The Palimpsest originally published as "The
Fourth of July" and "Harvest Time," by Lenore Rickels Salvaneschi, The
Palimpsest (1984): pp. 118–23, 207–13; copyright © 1984 State Historical
Society of Iowa; reprinted by permission of the publisher. Lyrics to "American
Pie," words and music by Don McLean © 1971, 1972, Music Corporation of
America, a division of MCA, Inc. and Benny Bird Music; all rights controlled
and administered by Music Corporation of America, a division of MCA, Inc.;
all rights reserved; international copyright secured; used by permission.
Hadfield's Cave, David W. Benn, reprinted by permission of Office of the State
Archaeologist, University of Iowa.
Brief quotations appearing in the text are from the following sources: page 123:
"1910 History of Jones County" edited by R. M. Corbit; page 126: Record of
Iowa Supreme Court, December Term, 1870; page 152: G.W.F. Hegel, The
Phenomenology of Mind; page 157: Gerard Manley Hopkins, "God's
Grandeur"; page 191: Truman Michelson, The Autobiography of a
Fox Indian Woman.

In memory of my mother,

KATHLEEN HUGHES NORRIS

1905–1963

Contents

Prologue   3

(1) Honour Thy Father and Thy Mother   5

(2) The Homecoming   23

(3) The Holy Farm   40

(4) The Scots   60

(5) Faith of Our Fathers   83

(6) The Historical Society   97

(7) Women's Work   119

(8) Cry Softly, Swallow   148

(9) The Fire of the People   172

(10) Reunion   200

Photographs   *following page* 216

Epilogue   217

Family Tree   222

Maps   225

Acknowledgments   227

Additional Sources   229

Prairie Reunion

Prologue

—let all go
dear
    so comes love

—E. E. CUMMINGS, XXIX, *One Times One*

For a long time I did not look back. During those years I could not have said exactly why. When I thought of the Scotch Grove Presbyterian Church community or the brown Victorian farmhouse, I thought of them with love. When I did return, in 1983, it was too soon. I brought my young sons and my husband, with whom I had wanted to share my love for the place of my childhood. But I showed them mostly my pain. Uncle Jim was still alive then, a querulous thin brown ghost. The big house was settling into ruin, weeds growing through the porch, raccoons in the attic. Somewhat reluctantly, my uncle let us enter so I could show my family the house in which I had been a child.

In the blue room where my mother had slept, my uncle's voice changed to the tone I remembered. "I think there is something here your mother meant you to have. I've saved it until you returned." He pointed at the black-and-brown trunk under the east window.

While my children scampered to the attic, searching for scenes from the stories I had told them, I looked quickly through the contents of the trunk to decide whether I should carry it back to Oregon. My uncle was right. It had definitely been left for me. Odd that I had not claimed it when I moved away. I can only explain this by saying I took nothing from that house, for we had never belonged there, my brother and I, and nothing there was really ours.

The trunk was filled with various paraphernalia of my youth, including my braids. At the bottom I found a blue satin gown. It was not neatly folded; instead, it was wound around a brown stationery box and some pictures. Even a quick perusal of the pictures and the letters contained in the box told me that my mother had left me the story of her brief marriage and its painful unraveling. The pictures were of the wedding, of her in the blue satin gown. The letters were my father's, first drafts of hers, and other relatives' correspondence that detailed for me, when I read them carefully later, a poignant and mysterious story. At the bottom of the box of letters was a note on a pink-orange piece of Rainbow pad paper. It contained three evenly spaced lines:

What do you think?

You don't understand.

You'll never know how much.

I closed the box. Even when we returned to Oregon I did not open the trunk for several years.

Finally, in the spring of 1993, I was ready. I reopened the trunk, carefully read all the letters, and puzzled over the note. I felt the pain; I felt the love. I also felt a confused resentment that I needed, at last, to resolve. So in early summer I returned again to the brown Victorian farmhouse.

The quest began as an attempt to understand my mother. It developed into a quest to understand myself and my own connections with the people and place of my childhood. Finally, it became a search to connect to the past of the land itself.

The story that follows is as true as memory and investigation can make it. A few names have been changed. I offer this personal journey humbly, knowing that your history is as interesting as my own. For you—or others in your family—come from Scotch Grove, Iowa, too, or someplace like it.

1

Honour Thy Father
and Thy Mother

Honour thy father and thy mother: that thy days may be long upon
the land which the Lord thy God giveth thee.
—Exodus 20:12

I had only two newspaper clippings about my father to
guide me that early morning in June as I sat at a Burns Brothers
truck stop east of Council Bluffs, Iowa. The attendant had just
refused to let me buy a shower. "Are you a trucker?" the young
woman had asked suspiciously, scanning my grey-haired female
form.

"No," I answered truthfully, "but I need a shower. Last night's
campground didn't have any." I had been driving for four days from
Oregon.

"Sorry, ma'am. Our showers are only for truckers." The matter
settled in her mind, she turned to wait on a more promising cus-
tomer. I returned to my camper.

The yellowed articles were wrapped in a piece of paper. I had
found them at the bottom of the cardboard box of memorabilia that
was fueling my quest to understand my mother.

MAN FOUND DEAD

IN PARKED CAR

BLAIRSTOWN —A man identified as Bob Norris, 37, of Luzerne was found dead early Tuesday morning in the front seat of an automobile parked on a side road near here. The car bore Colorado license plates.

The death was pronounced a suicide by Coroner John Burrows of Belle Plaine. A rubber hose was attached to the automobile's exhaust and extended through the front window.

Norris was found by a hired man on his way to work at the Waldo Niebuhr farm. He called Dr. R. A. Seiler of Blairstown and Coroner Burrows.

The body was brought to the Dewey funeral home here.

Norris is survived by his wife Edith and three daughters Sallie Mae, 5, Annie Sue, 4, and Ellie Jane, 3.

His wife could give no reason for his act.

Edith was not my mother. She was the woman with whom he had gone to Colorado. And my name was not Sallie Mae, Annie Sue, or Ellie Jane.

A smaller clipping was included in the wrapped packet.

Harold and Howard Norris of Hawick and Painesville, Minn., were brief callers in the homes of relatives here and Monticello during the past week. They attended the funeral services for Robert C. Norris on Friday morning at 10:30 in Blairstown from the Dewey funeral home and the burial which was in Luzerne. Mr. Norris died Tuesday morning.

The C. was wrong. My father's name was Robert George from his grandfathers. Harold and Howard were my father's younger brothers. His mother was not at the funeral because her husband would not allow it. I was once told that she cried all day when her eldest son was buried. The letter she wrote in response to my mother's note, which must have described the service, ended with the statement: "I've felt so nervous since this all happened it seems hard to work but I must get at house cleaning."

The paper in which the clippings were wrapped had the following written on the inside in my mother's hand. "Robert G. Norris was born on Oct. 5, 1912 and died on Mar. 28, 1950. He was married to Kathleen Hughes on Nov. 25, 1939. He is survived by his wife, a son, Robert Hughes Norris who was born Sept. 8, 1940 and a daughter Barbara June Norris, who was born Feb. 16, 1942."

I had decided to find his grave. Getting out the map, I found Luzerne. The dot on the map was only about thirty miles west of Cedar Rapids on the old road north of the Interstate. As I was not expected in Cedar Rapids until evening, I had time to make the trip. I was a bit disgruntled with the woman at Burns Brothers. Two days without a shower had left me rather disheveled. It occurred to me that I would like to look nice at the cemetery. My father was, after all, a man I had never actually met. Luckily, I found a private campground as I headed off the Interstate just before Newton, and the attendant sold me a shower for a dollar.

The bathroom was clean and warm. I turned the steamy spray full stream on my stiff neck, reviewing the last few days in my mind. I had left my home in Portland later than I intended on Monday and had to settle for camping near the noisy Interstate the first night. But by the second night, in Idaho, I found a beautiful, isolated campground in the Sawtooth Range called The City of Rocks. The sunset had already darkened when I wound up the seventeen-mile gravel road to a strange collection of walls and pyramids, so I did not really see them until daylight.

Such a beautiful morning it was, too: cold wind, soft new sun on silver granite domes, and clear notes of a canyon wren, sliding down the scale. The park had been deserted except for sleepy rock climbers holding coffee cups and planning their routes for the day. They could have been my sons, for I recognized their carabiners, brightly colored ropes, and dirty sweatshirts as kin to those that had littered my upstairs as recently as a year ago. I was sorry to leave. Yellow paintbrush quivered in the wind. But I had little time to spare. The Hughes family reunion was scheduled for Saturday in Cedar Rapids, Iowa. I descended onto a level sweep of colorful desert where plains prickly-pear cactus blossomed with pink and yellow cups.

Not until I began to see signs for Cheyenne, Wyoming, did I first think of my father—with a little annoyance. His suicide prompted the association, for I, too, had tried to die, not in Iowa, but in Cheyenne. Exactly twenty-three years ago, I calculated as I drove along. Pregnant, in a marriage that was sliding precipitously downhill, I had tried to die—like him, I thought, with an old rise of anger. He was not going to usurp my mother as the primary object of this search, I promised myself firmly. To understand my mother's loyalty, however, I would have to know more of him. "She loved him still," my grandmother had said on the day of his funeral, when I feigned a headache and stayed home from school.

Abruptly and completely the water in my shower turned cold. I jumped out of the spray and spun the handles.

Driving through Newton seemed a return to my Iowa childhood of the forties and fifties. The main street sported a Maid-Rite, the Shirt Shoppe, a Hearing Aid Center, and the *Newton Daily News.* Next to the Heart of the Home Kitchen Center the Corsette Mansion Bed and Breakfast resembled the house near Scotch Grove in which I had lived until I went to college. Both the Hitching Post Auction and Red Pump Antiques looked familiar, but I was not prepared for the Wal-Mart Discount City on the east side of town.

A sign indicated the mileage to Grinnell. The road proceeded past rolling fields. Corn plants were small and sickly-looking after an unusually wet spring. Large oaks stood on isolated grass islands in plowed fields. I crossed the North Skunk River, which brimmed over its banks. The road followed the Hiawatha Pioneer Trail. In Grinnell I passed the brick college buildings and Lang Bros. John Deere Implement Store. The familiar yellow deer leapt on a green sign. Nutrena Feeds. "Feed your hogs Nutrena, Nuu—treeen—a, the best feed that money can buy." Every morning I had heard the song on WMT with the seven o'clock news, accompanied by grunting hogs. Or clucking chickens. Sometimes they sang "Feed your chicks Nutrena." I turned on E66 toward Belle Plaine.

The Iowa River was well beyond flood stage. The flat plain had become part of the river and the sign saying PUBLIC AREA was almost submerged. Picnic table benches were under water. I was beginning to understand how wet the spring had been. On a side road an abandoned automobile leaned precariously into the ditch.

In Belle Plaine I turned right, following the map. I slowed down as I passed a large cemetery. How does one find a person who has been dead for over forty years? Framing the question in my mind, I decided I would say I was looking for a relative's grave. I would not have to say he was my father. An impatient farmer in bib overalls and a pickup truck honked and passed me on a hill.

Then I came to the Lutheran cemetery. This stand of stones looked more promising, but the driveway was on a hill and there was no place to park. A farmer in a hurry could damage himself and my camper if I simply left it at the side of the road. The road curved. Surely I was close to Luzerne.

The next cemetery was small and unmarked, off the road to the right down a grassy lane. Two brick pillars with odd dome caps framed the gate. Certain that this was it, I did not hurry. The wind blew hard, but the direct noontime sun shone with uncomfortable warmth. I took off my denim jacket and from habit slung my binoculars around my neck.

The graves covered a little rounded hillside. A cedar windbreak lined the west fence, and below it was a pond with a collection of abandoned cars, including a rusting blue school bus. Red-winged blackbirds called in the reeds with their raspy song. *Chur-reeeee-a.*

I strolled slowly to the oldest stones, highest on the hill. Some were quite difficult to read . . . Addie Joachim Schuett/Geborn den 11 June 1879/Gestorben den 9 July 1881 . . . a two-year-old child. Another with an undecipherable name read Wife of Mads Hansen/Born in Danmark 1822/Died 1874. One year older than my present age.

I worked my way down the hill. Corrine Reich, said a stone with a lamb on it. Feb. 9 1921–May 21 1921. Across the field to the north of the cemetery a meadowlark's song fragmented in the wind. Plastic flowers decorated many of the more recent stones. A lone peony bush with pink blossoms whipped fiercely, dropping its petals. The insistent haunting whistle of the cardinal came from the large oak by the pond. *Whit-whit-cheer-cheeerr-cheeeerr-cheeerr.*

I saw the grave out of the corner of my eye before I focused on it clearly. I chose to watch a turquoise dragonfly with fragile wings land in the lee of the taller stone next to it before I shifted my attention fully. "Robert G. Norris" read the grey, flat stone. Under the name were the dates 1912–1950. That was all. I stared silently. Then I had an idea.

I put my binoculars on the stone as a promise to return and ran down the hill. Realizing a farmer across the road was looking my way with shaded eyes, I slowed to a walk. This was not the kind of scene I wanted to explain to anyone. Opening the side door of the camper, I got out bread and peanut butter. I made a sandwich and took a small jar of apple juice from the softly humming refrigerator. Then I put everything in my leather pack, wrapped a paper towel around the sandwich so I wouldn't get peanut butter on my bird book, and returned to the cemetery. "Lunch with my father," I said to myself, more amused than sad at the moment.

I sat down on the stone. The smooth surface was hot, almost too hot on the backs of my thighs. Like the smooth oven door of the old Majestic Range in my grandmother's kitchen on which I'd sat on cold mornings. I drank the apple juice too quickly and was left with sticky sweetness on the roof of my mouth.

I glanced across the field. The farmer who had been watching me suspiciously was nowhere to be seen. Stretching full-length up the incline, I put my head on my leather pack.

The phone rang early in the morning. Five long rings. That was our ring, just as four long rings meant the call was for Fannie Henrichs and two long and two short rings the signal for Bert Clark.

I was eating my oatmeal, sitting on the open oven door of the Majestic Range.

I had learned to time it just right so that the oven door was cool enough to sit on by the time I was ready to eat. I always woke when my grandmother got up to start the fire. First, the metallic sound as the grate was turned to spill ashes into the long box with the nickel handle that was in the bottom of the stove. Next, paper would be crumpled. Then I would hear the stir in the cob box, red corn cobs that I had gathered in the summer. I would lie very still, for to move would be to touch the coldness in the covers beyond my curved nest. For a while I would hear no sound, but I knew the fire was burning. My mother was awake, too, for soon I would hear her slippers whistling slightly on the carpet. The voices murmured before my mother went to the basement to stoke up the furnace with the big arms. Just then I would get up. By the time I went downstairs, the oven door was open and almost cool enough to sit on.

The phone rang again, the five long rings, before my mother answered. How unusual that someone would call so early in the morning. Warmth from the oven seeped through my flannel shirt. My mother returned and stood in the doorway, her eyes bright. "Well," demanded my grandmother, scraping the last of the oatmeal into my brother's bowl. "Who was that ringing up at this time of the morning?"

"Ella Clark . . ." My mother filled the kitchen doorway. "Bob's dead."

"Dead?" My grandmother put down the pan.

"She thought I might want to keep the children home from school." The women looked at each other silently. I did not speak. Bob. Daddy. Daddy ran away. In my mind was a picture like the one in the storybook: a long-legged man with coattails and a tall hat was running down the road with a spotted dog snapping at his heels. His hat was flying off his head. Daddy ran away.

I did not move from the open oven door of the Majestic Range where I was sitting, even though the creases from the shirt were uncomfortably hot on my back. I watched my brother, who put his spoon on the table.

"Bobbie, Barbara, listen to me." My mother spoke very fast, with the words running together. "Your father is dead. He died last night. God wanted it that way because he was not a happy man. He will be happier with God. Ella Clark called me now in case I would want to keep you home from school because other children might say something to you. There is no reason to stay home, because you never knew him. If anything is said, say you never knew him. Do you understand?" Her eyes flickered, reflecting the glow of fire that showed around the circular lids on the stove top. Then she turned and left the room quickly. The teakettle made a hissing sound. My grandmother came to life and began scolding about coats and overshoes.

The large yellow bus lumbered to a stop in the gravel. I wanted to find a seat by the window so I could wave to my mother. It seemed especially important to wave this morning. Only one seat was left in the back, but the frost on the window was so thick that I could not scratch it clear in time to wave.

One time a large cardboard box had come a few days after my birthday. I was mystified, even a little afraid. A box had never come for me. The only boxes that came were from Sears and Roebuck for my mother. "Go ahead and open it," my mother said.

"How do you know it's for me?"

"It says so, silly," said my brother impatiently. "Come on, open it." No box had ever come for him, either.

"Who is it from?"

"It doesn't say." My mother brought a knife to cut the string. I moved very slowly. She carefully pulled off the brown paper. Inside was a box held together by tape. My mother cut the tape with the knife. Slowly I lifted the lid. I saw only newspaper.

"There's nothing there."

My brother pushed me aside and lifted the paper. Underneath was a doll, a soft doll, with a long face and hair made out of yarn. I picked it up, wonderingly. "Where did it come from?" My mother found the card under the doll and opened it. She read it aloud.

"It says, 'From your daddy Bob.' " My grandmother snorted, but my mother turned to her and she was still.

"Is that all?" asked Bobbie, pawing through the paper. But that was all. I did not feel quite right about the doll. I propped it up on the big wooden box that held the extra blankets, rather than set it at the foot of my bed with the others.

The children poured out of the yellow bus. I wished I still had Mrs. Shover for a teacher. In second grade Mrs. Shover had given my papers back to me with gold stars on them. She told my mother that she thought I was good at writing rhymes and put my rhymes on the blackboard for everyone to see. In third grade, Miss Nelson had scolded me for writing rhymes during arithmetic class. I would not tell Miss Nelson the rhyme that had formed in my head on the way to school.

> *My mother said*
> *my daddy's dead*
> *I want to cry*
> *I don't know why*
> *I didn't know him anyway*
> *They said that he had run away.*

I hurried to copy the rhyme into my notebook before school started. I didn't want to stay in for recess to finish my arithmetic.

During the spelling lesson I thought of one other time. I was not quite sure whether it was real or part of a dream. I had been walking down the main street of the town with my mother. The street was quite dark, so it must have been a Saturday night. A man who had on cowboy boots was facing us. My mother said something to the man and was very angry. Afterward, she was crying. She put her head down on the steering wheel in the car. Don't cry, Mama. Mama, don't cry. Was that my daddy?

I walked beside Bonnie Smith on the way to the Masonic Temple for lunch. Bonnie's mother and father were divorced. That's what it was—my mother and father were divorced. That meant not married, not having babies together anymore. That meant no man stood in the picture throwing the stick for Spot. Run, Spot, run. Ahead of me walked Janet White. Janet's daddy had been killed in the war. Something was better about Janet's father than Bonnie's or my own.

When I was very small, my mother rocked me in the old wicker chair and sang to me before I went to bed. It was in the summer and the long shafts of light came in the golden brown window in the west. "Baby's boat's a silver moon . . ." I knew what that meant. It meant the new moon was curved like a heavy-sided hoop, and up above you could see the rim of the old moon. "Far across the sea . . ." The sea was what was in the Peter Pan book where the lost boys and Wendy were in the boat and the picture was full of clouds and swirls. "Only don't forget to sail . . ." my mother's voice broke a little . . . "back again to me . . ." It had to do with my daddy. The song started again. The wicker squeaked, and where the weave was broken, it pressed against my leg. I could not bear to hear the sad part again. "Stop, Mama, my leg hurts."*

Nancy McDowell sat across from me at the lunch table. We sat on either side of Miss Nelson. Nancy was the prettiest girl in the class. Her black curly hair formed soft waves around her face. I stood on my tiptoes to look in the mirror above my grandmother's dresser to smooth the braids that framed my face. I looked nothing like Nancy McDowell.

The plates were flecked brown with three divisions. Every day the routine was the same. Today was my turn to pick up the plates when everyone was done eating. As I was waiting for the boys at the end of the table to finish, a thought occurred to me. Now when anyone asked what does your daddy do, I could say, "My daddy is dead." Like Janet's daddy in the war. Yes. I would never have to say "My daddy ran away" again. The man with the coattails flying and the top hat came to a halt. He took off the hat and smoothed his coat. I imagined him lying down. Dead.

*The Violet Shyness.

I looked timidly at Miss Nelson and smiled. Miss Nelson smiled back. The boys had not finished eating. I began humming softly. Nancy McDowell looked at me sharply. "Barbara!" I looked around quickly. "I wouldn't be singing if my daddy killed himself."

All conversation at the table stopped. I stared hard at my plate. I had not noticed before that the speckles made a sort of pattern. Miss Nelson's eyes were fixed on me. My chest tightened.

"Children," said Miss Nelson briskly, "line up. It's time to go." I could not move. I sat with my head bowed in shame. Somehow the other children were all gone. The plates were there and I knew it was my turn, but I could not get up from the table. Then Miss Nelson was back beside me, kneeling.

"Barbara, did your father die?" I regarded her gravely. The teacher's eyes were very soft, not at all as they were when she made me stay in at recess because of arithmetic. Some of the shame subsided.

I did not know how to answer Miss Nelson. This must not be like Janet's father. It was good that Janet's father was dead. I was not sure what Nancy McDowell had said, but it was very, very bad. It was worse than running away. It was worse than divorce. It was like the time in first grade when I had to go to the bathroom for a long time but the teacher didn't see my hand. Then there was the wetness and the smell and the older boys had teased me on the bus. It was even worse than that. Somehow I must answer Miss Nelson, who had slipped a comforting arm around me.

"I never knew him," I said softly. Then I began, uncontrollably, to cry.

I sat up suddenly. My hair was slightly damp from the heat and the wind caught it, making cooler lines on my head. I could feel sun in hot stripes where the sandal straps did not cover my feet. On the slightly crooked wooden flagpole that looked too fragile to withstand the wind perched a bird I didn't know, black with a narrow bill. Its snowy breast was accented by a white band at the tip of its tail. I got out my book. Eastern kingbird. "The white band across the tail tip marks the Eastern kingbird." Could that be right? Western kingbirds have a light golden breast. Why had I never heard my mother speak of it? She was always naming birds. I looked in my other book. "No other songbird has a complete broad, white terminal band on the tail."

I had come to this grave to honor my mother. Her love for this man had been deep, unconditional, and maddening, as far as I was concerned. I felt a rise of anger again as I thought about it. To bear humiliation bravely was a virtue, I would grant that. But to continue to love a man who humiliated her? Never to speak ill of him, indeed never speak of him at all for almost twenty years, carrying that love to her own grave in dignified silence—was that a virtue, too? A rush of guilt at my own disloyalty swept through me as I stood up to return to the camper, for I had loved her intensely. Nevertheless, as I drove along thinking of her, my mind repeated the question: Was it a virtue—or was she merely playing the fool?

. . .

My mama was a teacher. And that is why we sat on the slab at the end of the cement walk waiting to see the walking stick at the top of the first hill. We must not go in the road. The road was for cars, and if we went in the road we would be run over like the grey cat.

My mama was a teacher. At the number five school, which was three hills toward the church. In the morning she walked into the sun to go to school, but in the afternoon the sun came from the other way. If I watched carefully, the stick that was walking would become my mother and then she would wave. But I must not go in the road.

At the number five school was a big bell. I could hear my mama ring the bell, but I could not go to the school because I was too little. Next year my brother could go to school, but I would still be too little. "Whoever heard of such a thing," said my grandma. "You shouldn't teach her to read so young. What will she do in school?"

But my mama smiled. She let me read the words to her from the books she took to school.

Now the stick was on the very tiptop of the first hill. I jumped up and down, and my brother jumped up and down. The walking stick became my mama and what was black now had a blue coat and we could see my mama wave. We waved and waved.

We liked wash days, for we could play in the cellar, riding the scooter around the furnace with the huge arms. We could play in the cob pile with the clean red cobs, but we could not play in the coal bin because of the black dust. My mama would heat the water on the black stove in the kitchen and carry it down the stairs. When the sheet went through the wringer, it would swell in a balloon where the air was trapped. It was like the cow, my brother said, like underneath the cow. "Udder," my mama said, "it's called an udder." We laughed and laughed and laughed.*

The breadboard was a special board that stood on one end behind the buttery door. My mama would put the breadboard on the wooden counter above the flour bin. The flour bin swung out if I hung on the handle, but then my grandma would scold. When my mama made bread, I would sit on the warm oven door of the old black stove. "Now?" I would ask, and she would shake her head, as she folded the dough over on itself, coaxing it to life. "Now?" I would say again, and she would shake her head again. "Now?" I would plead, and she would smile. Then I would pull the chair over so I could stand on it beside her, burying my hands in the dough that was alive.

When I went with my mama to the henhouse, I would carry the lard pail with yellow straw that was like the gold in the Rumpelstiltskin book. I did not want to reach under the hen, but my mama said if I did so quickly and gently the hen would not strike at my arm. Under the hen the warm softness closed over my hand and

The Violet Shyness.

around my fingers until I found the hard smooth shell of the brown egg. I did not want to move my arm, but the hen who had at first just cocked her head pecked swiftly at my elbow. I jumped and dropped the egg, but it did not break when it fell into the straw below the nest. "Shush, you'll scare the hens," said my mama. "I told you to reach quickly."

Mama carried the big hoe and the little hoe. My brother carried the little toy tractor and the cardboard box of little cars, but I carried only the big empty pail. To reach the place-where-the-garden-had-always-been we went across the road not holding hands, because our hands were full, but stopping to look both ways. No clouds of dust churned in the distance. We said together, "No cars." We passed the windmill, which creaked as the shaft went up and down when the high wheel whirled against the sun. Then we were in front of the brown house. Where the John Deere tractor stood. The brown house smelled of oil and dust. The plow was behind the John Deere so I put down the bucket and knelt to see my face in the blade. In the silver mirror I could see the wisps of hair that were loose from the braids and the clouds reflected behind my curved face. My mama hoed the rows of beans and corn. My brother and I made roads for the toy tractor in the part of the garden where the watermelon vines would later spread.

The quilt that was laid out on the large frame had pieces from my mama's apron, my grandma's dress, and my brother's shirt. One pattern was my pajamas, but the colors were bright instead of faded. Aunt Frances came with Denamae and the women tied knots while we played under the tent of the big quilt. "Now, Kate," said Grandma, who had stepped on the toy car again, "this will not do." So my mama let us take the blankets from the big wooden box. She helped us build a cave over the radio table by the warm-air register in the sitting room. She gave us the blurry cards with the double lines and the viewer with the lens that fell out when it was tilted.

The raspberries drew black lines on my mama's hands. First she brought in the large dishpan which she had filled with berries. My brother and I dumped the little coffee cans of berries which we had picked into her pan. Then the berries bubbled and bubbled until they disappeared. My mama skimmed pink foam into the cup. She poured the thick purple liquid into the clean jars. When the sun slid across the kitchen from the dining-room window, light came from inside the jars. In the evening when we rocked in the wicker chair with the broken weave my mama would stroke my legs. She had purple hands and knuckles ringed with black lines.

In winter my mama would have to soak her feet because of the chilblains. That was because her feet had gotten too cold when she was a little girl, so I must always wear my boots in the snow. When she soaked her feet, the scars from the bunions turned bright red. After the operation she could not come to see where I had learned to climb on the monkey bars. The monkey bars were behind the school-in-town where we got off the long yellow bus. She could not walk for a long time without using crutches and we had to be careful not to bump her feet. I could not sit on her lap for the story.

When snow curved in a huge wave like the sea in the Peter Pan book, my mama would take fat from the meat and some chicken feed and scatter it all by the raspberry bushes that twined like tangled hair. "Now, that is a black-capped chickadee. And that is a junco. The one with the black-and-white flecks is a hairy woodpecker. See how the nuthatch comes down the tree? The beautiful red is a cardinal." She would carry the big teakettle to the henhouse to turn the ice to water. The chickens stayed inside all day. The snow began again and turned the tangled bushes to an igloo like in the picture. "The birds are inside the igloo," she said. "They are Eskimo birds."

On certain Sundays my mama would bring the black book with the red binding because it was time for the meeting. That meant we would not have Sunday school with Ella Clark. But Bert Clark, who was an elder, would say, "Now we will have the minutes of the last meeting read by Kathleen Norris." That was my mama, even though Grandma called her Kate. My mama would stand up and read in a loud, clear voice. And when she sat down she would whisper that I must not lean on her arm or she couldn't write the minutes. The minutes were on the clock. But even if I was very sleepy I should not lean on her arm. "Lean . . . ing. Lean . . . ing./Leaning on the ev . . . er . . . las . . . ting arr . . . ms." But I was not leaning on Jesus, I was leaning on my mama because I was so sleepy. She could not write the minutes from the clock if I leaned on her arm. If I put my head on the pew, everybody was leaning like the song. If I fell asleep on the seat, my mother would carry me with her everlasting arms to the car when the meeting was done.

·　　·　　·

"Perhaps," suggested the grey-haired woman kindly, "you should begin with the beginning as it seems to you."

"In the beginning God created Heaven and Earth and Scotch Grove, Iowa. Not Scotch Grove the village, for that was just a corner of commerce laid out at the crossroads by the Applegate brothers when the railroad came through in the 1870s, at first called Scotch Grove Station. But the Scotch Grove Presbyterian Church. And Gideon Hughes. Even the post office had been in the Old House on my grandfather's farm before the village began, my grandma said as she rocked by the window.

In the beginning God created the Land and the Scotch Grove Presbyterian Church. And the Land was our grandfather's. As far as I could see to the east all the way to the Church. The Church was at the end of our grandfather's land and that was where he lived now, for he had died on Christmas Day when Jesus was born. That was the Resurrection.

In the beginning was the Word. And the Word was God and Gideon Hughes. "Why don't you build the manger by the barn?" I asked my Uncle Jim, who was nailing the long boards in place in huge Vs. "You wouldn't have to carry the bales of hay through the mud." He had brought the boards from the sawmill in the timber where he had cut the tree. He stared at me silently a minute. "It has always been here," he said. As it was in the beginning. "My Father put it here." And the Word was God.

God the Father. In the Father's house are many mansions. The attic with the dead bees under the window where my brother and I play when it rains is a mansion. The cornbin, which is on the back stairway landing, and we have to boost each other up to crawl in the door. The hired man's room, which has only cardboard boxes on the bed and our grandfather's cane in the closet. And the west room which is the warmest where I sleep with my brother in the winter before we are old enough for rooms of our own is a mansion. "It is only our mother," I said as we lay there in the darkness. "She buys the things in town." My brother was older than I but he refused to give up believing that Santa Claus came. He did not answer. A car came from the west and threw shadows of crooked limbs across the wall. I said it again. "No," he said, finally. "There is a man who comes. A big man who carries all the presents."

"This is my Father's world./And to my list'ning ears,/All nature sings, and round me rings/The music of the spheres./This is my Father's world/the birds their carols raise,/THE MORNING LIGHT, THE LILY WHITE . . ." "Shhhh," my mother whispered. I was singing too loud again. Make a joyful noise. "Not that joyful," said my mother on the way home from church. "This is my Father's World./Oh! Let me ne'er forget." God the Father. God the Son. God the Holy Ghost.

My brother was the Son. I was the daughter. We did not have the Father. We had a daddy, but our daddy had run away. That's what our grandma said. But our mother did not talk of him. My brother and I did not talk of him either. When our mother talked of our grandpa she used the words. My Father. He was dead. Our Father who art in Heaven. And at the end of our grandpa's land was the Church. The Church was on the Land. In the beginning was the Land and the Land was God. In the beginning . . ."

It was no longer the beginning. It was 1972 in Portland, Oregon. I was afraid it was the end. I sat on the edge of the bathtub. With the razor blade I carved shallow triangles up the inside of my left arm. I did not want to die, but I was doing this anyway. But the triangles were not deep, so surely I did not mean to die.

"Who recommended me to you?" asked the psychiatrist. She had explained that she was a child psychiatrist who did not usually accept adult patients.

"No one," I said. "I tried to get into the Health Sciences crisis center but the man on the phone asked me if I was standing on a bridge. No, I said. He was sorry but they had a long list of people on bridges waiting to get in. I looked through the phone book for a woman." The fear that she might turn me away became a tangible taste in my mouth. "And the address said the Sylvan Medical Building," I added, the panic making my voice high and thin. "Doesn't sylvan mean woods?"

She did not answer my question, but leaned back in her chair. "Do you have any money?" she asked gently.

"No," I said, "but maybe I can sell some land."

2

The Homecoming

500 million years ago Iowa was covered by a shallow sea. The
Brachiopod Pentameras was particularly common. Occasionally
[the brachiopods] were rapidly buried by sediments and preserved
without disturbing the arrangement of their shells. These specimens
were formed when sediments filled the space between two shells
and hardened into forms superficially resembling hickory nuts or
pigs' feet.

—*from the label at the Natural History Museum,*
McBride Hall, University of Iowa

The descendants of John Hughes and Salina James were
being served barbecued ribs, roast beef, and chicken in the Hideout
Room of the Longbranch Motor Inn in Cedar Rapids, Iowa, on
June 26, 1993. I usually avoid eating meat. When I scanned the
banquet room, I recognized only a few of the forty people. A real
feeling of family or reunion for me would have to wait until I went
to the farm where I spent my childhood. I was conversing with Lois
Shover, my second cousin by marriage, who had been my teacher
in both first and second grade.

"I didn't actually know him," Lois Shover said. The "him" was
my father. "I'd met him, of course. He was good-looking, I remember that. What I remember best, though, is the time Kate
brought him to dinner at Mother Shover's. That was the custom
then—marriage partners had to pass scrutiny from the relatives."
She and her husband, Johnny, laughed. They must have a story of

their own about that. "Mother Shover was so proud of being a Hughes. And she was especially proud of your grandfather Gideon, who was her uncle. They all were proud of Gideon. He was important in local politics, you know, and such a wealthy man when he died. Mother Shover thought no one was good enough to marry a Hughes."

Forty-six years later it still seemed impertinent to call her Lois. She was being careful. I had put her in an awkward situation. She knew a story but didn't know whether she should tell me.

"Just tell me anything you know," I said, consciously making my voice sound relaxed. "I'm not sensitive about it, really I'm not. I'd just like some facts about the man. I'm aware he had a lot of problems."

"Your mother was a wonderful woman. Everyone—including Mother Shover—loved her."

"Thank you." Whenever I asked about my father, people invariably told me what a wonderful person my mother was. I tried to redirect Lois's attention. "What did your mother-in-law say?"

"Oh, I don't know now. I just remember her thinking that Bob wasn't good enough for Kate. I was a little threatened by that because I wondered what had been said about me at first." She smiled at her husband, who smiled back.

"Is that all you remember?" I persisted. She had dropped the story again. I was quite sure I hadn't heard it all.

"She didn't like him, I knew that. But I thought it was because of that Hughes pride. She absolutely revered her uncles and your grandfather Gideon most of all. She always said if Mabel Krause had lived, Gid would have been President of the United States. You do know about Mabel, don't you?"

"Yes—the first wife, who died in childbirth." This wasn't the story I was after at the moment.

"Mabel was extremely talented and beautiful. Their wedding was a legend in the community—or at least it was to Mother Shover, who had been a bridesmaid. Both bride and groom were musical, and after the ceremony the wedding party entertained the guests with songs all evening. Mother Shover absolutely adored Mabel.

I'm afraid your grandmother Dena never had a chance with her."

I felt a rush of sympathy for the tiny white-haired woman who had been my grandmother. Grandma had been working as a hired girl for a neighbor when the widower Gid Hughes married her three years after Mabel Krause had died of complications following childbirth. He was almost fifteen years older than my grandmother. "I suppose Mabel was hard to follow."

"Well, yes. And Dena's family was so poor."

I could see I had lost my chance with Lois. A cousin from Indiana glanced at my plate disapprovingly.

"Don't you eat any meat at all?" he asked.

"Sometimes," I returned noncommittally. The conversation moved on to other things. When I stood up to fill my punch cup, Lois followed me. I felt a little chagrined that I hadn't offered to serve her. Ahead of me in the line a woman I did not recognize turned to me suddenly, as if she remembered something.

"Didn't Kate have two children? Wasn't there a boy, too?"

I was prepared for this. I had imagined answering this exact question. I met her eyes directly. I was not going to resort to polite euphemisms when I was searching for the truth myself.

"Yes," I said. "I have a brother, but I haven't seen him for years. He had difficulties with alcohol and dropped out of touch." The woman stared briefly in shocked silence at my rude honesty.

"Oh, I'm sorry to hear that," she murmured uncomfortably. Lois turned discreetly away. We returned to our seats with filled glasses.

When we sat down, Lois turned sideways, directing her conversation exclusively to me. "Barbara," she said, "I do know another story, but I'm not sure it's the truth."

"Please tell it anyway," I said, keeping my voice absolutely even so she wouldn't back away again. "I'll sort it out later. I'm not sure there is a truth so many years after it all happened."

"Well, what I heard was this. The reason Mother Shover was suspicious was that the aunts had done some research. Your father had been gone for a long time and had come back with a short haircut. The story he told was that he had been in the military, but they found out he had been in jail." Johnny apparently nudged her under the table, because she turned to him. "Johnny, she has a right to know what people said. She's not a little girl, you know." Lois leaned over and patted my hand. I smiled reassuringly.

"He certainly ended up in legal and financial trouble later," I volunteered.

"Yes," said Lois. "What Mother Shover said is that the relatives went to Gid Hughes with this story and he told them to mind their own business."

I was surprised at her comment. "I've heard he was quite dictatorial with his children. I wonder why he didn't interfere with this marriage."

"Well, your mother was older by that time, you know. All the others were married and even had children. Surely he had seen her happiness. She was positively radiant that night at Mother Shover's. Gid Hughes didn't live long enough after the wedding to regret his lack of action."

"I know. I remember my mother saying once that she was glad he never knew how badly things had turned out."

"No one blamed her, you know. No one ever blamed her, not for any of it." Lois was suddenly curious. "Your father was from somewhere else originally, wasn't he?"

"Yes, Minnesota," I told her. "But his parents were from Scotch Grove. His mother was a Clark. Bert Clark's sister Mary. Relatives called her Kitsy."

"A Clark! Your father was a Clark?" Lois was astounded. "I never knew he was a Clark! Why, Barbara! They were such a *good* family." Then she looked a little flustered, because the implications of her remark were obvious.

"Even good families have black sheep," I assured her. She smiled gratefully.

"Do you know, Barbie," she said, unconsciously using my childhood name, "there's one thing I'll never forget about you."

"What's that, Mrs. Shover?" I asked, as if we were still in school. I felt a nervous twist in my stomach.

"One morning I read a story aloud about a boy who had taken something from his little brother and made him cry. In those days we still tried to incorporate some moral instruction in schoolwork. Afterward I went around the room asking students whether they had ever taken anything from anyone else. Most children do, you know, it's such a natural thing. But when I got to you, you said very solemnly—I can still see your brown eyes welling up with tears— that you had never, ever taken anything that belonged to someone else and you never, ever would. I was so struck by your sincerity that I have never forgotten it."

"I was undoubtedly telling a lie," I said, and we both laughed.

But I *was* telling a lie. The memory that had flashed through my mind when Lois Shover began the story was that I had once taken half a stick of gum from the top of Jerry Eggiman's desk and hidden it in my coat. I had been afraid to chew it even on the bus for fear my brother would ask me about it. After I got home, having already wallowed miserably in my loss of innocence, I pretended to go outside to play. I actually went to the far northwest corner of the orchard and buried the gum, wrapper and all. For years I watched fearfully for the silver paper to surface, but it never did.

•   •   •

Without a definite plan in mind I headed east from Cedar Rapids late that afternoon. I could have driven to the farm easily, but I was not expected for another night and did not want to show up unannounced. More to the point, I mentally needed a gradual approach to the world of my childhood. Highway 151 had been straightened, widened, and generally modernized beyond immediate recognition, although I could often see the old highway meandering to more familiar farmsteads along the way. Some of the houses appeared deserted and the farm buildings seemed unused. I saw almost no animals, but two large plastic cows stood on a closely cropped lawn. I turned off the new highway at a sign for the Hillcrest Motel because I recognized the old road through Anamosa and I impulsively thought of going to the Wapsipinicon State Park.

Plenty of rooms were available at the little motel. "You've been here a long time," I said to the woman at the desk. "This was the first motel in the area, wasn't it?"

She narrowed her eyes as if trying to recognize me. "We've only had it since 1974, but it's been here since the fifties." She was waiting for me to identify myself, but I decided not to, as my time in the area preceded hers.

I pointed across the road. "Is that big building the old skating rink?" That was where the town kids from Monticello went on Saturday nights when I was in high school, but I was not a town kid and had been only once or twice myself. For my first date, I thought suddenly, and he kissed me.

"Yes, it was a skating rink, but it's been a furniture mart for many years." She handed me a key to the room.

"I'm surprised you've been able to make a go of it since they changed the highway to bypass Anamosa."

"We were the only place in town, and we've kept it up, so we've been able to make a living," she said. "But they've finished us now. There's a Motel 8 under construction out by the highway junction. Nobody will bother to come here anymore. We're converting to condominium apartments."

I smiled. "I guess I got here just in time, then."

"Yes," she said, still puzzling over my identity. She glanced again at the registration card. The name Scot would mean nothing here, and I was glad. "Thank you for remembering us," she added.

The room was clean but smelled of cigarette smoke. I thought of asking for another, but no doubt the rooms all had been smoked in for years, so it wouldn't have mattered. I could tolerate the smell for one night. Confused, I sat down on the bed.

I wanted to walk to the park, but the air was unbearably hot and sultry. My energy level dropped in accordance with the rise in humidity. I'd forgotten the way the weather works in Iowa. Why hadn't it cooled down after all the rain of last night? I turned on the air conditioner. Then I brought a few things in from the camper. I should have just camped in the park, but I didn't want to back out on the woman now, who so obviously needed customers. Enticed by the cooling air in the room, I decided to let the park wait until morning.

The Wapsipinicon wasn't my river—the Maquoketa was. What I remembered from the state park on the Wapsipinicon was a small cave in a limestone bluff called Horsethief Cave. I lay back on the bed, reconstructing from memory the flared opening and the cool mud floor of a shallow room. My mind began to wander in and out of sleep. Disjointed clips from my memory flashed on the inside of my closed eyelids.

My mother and I stood in the little cave. "There isn't enough room for horses," I complained. I wanted a horse of my own more than anything in the world. "It's just called that," said my mother. "Indians used it."

The window air conditioner shuddered with a disquieting rattle. I did not open my eyes. The last line of the note my mother had left me, her usually neat cursive crowded on the narrow page of faded paper formed a clear image.

You'll never know how much.

I sat up and turned off the air conditioner, which had succeeded in lowering the temperature to an intolerable degree. How much what? How much she loved him? How much she suffered? How much it cost her soul to live through that humiliating experience in a farming community in Iowa whose core was still permeated with the Calvinist values of its founders? Then why did she stay?

I still felt an unresolved edge of anger whenever I thought of her quiet loyalty to my father. Was quiet loyalty the best example for a daughter who would later be left by a husband of her own, I wondered resentfully. How was I ever going to decipher her mysteries when I had chosen to disassociate myself early in life from the farm, the church, and the traditional woman's role—with its deference to men—which had been her existence?

I would start at the beginning of my understanding. I put my head in my hands for a minute.

"In the beginning God created heaven and earth and Scotch Grove, Iowa," I said aloud. I stretched across the bed again. The disjointed documentary of distant images resumed.

Science says that the oldest rocks in Iowa are between one and two billion years old, but these are not my rocks to understand. I attended the high school in Monticello, eight miles from my grandmother's house, from 1954 to 1959. There we were not allowed to learn about evolution because the superintendent saw it as antithetical to biblical truth.

"Nonsense," said my mother, whose own Christian faith saw no contradiction between science and religion. She was reading at the dining table, where my brother and I were doing our homework. "The Hebrews were an ancient people who recorded their religious faith in the symbols they understood. The truth of the Bible isn't challenged simply because the stories reflect the limited scientific knowledge of their time."

But it was not from her that I learned about the oldest rocks in eastern Iowa. I was taught by her brother, Jim, a strange man whom none of us, even in later years, understood. He said that he had wanted to be a science teacher, but as he was the only son, there was never any doubt that he would farm. And so he did, sort of, all the while I was a child. He lived up the road with his wife and two daughters at the west end of the horse pasture in the white house with the blue roof. He tended the acres of my grandmother as well as his own in a bizarre reversal of history, working backward to more antiquated farming methods as his life progressed. "Chains," our neighbor Paul Ernie Paulsen had told me once, "he wanted me to measure the fence lines in chains. 'Jimmy,' I said, 'what's a chain?' 'Four rods or 100 links,' he said."

My Uncle Jim drew a picture in the dust of the barnyard while I swatted mosquitoes and shifted from foot to foot. According to him, the oldest rocks in our world of northeastern Iowa were the limestone bluffs. "Notice," he said, making the line to the east slant upward, "that the lay of the land is such that eastern Iowa tilts and the oldest layers of rocks that are exposed are the limestone bluffs. They are more than 450 million years old." My time was measured in the length of sunlight hours left for riding the horse after the yellow bus had brought me home from school. He drew in the bluffs in squiggly lines with his stick. "These bluffs were once

the lime-rich mud on the bottom of shallow, warm-water seas."
Now I was interested in spite of myself, for I had seen the sea only
in books. What a romantic notion. That right here where the windmill spun its finned wheel, and where the soft warm necks of the
cows carved polished half-moons in the wooden slats of the hay
manger, once swirled waves with crests of foam.

The spreading fingers of the last great glaciers had split and left
the Cambrian limestone intact in well-defined delineations. Bluffs
of dramatic heights occurred in outcroppings along the Maquoketa
River like the one behind the house of Millie Kuper, a cousin from
my grandmother's side.

"Don't step on any rattlesnakes," said August Kuper, who was a
large, friendly man, amused that I had ridden the horse all the way
to their house again just to see the autumn leaves of the bottomland
hardwoods rippling in a thick textured mosaic of red and gold below
the bluff. I tied the horse to the fence and August watched me pick
my way through the undergrowth, his thumbs in the buckles of his
bib overalls.

In the limestone remnants the seeping groundwater made crevices, sinkholes, and underground caverns. Maquoketa Caves.

I had been sick in the car and the smell would not go away, even
though Grandma scrubbed me with a wet towel. I had to sit on the
bench with her while my brother and mother followed Uncle Jim
through the biggest cave with the lights where the water beaded and
dripped. I had never tasted soda water before, but my mother bought
some strawberry pop to settle my stomach and magic silver bubbles
climbed the inside of the glass.

Or Panther Hollow. Once a man had stayed too late in the woods
at night and took shelter in the little cave. He hung the deer he
had shot in a tree and tried to keep a fire going, but fell asleep. He
awoke to the scream of a panther who had pulled the deer carcass
from the tree. As his bullets were gone, he could only watch while
the panther ate his fill. My uncle had once found an arrowhead in
the cave.

I followed Uncle Jim because he said I could, but he walked so
fast it was hard to keep up. I carried the bag of rocks he collected

which had the fossils in them. They were lumps like the cloven hooves of baby pigs' feet embedded in larger hunks of limestone. "Brachiopods," my uncle said.

"Brak-ee-a-pods," I obediently echoed. The bag was very full.

"Why didn't you tell him it was too heavy?" said my exasperated mother, hoisting the sack. I did not tell her I was afraid to say so for fear I could not go with him again. When he walked, his stiff overalls made a sound like dry cornhusks rubbing together. *Swiss swiss swiss swiss.* And I did not tell her how I reached over the bluff where I could not see and Uncle Jim grabbed my arm, pulling me back before the rattlesnake struck.

"Never, never do that again," he said, and I didn't.

I sat up suddenly. Even after forty years my terror of the coiled snake had a sharp, metallic taste. Swallowing involuntarily, I shook my head to dispel the illusion of the snake's presence.

What do these limestone bluffs have to do with my mother, I asked myself, seeking to contain the memories that snowballed away from me with each association.

"Their mystery. They, like my mother, seem a remnant from another time," I said aloud. Then my memory spun away from me again.

My mother stood along the Mississippi, on a bluff at Eagle Point Park in Dubuque. She wore a red plaid dress which she had made, incorporating the remainder of the material into a dress for me that had a flared skirt with panels of white. She made all our clothes, for she was embarrassed to have us wear hand-me-downs from Jeanette Wilcox, who was a cousin on my father's side. We had packed the basket with the plate of deviled eggs and the fruit jars of lemonade wrapped in towels. "Where are the eagles?" I wanted to know as we watched the barges go through the locks on the river far below us.

"We've killed them off," she said sadly. "So many of the wild things are gone."

That must have been in the early 1950s, when so much DDT was used in the fields.

The room had become unbearably close again. Jerking up the window by the bed, I was pleasantly surprised. The air had shifted into an aching pre-thunderstorm coolness. The leaves of the silver maple trees turned inside out and their tops bent sideways before the rain began.

• • •

I left for Scotch Grove by midmorning, having taken advantage of the relative coolness of dawn to jog down the hill through the Wapsipinicon State Park. It was much as I remembered, with the small cave and the creek running over the road to make a shallow ford. The muddy flood of the Wapsipinicon River churned barely below the bridge floor in a turgid flow that looked like liquid topsoil. The bottomland, including a baseball diamond on the north side of the bridge toward the town, was completely submerged. A news commentator on the radio talked of natural wetland reassertion. To my surprise, a great blue heron glided above the water.

Just north of Anamosa at the top of a long hill a sign for E23 proclaimed JONES COUNTY CARE FACILITY FOUR MILES. COUNTY HOME ROAD announced another sign. "Poor Farm," my grandmother had called it. It was one of those places, like hell, about which I didn't know very much except that I didn't want to end up there. "If you don't save your money, you'll end up at the Poor Farm. There'll be nothing left but the Poor Farm for you if you act that way." This road was unique in an area laid out in checkerboard grids. It wound along the ridgeline with a commanding view.

The site of the Poor Farm was the place where the first party of Scots had planted tentative roots in 1837 before they built the more substantial Scotch Grove Presbyterian Church on the corner of Ebenezer Sutherland's land. Edinburgh, they had called the first settlement where they had erected a courthouse. Now nothing was left but a little cemetery with the oldest Livingstons and Sutherlands. I'd heard that Jones County had established a historical museum nearby and I wanted to see it.

But the museum grounds were closed and the gate was secured with a chain. A sign announced summertime hours of 1–5 on

Sunday. A warning sign on the County Home read, NOT RESPON-
SIBLE FOR VEHICLES IN COUNTY CARE FACILITY PROP-
ERTY. What could happen to them out here in the middle of the
country? Did poor people steal them trying to get away?

I continued toward the house that had once been my grandmother's. Inevitably I felt a twinge of nervousness when I returned,
even though it wasn't painful now, as it had been after I had stayed
away so long. I'd been back several times since then. Yet each time
it jolted my sensibilities to come to the house of my childhood and
find it a bed-and-breakfast named Sweet Memories.

My cousin Vaneta, whose father was Uncle Jim to me, was the
proprietor of Sweet Memories. She actually counted her residence
in Arizona with her husband. She operated the B&B during the
summer months in anticipation of an eventual move back to the
area. Vaneta was not at all enamored of the idea of natural wetland
reassertion. I was repeating what the radio news commentator had
said.

"Don't even mention wetlands to me," said Vaneta. "I'm mad
enough to spit." The idea of Vaneta spitting made me laugh. We
had emerged from the farm experience at opposite ends of the
spectrum and our attire illustrated our differences. I wore blue jeans
and Vaneta wore a skirt with high-heeled pumps. I had arrived a
day ahead of the other relatives she was expecting. I sat at the end
of the Majestic Range in our grandmother's old rocker while she
fixed a pot of tea.

"Where's your wetland and what's the problem?"

"It's in that low part of the old Henrichs place, right next to your
eighty acres. Dad let that area go back to slough grass and I had to
tile out part of it. But now with all this rain a swamp has surfaced
in the rest. The renter got his tractor stuck in there this spring. He's
likely to pull out on me if I don't get it retiled. Or even worse, the
Department of Natural Resources will fly over in a plane and try
to reclaim it as a natural wetland."

I had a sudden intriguing image of a map of northeastern Iowa
completely underlaid with vast spiderwebs of brick-red tubes of clay
drainage tile. No wonder the wetlands were gone. Probably some

kind of plastic pipe was used now, I thought. "Are they reclaiming wetlands?"

"There's talk of it. And some of my land is really borderline."

"So why not let them?"

"Barb, we're talking about a 60-acre piece. If I tile it, I can get $100 an acre rent a year. And I need it. My husband's company is downsizing—facing bankruptcy even—and we may need every penny for retirement. Your land, by the way, is a little soggy, too."

I hadn't thought to ask, not having much sentiment for the piece of ground that had become mine in 1968, when Grandma died. "It can't be cheap to retile it at today's prices."

"It's *not*. It'd cost about twenty thousand."

"How can it be worth it?" I didn't want her to retile the piece—not that it was my business, of course. In his last years, Uncle Jim had deliberately let much of his land return to natural growth.

"It's not really worth it, but I'm over a barrel. I need the money and I want a reliable renter with a going operation for the rest of the land. You never know who's going to go under these days."

I changed the subject. "The place looks beautiful. Sometimes it's hard to believe this is the same house where I spent my childhood."

"What do you mean? I've restored it almost exactly the way it was in the beginning—I've even used old pictures to be sure I was getting things right."

"But that's not the way it looked when I lived here. Nothing worked right by then. The toilet didn't flush unless we dumped an extra pail of water in. We mostly used the outhouse. The cistern ran dry every winter and that was the only source of hot water through the boiler that used to be connected to this range. We had to heat all the other water on the stove. Mom carried the wash water to the Maytag downstairs. Then back up the stairs to throw outside because the drain in the cellar didn't work. I don't think a single repair had been made since the house was first built."

"I know. It was even worse when I got it, believe me. After Grandma died, Dad just filled it up with junk. You wouldn't believe what all I hauled out of here."

"Yes, I would. I was back here a few years before he died. He let me in the house because I wanted to show my husband and kids where I grew up. We had to fight our way in through the weeds. He had one whole bedroom practically filled with antique barbed wire."

She sighed. "He was making a *spinning wheel* when he died. A few more years and he would have been living back in the caves by the Maquoketa River." Senile dementia, the death certificate had said, but we knew it wasn't that. Always unhappy with the present, he was just continuing the strange reversal of time he'd always lived. "The carpenters advised me to tear the house down and start over if we wanted to retire out here. People in the neighborhood thought I was crazy."

"Well, you were, of course," I said affectionately, "but I'm glad you salvaged the place. I always loved this house—even though I knew there was something sad about our living here. It was the showcase of the neighborhood when it was built—and this was the most progressive farm."

"Well, it didn't take my dad long to reverse the pattern."

"No, it didn't." When our grandfather had died in 1940, everything stopped on the place and we all grew up knowing we were living in suspended time because the force that had relentlessly driven everyone was stilled. "I can't get over all the big empty farmhouses I saw as I was driving through Iowa. Big old houses with the paint peeling. They'd sell for two hundred thousand dollars in Portland. They're beautiful old houses, built to last centuries with all that lovely wood."

"They're not *in* Portland, sweetheart; they're taking up good corn land."

"Is that why the barns have been bulldozed?"

"Certainly. Who needs barns? Nobody keeps livestock around here—except a few keep pigs. My renter keeps pigs. Some farmers make liquid fertilizer from the manure. Although I'm told the ground is so wet this year that it's all running off instead of soaking in like it's supposed to." Vaneta was doing her nails and I was watching, fascinated.

"At least that's somewhat organic, then. I thought they just used chemicals."

"Mostly they do." Vaneta waved her nails back and forth to dry them. My eyes followed the red and she laughed. "My mother-in-law was doing this once at our place in Arizona, and a hummingbird flew right up to her nails," she said. "You looked hypnotized—like a hummingbird. Don't you ever do your nails?"

"No." I knew she was about to start in on my appearance. We had this discussion each time we saw each other.

"Honestly, Barb, there's a place in Cedar Rapids we could take you. They make you over totally—a new hairdo and makeup—and then take your picture."

"Vaneta, if anyone else said that to me, I'd take offense."

"But you know I love you, dear," she said, putting the top back on her nail polish. "I just don't see why you let yourself look old on purpose."

I smiled at her. I loved her, too, even if we were monumentally different and hadn't been close as children because she was seven years older. "I like grey hair. Which room do you want me to take?" I asked.

"I decided to put you in your mother's old room," Vaneta said, "the blue room. I've got all my own stuff in the south room, where you slept as a kid, anyway. Aunt Em and Marge are coming tomorrow, so I'll put Aunt Em in Grandma's room and Marge in the brown room. They'll just stay here one night and head back to Indiana. I might as well put you where you can stay the whole time."

"Fine," I said. After my mother died I'd stood in the middle of her room, holding her pillow to my face and wondering how long it would take before all the smell of her faded. No one had died for me before except my father, who left no smell at all. "That'll be fine."

•   •   •

This is my mama's room, but I sleep in the crib . . . "You are too big for the crib," my mama says, but she lets me sleep in the crib because I cry when she puts me in the bed. I like the crib.

Seek-a, seek-a, seek-a, seek. When I rock, it makes a funny noise. *Seek-a, seek-a, seek-a, seek.* "Barbie, stop," my mother says gently in the darkness. *Seek-a, seek-a, seek-a, seek.* And early, early, when the sun comes through the window to the east, the room turns yellow. My mama is sleeping. The sun is on my mama's hair. My pajamas have feet in them. *Seek-a, seek-a, seek-a, seek.* My mama is awake.

Before we go to bed my mama reads a story. If we sit in the wicker chair, there is room for us both on her lap. When the story is done we put the water in the pan for the hot-water bottles. "Spank the baby's bare butt," says my brother, who is silly when she has squeezed the air out the top and given him the jiggly water bottle. I am not silly. I hold the water bottle under my flannel shirt, which I am wearing over my pajamas. It is Bobbie's turn to sleep with Grandma and my turn to sleep upstairs with my mama. The other rooms are cold. My mama carries me up the stairs to tuck me in. On the stairway landing we stop at the window to look at the moon. My old pajamas line the windowsill to keep the draft from coming in. "See how the tree reaches its black arms," says my mama, for the wind is blowing. The snow shines with ice and the moon is as white as the snow.

When I have the headache I can stay home from school. And after I have been sick to my stomach and the light has changed color, I lie quietly in my mother's bed with the flannel sheets and both pillows under my head. The blue flowers on the wallpaper, which seemed like grey circles before I threw up, have come back. The glass of water on my mama's dresser has bubbles on the side. Under the window is the brown-and-black trunk which is never opened. "Is it secrets?" I ask. "Just sadness," she says. In the chest of drawers are the games for when we are sick and the basket of souvenirs from Yellowstone National Park. When I feel better and my eyes have come back right, my mama will let me look at the book with the buffalo that is covered with snow.

———

Now I am a big girl so I am not afraid when the wind in the wire outside the window sounds like wolves. But why is my mama staying downstairs so long? If I go to the bathroom, my feet will be cold again, for there is no heat in the hallway. I know that sound is the wires. That is not wolves. I am a big girl. I am not afraid. Even if there were wolves outside, they could not reach to the porch roof and come in the window. Are the wolves in the front yard? But they cannot come up here. Mama says there are no wolves, but why is she staying downstairs so long? Maybe the wolves are down there. Mama, Mama, are you all right?

(3)

The Holy Farm

The great cities rest upon our broad and fertile prairies. Burn down
your cities and leave our farms, and your cities will spring up again
by magic; but destroy our farms and the grass will grow in the streets
of every city in the world.
    —WILLIAM JENNINGS BRYAN, *"Cross of Gold"*

For a brief moment after I awoke I had absolutely no
idea where I was in either geography or time. Then I remembered.
Sweet Memories. The "Exquisite Blue Honeymooners' Room,"
according to the brochure. The irony seemed too great in the dark.
Sitting up, I switched on the light. My mother and father gazed
benignly from their wedding picture. I had the colored version in
Portland. I had found it, wrapped in the wedding dress with the
box of letters, in the trunk I had taken from this very room. The
glass from the colored picture's frame was broken in a rayed pattern,
as if it had been struck.

"Are you being facetious calling this the honeymooners' room?"
I asked Vaneta carefully the first time I saw the redone house. I
didn't want to hurt her feelings. The decor was tasteful, with several
shades of blue blending and casting cool shadows. She looked at
me in genuine surprise, almost alarm, as if she didn't want to hurt
my feelings, either.

"No," she said, watching my face. "You know how Aunt Kate
loved blue. I think she would have loved this room. Don't you?"

"Oh yes," I hastened to assure her. What did it matter; it was all in the past. "She loved blue and it's a beautiful room. I just mean the honeymoon part." I tried to make a joke of it. "You don't want to jinx anyone's marriage."

"I'm not. I think the depth of love she felt was beautiful."

I didn't answer. I picked up a picture from the bureau. "Who's this?"

"Don't you know?"

"No." I looked at it again. "I don't. Who is it?" The face was familiar, but not really. The woman's head was tilted at a jaunty angle, a flapper-type twenties hat over her straight bob.

"That's your *mother*. Don't you recognize her?"

"No." I looked at the picture closely. "I think you're wrong. I have pictures of her at this age and her hair was wavy. Her eyes were always soft and fawn-like. This young woman looks much too self-assured for my shy little mother. Maybe this was a college friend?"

Vaneta was irrefutable when she had an idea in her head. "I know I'm right. I asked several other relatives and they agree." I didn't press it, but I wasn't convinced.

Now, after thinking through that scene, I was solidly awake. It was only one o'clock. I stepped out of the bed onto the deep carpet. My mother would have loved the softness. Her feet were always cold. For years and years her Christmas present from my brother and me was a pair of mail-order bedroom slippers that Grandma helped us wrap. Padding around the room to the dresser, I picked up the photograph that had troubled me.

Why didn't I recognize this likeness as my mother if it was really my mother? I held my hands around the woman's face, blocking the hair. Well, maybe. The picture resembled her a lot more that way. But the eyes were different. I glanced back at the wedding picture. Those eyes held the soft vulnerability familiar to me. "Mom?" I spoke silently to the self-assured countenance. But the woman with the mysterious eyes was not looking at me.

I sat down on the bed. Perhaps I did not know her at all. I was only twenty-one when she died. How much do my own sons, now in their twenties, know of me? I thought about that a minute. A lot, I decided. I had known a lot of her, too, but not what she'd gone through with the marriage. She'd spoken of that only once. I was home from graduate school preoccupied with my own pain over a broken engagement. That was shortly before she died. I hadn't even seen the letters until a few years ago, when I'd returned to show my family the farm of my childhood and had taken the trunk to Oregon.

I shifted the cardboard box with the letters from the nightstand to the bed. At the bottom I had placed a few pictures of relatives. In one my mother, my brother, and I were grouped on a little bench. Judging from my diminutive size, the picture must have been taken soon after we moved in with Grandma. My mother had dark hair and the soft eyes of the wedding picture. I placed the note with the three short lines beside the picture.

What do you think?

"What do I think?" A guilty clutch tightened my stomach. I was about to be untruthful to my mother. "I think you were a loyal, sensitive woman who loved a man deeply." A man who was a crook and took you for every penny he could. "And when he left, you were humiliated and retreated in silence." And covered his bounced checks, paid off his notes penny by stinking penny, until you had saved that damn farm for my brother and me to lose in our own divorces later. "You lived your life quietly, traveling only to town for groceries, to the woods for picnics with your children, and to church." For twenty years every Sunday unless the road was blocked by snow. Ladies' Aid. Sunday school. You were a Presbyterian nun. "Never saying a word against him."

You don't understand.

"You're right. I loved you. But I don't understand." I really don't. Why did you stay? You had a college degree at a time when many teachers didn't. You drove a car when many women were afraid or too controlled by their husbands. "I don't understand the whole lot of you." Why was it so important to stay on the farm? The farm. That hallowed ground. The father, the son, and the holy farm. "Were you trapped or were you here by choice?"

You'll never know how much.

I put the box back on the table and turned out the light. Until I understood, I could not possibly know how much.

•　　•　　•

Outside the window of the psychiatrist's office in Portland one massive tree screened the freeway, creating the illusion that the red Sylvan Medical Building stood in the woods. The small middle-aged woman who sat between me and the window did not exude personal warmth, but I found her solid grayness comforting. Occasionally she would interrupt my monologue with a soft question and record my answer in an abbreviated note. "Do I understand you correctly," she asked, "that your mother's farm was separate from the land surrounding your grandmother's house?" Her form silhouetted against the branches which whipped wildly in the autumn wind.

We could not see the Farm from my grandma's house. But sometimes my mother would say, I think that must be stored at the Farm. So we would get in the green Ford that had been my grandpa's and we would go to the Farm.

Now, the Farm was not the same as the Land. The Land was my grandfather's: the Yerrian place, the Henrichs place, the Ebenezer Sutherland place, and the place that my grandfather had bought when he was just a boy and his father signed the note. That was the Land, which belonged to my grandpa, even though he was dead. But the Farm belonged to my mother.

When we came to the Farm we would drive up the shady lane with the big elm trees joining at the top like a tunnel. To the faded yellow house which was the biggest house in the world, even bigger than my grandma's house. My mother would knock politely on the door. The house, a sad, dark house with brown beams on the ceiling, had big brown window seats that were not for children to play on. When we went in we had to walk quietly, as if we were in church. The house was so big that the renter did not use the upstairs, so we went through a row of brown doors all just alike and up the stairs to mysterious rooms that held mostly cardboard boxes, one of pots and pans and another that my mother said held wedding presents. In one room stood a green couch with a rounded hump on the end.

To come back outside felt a relief and we would want to run, but still my mother said no, this was not a place to play. But my brother always ran to look in the barn. On the side of the barn where the paint peeled hung big white letters: THE ELMS. When I asked what it meant, my mother said it did not mean anything. So later I asked my grandma.

She sniffed. "Humphf!" She said it did not mean anything. She said that the Farm was the old Livingston Place and that Grandpa had bought it during the Depression because the Livingstons did not work hard enough and had racehorses. My grandpa had given the Farm to my mother when she was married, but my father ruined it. "It was a terrible thing he did to her, a terrible thing." She stroked her chin and rocked so hard that her feet came up from the floor together.

But in spite of the terrible thing, my mother kept the Farm. She went to Ed Zirkelbach, who was then one of the most successful farmers in Scotch Grove, and owned the place where the old Hoyt nursery had been, and she asked him to help her manage the farm. He was a large man like her father. "She came to me," he told me after she died, "and she said she needed advice. I didn't want to cause any bad feelings in the family, you know, so I said what about Jimmy, couldn't you have him manage it, but she said, 'My brother has troubles of his own.' And I knew what she meant, so I helped her. I had to pry every penny out of her to invest in it, because all she could think about was paying back those debts. And she did. She was quite the woman, your mother was, Barbara. To pay that all back from the rent and get that farm back on its feet and raise you kids besides. I don't think she ever bought anything for herself. Ever."

I counted the windows on the house at the Farm the year my brother and I painted it. Forty-two, I believe, or was it forty-eight? The year before, we had painted the barns. Finally, finally we covered up the faded white lettering that said THE ELMS. That made my mother inordinately happy and she stood looking at that side of the barn for a long time. At church people would come up and say with surprise in their voices, "Why, Kate, your farm looks so nice!" and she would smile shyly.

"How can I even think of selling the Farm?" I said to the psychiatrist.

All through the heat of July and August we painted, and whenever the Everly Brothers sang, I climbed down the ladder and held the transistor radio to my ear. "Darling, you can count on me/Till the sun dries up the sea./Until then I'll always be/Devoted to you." Always. Devoted.

But my husband had gone away. Mr. Morf had called from the Monticello Bank because the note was due. Could he in some way be of assistance to me, he inquired, for he was a kind man who knew me personally and trusted me. I had taken the rent check from the farm and paid the half that was assigned to me in the divorce papers that were waiting for court action. "Thanks for offering to help," I said. I flushed hot with painful embarrassment, for I had taught his daughter in school the year I stayed in Scotch Grove to take care of Grandma. I would pay the rest somehow if my husband didn't, I promised, I would even be willing to have the next rent check deposited directly with him, but I thought my husband should have to pay. "We'll do our best to get it from him," said Mr. Morf. "How strangely history repeats itself."

I was living my mother's life.

· · ·

The next day was another Hughes family reunion as far as I was concerned. I had timed my pilgrimage to Iowa to coincide with the visit of my mother's one remaining sibling and her children, my cousins. Aunt Em was eighty years old and functionally blind. Her older sisters—my mother, Kate, and my Aunt Bess—had died young of heart attacks. Aunt Em had survived her heart attack and lived on. Although she had diabetes and a host of attendant health problems, her mind was keen and she liked birds.

We had a long discussion about sandhill cranes. No, there hadn't been any in Iowa when she was a child, either, she informed me, but it was a regular flyway before all the sloughs were drained for agriculture. "I never saw them—or many ducks, even, but the old folks talked of them sometimes—and they still talked of prairie chickens. I remember Uncle John describing how they sold them in the market, even. The eagles were mostly gone—even the Canada geese. They've come back in Indiana," she said. "Lots of geese now, and even the sandhill cranes. But the prairie chickens are gone for good."

"There isn't any virgin prairie left."

"There wasn't any when we were kids, either. Or much wildlife. We never saw any deer."

"Neither did I."

"I can't read anymore, but I listen a lot. I get those talking books and I like the ones on wildlife. I've been following the whooping cranes—and other species that they try to reintroduce. If only people had thought a little more before they killed everything—and drained all the sloughs. That's what this flooding is about, you know. They drained a lot of land that should have been left alone."

I felt a rush of warmth. "You sound like my mom," I said, and hugged her. "Tell me something, Aunt Em."

"What can I tell you? I'm an old lady and I can't see." But she laughed when she said it.

"I want to know if she ever went out with anyone but my father. And if she didn't, why not, when she was so pretty."

"Barbara, we all wondered that ourselves. No, I don't think she did. I think there were at least two reasons, maybe three. One, she was so smart. Men were probably afraid of her. She was determined to get a four-year college degree, and she did. The only other one to do that at that time was Esther Sinclair, and she didn't marry at all. The second reason I'm sure of is that she was shy. That probably made her seem kind of standoffish, you know what I mean?"

"But you and Bess weren't shy. Especially Bess. I've heard great stories about Bess."

Em laughed, not contradicting me. "We came later. The folks treated us differently than Jim and Kate. Your mother was trained very strictly into a woman's role. In fact, she looked after us little ones, especially me, as I was almost eight years younger."

"But most women didn't go to college."

"That was the Hughes part of it, and the church, too. Lots of those women were quite well educated—certainly all the Clarks."

"What was the third reason?"

"Well, there was our father, you know."

"What do you mean?"

"We loved him and almost worshipped him in a way. I don't think Kate would have spent time with anyone if she thought he wouldn't approve."

"Weren't there several reasons not to approve of my father?"

"I was gone by then, married and in Illinois. I really didn't know your dad."

"Aunt Em, that's not fair. Of course you did. He came to Chicago and worked for your husband one winter."

"No, I was too busy with babies then. He was a talker, though, I'll say that. Full of big ideas." Her face closed. Whatever else she knew, she wasn't telling.

I wasn't getting anywhere, really. "Why was my mother's childhood so unhappy?"

"Did she say that?"

"Yes. I'd ask her to describe something from her childhood and she'd shake her head. Once when I was home from college I asked why she wouldn't talk about it. I can see her sitting under the green lampshade, her eyes brimming. 'I couldn't talk about it if I tried,' she said."

"I don't know. I really don't, unless it was because she was so shy." Aunt Em was suddenly apprehensive. She didn't want me to think her father cruel. "Our dad never raised his voice to us. In fact, the only time I remember him shouting was when a hired man had whipped the horses. We just had the normal childhood every-

body had in those days. You didn't expect all the praise kids want
today. You just did what you were told. Marriage was like that, too.
You just got in the harness and you pulled your load. And the men
did their part, too. My father was a stern man, but there was never
a doubt that we'd eat. He said he married my mother because he
liked the way she baked bread."

"Well, look what happened to my mom."

"That was because your dad didn't do his part. She did hers."

"What did he . . ."

Aunt Em interrupted. She didn't want to deal with questions
about my father. "I don't blame you girls for wanting more and
kicking up your heels. But don't forget, it was a different world for
us. Just like the farming."

I didn't want to talk about farming. Here was one person who
knew both my mother and my father well and she wasn't going to
tell me anything. I wondered what she knew but would never say
because it didn't fit her idea of what you told a daughter about her
father.

Aunt Em continued, launched on a favorite tirade. "The farms
are all chemicals now. Even the chickens. We were talking about
prairie chickens. Imagine how something tasted that had a life of
its own. The kids got a batch of chicks for me a couple of years ago
when I could still see to feed them. They had me pumping stuff
in those chicks that got them ready for market in just a few weeks.
Those chickens grew so fast the bones in their legs didn't even hold
up their bodies. They just rolled around on the floor."

"Aunt Em," I said, "that is a positively disgusting story."

"It must be all the hormones they put in chicken feed these days.
It's the same way with the corn. Take your grandfather. When he
died he was one of the richest farmers in the county and his land
was the best land. He used to go around to the neighbors and ask
them if he could haul the manure out of their yards. He built up
his land so he had a yield of sixty bushels an acre. Now, to break
even, a farmer has to produce one hundred bushels an acre, even
try for two hundred, and the only way he can do that is chemicals.
We all thought my brother Jim was crazy," she said, looking in the
direction she'd heard Vaneta's voice. "He let some of the land go

back natural. He was the only sane one among us." We all sat quietly a minute, thinking of him.

"Barbara," said Aunt Em suddenly. "Where's that poem you wrote for Jim's funeral? Would you read that to me? Marge has it in the Hughes genealogy book."

"Do you really want me to read it, Aunt Em?" I wasn't enthusiastic. The poem had been hurriedly written for sentiment. Marge signaled that I should read.

"Yes, please. Your mother would have liked that poem, Barbara. She felt that way about things, too."

Marge handed me the book. I cleared my throat a little nervously and looked apologetically at the cousins, but no one seemed embarrassed. We were all at Aunt Em's command, for she was the oldest relative.

In the first part of the poem I described Uncle Jim coming across the field in the first light of morning, yodeling. I was up early, too, hoping to see the red fox loping toward the creek. I'd hear Uncle Jim's yodel and see the barn cats all lined up on the fence, waiting for him.

In the next stanza I listed things I learned from him as a child. Suddenly I was embarrassed. I didn't want Vaneta to feel as if I'd had more of her father than she had.

> . . . *things he showed me—*
> *fossils from a long dead sea,*
> *Orion's sword—which clouds meant rain—*
> *where to find the wild lady slipper in the spring—*

Vaneta smiled at me, because she knew what I was thinking.

"Go on," said Aunt Em, "there's more."

> *I see him in my childhood summer evenings,*
> *standing by the windmill in the slanted light.*
> *He reaches up, unhooks the motor pin,*
> *and pulls the wind-drawn shaft in line,*
> *to utilize the natural power.*

Aunt Em interrupted me. "That's it. That's the line I wanted. 'The natural power.' Men like my father made good livings for their families. And my brother, Jim, wasn't crazy. If anything, he was the first to see the craziness around him."

We were all descendants of Gideon Hughes, who for one brief moment in time had built a farming empire in that area. Of course we wanted to ennoble what had been done. I did, especially sitting there with all my relatives, who were smiling approvingly at what seemed a validation of my Uncle Jim's turning back to the time when farming made sense, when people were in touch with the land and were at least minimally integrated with nature.

But a claustrophobic tightness rose in my chest. I wanted out of the room, out of the house, out of the farm. Had the horse not been long since dead I would have bolted, leaping the porch steps the way I had as a teenager.

I could feel the wind lift my shirt, feel the sticky warmness of the horse's back clinging to my jeans, feel the soft give of the gravel as the hooves bunched and struck. We were galloping, galloping, escaping the prairie for the woods. The yellow-green light slanted through the timber, insects droned in strange whispers, the soft mud sucked at the horse's feet where the seepage crossed the narrow wagon road. Leaving the horse at the last barbed-wire gate where the trees parted to park-like meadows, I began to run, harder, harder until I could see the river. The tightness burst and I sank to my knees in the soft, black earth, threading my fingers through the long, flat grass.

Who were we, really?
What was this land we called home?

•   •   •

In October, when the cornstalks turned dry blanched gold after the first frost, Uncle Jim harnessed the workhorses to the high-sided wagon. First the collar, the large oval, oddly rounded and smooth, the leather faintly sour-smelling of old sweat, but slick-black and slippery on the inside where it rested on the horse's neck. Next the hames, the curved sticks with the metal balls on the ends that rested on the collar. Then the tangle of straps that stretched over the horse's back, the metal rings jingling when they struck each other. "Does your mother know you're here?" Uncle Jim asked.

"Yes," I said truthfully, for I had seen her looking through the window, so she knew where I had gone. I followed him all afternoon as he opened the field for the rusted one-row corn picker. He did not talk or tell me things, only "gee" or "haw" to the horses as we followed the wagon and broke the corn from the stalks. Under the glove the hollow between my thumb and finger was bleeding, but I did not tell him. The sky was the hard blue of late fall and the corn leaves clashed like long knives sharpening in the wind.

When wild bluebells stood under the lilac bush that Grandma said was older even than the house, my uncle would hitch up the plow behind the John Deere. The blades of the plow were hard like the mirror, but my wrist turned as I followed the smoothness. My fingers left smoky marks, which I rubbed with my shirt. I stood beside the large cottonwood at the end of the field watching the plow cleave the soil in long, thick ropes, fighting the urge to press my body facedown into the blackness, wanting to touch that satin shine, wanting even to taste the cool dirt, wanting the feel of the earth against me.

When we made hay my brother drove the tractor and my uncle walked along beside, swinging the bales to the wagon. My cousin Denamae and I pulled the bales to the back of the wagon or lifted them together, alternating sides so the wagon would not tip. Uncle Jim had made the wagon with a tree he had cut in the timber and had taken to the mill. But he did not make the wheels. The wheels were rubber and not wooden like the old wheels leaning on the woodshed. The bales were heavy and the sun was too yellow. But when we brought the load to the barn, we stopped in the shade of the large maple. My mother brought our lunch in the big white dishpan, sandwiches wrapped in waxed paper and small fruit jars with ice cubes and yellow lemon rinds. When I was done I lay back on the bales, feeling the stiff hay prickling against my shirt. The sun and the leaves made warm and cool patches on my face and arms.

In late summer the gold braid topped the tall corn. The wind blew hard and stalks swayed like dancers flinging their skirts and arms in a fluid wave. Once when I was a little girl I had been lost in the corn, which interlaced above my head in a canopy of magic light. White morning-glory blossoms twined up the stalks. A silken house of interwoven moving walls sighed and whispered. Unafraid, I had not once thought of being lost, but had gone to sleep. I did not hear their anxious voices, calling, calling.

•   •   •

A copy of John Newton Hughes's memoirs, *Iowa Sketches*, edited and privately published by a distant cousin in 1992, graced Vaneta's coffee table at Sweet Memories. Intrigued by my great-uncle's lyrical account of Scotch Grove life in the late 1800s, I stayed downstairs until late in the night. I read the slim green volume twice, enjoying his descriptions of the varied pitches of bells during bobsled races on the road to the timber and the seasonal variety of wildflowers in virgin prairie sod. But by the second time through, I resented his romanticism about agricultural ties and his equation of good farming with a good course through life. John Newton Hughes described his father arranging a common bedsheet into a sling to pocket the seed, then striding purposefully across the land.

Stripped of coat and vest, and dressed in a hickory shirt and blue overalls, his athletic form appeared at its best. With a steady and confident step, he went forth and back across the field. As one limb went forward the hand reached into the bag. As the other limb moved, the hand was withdrawn and with a firm wide sweep of the arm, the grain was broadcast over the ground about 10 feet in width, falling always immediately ahead of the sower. In all his work he would no more tolerate a crooked row than he would tolerate a crooked act in his business. If the field was a long one, stakes with small white flags would be set as frequently as necessary. With these as guides, he had no difficulty in steering a true course from one end of the field to the other.

Agriculture as the basic metaphor for good living was no surprise to me. I'd gotten it in reverse.

"I don't know what will become of us, Kate," said my grandma when the early snow swirled through the corn still standing in the field. "We just get further and further behind. It's such a shame, such a shame." My mother looked silently out the window, her eyes sad. The shame had to do with my father, who had run away, and my uncle's sons, who had died. That was why Uncle Jim was always behind. Why it always rained on the cut hay. Why the tractor which had stopped running sat apologetically in the middle of the farmyard with grass growing around it. Why the roof of the shed which blew off during the tornado did not get replaced. "We just get further and further behind," my grandma said again.

The surprise in my great-uncle's memoirs was not the underlying metaphor but the briefness of the family ties to the land. My great-grandfather, the first Hughes to come to Iowa, was not born a farmer. He was a shipwright, a trade he had learned from his father after the family moved from Wales to Liverpool. Then twenty-four, he sailed to New Orleans in 1846 and continued inland to Illinois, just east of the Mississippi River. The young man, still not a farmer but a wagon-maker in a county with no ships, married a woman from Cornwall. Her English childhood had been spent in the little village of Tywardreath on Falmouth Bay. The street in front of her home "ended in a broad sheet of shimmering water where she and her companions raced back and forth with the tides." Her parents made their living from the sea instead of the land.

Near Galena, Illinois, my great-grandfather bought some land, a place of scenic beauty with "hills and hollows," timber and a creek. My grandfather Gideon, who returned to see it, pronounced it "not much of a farm," incapable of growing anything but mustard. The "attraction for the picturesque" instead of more practical acreage was due to the "wild country" influence from childhoods spent in Wales and Cornwall. They sold their land to some others who were in love with the picturesque and headed across the Mississippi on the ice in 1870 to try to get it right with the farming.

My great-grandfather's real craft was working with wood, not the land. As a child, John Newton Hughes watched his father with his tools:

> He loved his woodworking tools and could use them with great accuracy and skill. He was continually shaping some timber. I would stand for long periods only to watch the long strokes of the wooden jack plane as he smoothed the surface of some flawless piece of fine oak timber. Then I would pick up the long ribbons that fell in heaps at his feet or beneath the carpenter bench at which he stood, and wear them about my neck.

So this misplaced shipwright, in a sea of grass, is as far back as I can possibly trace the Hughes family in farming.

Of John Hughes's four sons, one, John Newton, became a lawyer and another, William, a newspaper editor. But two actually stayed in farming, and the one who was my grandfather did not take over his father's farm. He bought land of his own.

> Gideon, our oldest brother, was, I believe, most ambitious of all. At ten years, while father was lying very low of pneumonia, [Gideon] harnessed a team and did ten acres of fall ploughing. When a mere boy, with only the help of father's name on the note, he bought a hundred acres of land. He had it free of debt within two or three years. It was stated in the news at his death that he owned in Iowa twelve hundred acres.

My grandfather Gideon was the Hugheses' ticket into the new culture's complicated agrarian myth with its biblical imagery. The most dignified and worthy of callings was the land—a land rightfully assumed because of a promise to people far distant in time and place. Once on the land, you and your progeny were part of a succession that was not only grounded in the Bible, it was meant to endure until Judgment Day. On the family farm.

John Newton Hughes enshrined the small family farm in his account of family and Scotch Grove history, even as he admired the 1,200 acres his brother Gideon amassed. "The farms were surprisingly small, each head of a family desiring to own only so many acres as he and those of his family could farm . . . The greater number of farmers had eighty." This he recorded in a passage that extolled the self-sufficiency of the earliest settlers, those who had made the oxcarts in which they arrived with their own hands. These "steady, hard-handed folk" with "pluck, spirit . . . and a firm grip upon the purse strings" replaced their early log cabins with white green-shuttered houses and wisely planted windbreaks northwest of them.

When I came home from college with Richard Hofstadter's *The Age of Reform* in hand, talking about the "agrarian myth," my mother's hostility was tangible. I might as well have been attacking the church. "It isn't a myth," she said with fierce conviction. "I don't care what those Democrat professors from the cities say. The farmers are the backbone of the country." She quoted William Jennings Bryan from memory: "The great cities rest upon our broad and fertile prairies. Burn down your cities and leave our farms, and your cities will spring up again by magic; but destroy our farms and the grass will grow in the streets of every city in the world."

"Bryan was a Democrat!" I mocked her seriousness. "And you'd never agree with what he said about evolution." I was a sophomore in college and knew everything.

"I don't care." Her chin tilted. "He may have been wrong about evolution, but he was right about the farms." It was a religion with her—or rather, part of the religion that she lived. "You must always be proud of your heritage from the farm."

And I was. I pictured fathers passing their farms forever to their sons in some sort of holy ceremony that went back to Abraham and Isaac.

When my mother married, her father had given her a farm for a wedding present, free and clear of debt—the old Livingston place. But what an embarrassment the letters she left for me in the stationery box revealed. Two years after her marriage, she received an unsolicited inquiry from her uncle John Newton Hughes. He asked whether he could be of financial assistance to her. At first she did not answer.

John Newton Hughes, then a well-known attorney in Des Moines, had been alerted by my mother's brother, Jim, about a notice for delinquent taxes, a lawsuit brought against my mother's land for debts by a lumber company, and a rumor of an impending mortgage. When my mother did not respond to his letter, he tried again, for he was aware that his niece had married a man who had aroused suspicions in the family. Her reply began, "I didn't answer your other letter because there wasn't anything to say."

Her letter must have been extremely painful to write. "Thanks for offering to help. I'm awfully ashamed of the way things have gone, but we got ourselves into this mess and I guess it's up to us to see it through without dragging anyone else into it." She outlined the extent of the debt my father had incurred against the farm that made the mortgage inevitable. Her words cry with the disloyalty she felt in the confession: ". . . but he is so good to me otherwise and we are so happy together when we don't think about business that I couldn't do anything that would be disloyal to him or hurt his pride."

John Newton Hughes knew immediately there was nothing he could do to save the farm. In a letter to the concerned family dated November 15, 1941, he enclosed my mother's letter as evidence that it would serve no purpose for him to come from Des Moines and try to straighten things out. "Her affection for him is so strong and so sincere that so long as she can raise a cent for him she will do it. I am not blaming her. It is a condition that no one can help and never could. It is certainly a crime for that property to be dissipated by him and so unnecessary. I am very very sorry for it all."

But even in the face of what seemed the inevitable loss of the farm, the need to retain the tie to the land for the son was in evidence. John Newton Hughes proposed a plan to fulfill the necessary obligation to the next generation. "Jim, do you think Kate would be willing to place with you . . . a deed to the property she will inherit after her mother's death 'In trust for the benefit of their little boy Robert'? . . . Maybe we could save this property in this way." He was afraid some enterprising lawyer familiar with the extent of the previous generation's fortunes would recognize that a "future interest" in land could be "subject to sale for debts." My brother, for whom this future interest in farming was to be secured, was then a little over a year old.

My father did not stay around long enough for my great-uncle's fears to be realized. The land which was the subject of this last piece of advice came to me in 1968, when my grandmother died, for my mother had preceded her in death. Still mine, the land was rented to a neighboring farmer.

"It was really only one generation," I said to myself. Then I had to say it aloud, for the other reality was embedded in my consciousness in spite of the fact that I had heard the stories of ancestors before and I had known of the shipbuilding, the wagon-making. John Newton Hughes, who went away to successfully argue a case before the United States Supreme Court for the railroad, could safely romanticize his ties with the land. That tie did not bind him as severely as those still on the farm for whom it could quickly snarl into a knot of Gordian proportions. And Adam begat Seth, and Seth begat Enos, and Enos begat Cainan, and Cainan begat . . . and they all were named Hughes and they all were farmers. Or so I thought, or rather felt. For it is what I felt, not what I knew, that determined my reality and my family's reality as well.

A great sadness had pervaded the brown Victorian house in my childhood, and I felt it again, seeping out of the old pictures Vaneta had so decoratively scattered about the not-quite-familiar room in Sweet Memories where I sat. My grandfather Gideon was dead. He died on Christmas morning of 1940. Especially on that morning, when colored lights reflected in the blank windowpanes of our quiet house, I felt the sadness—not just for his death, but for our failure.

The most worthy of callings was to till the soil, and it was the natural order ordained by God that the farm would pass from father to son. My brother and I grew up in the fierce shadow of those beliefs, knowing that our father had failed, that our Uncle Jim had failed, and that maintaining the family farm was that duty-at-which-we-were-all-failing. And we were very, very sorry for it all.

•　　•　　•

Once six horses must have stamped their fringed hooves in the stalls in the old barn, for each manger had a smooth crescent where the necks had rubbed. Once the cutter that stood on the landing in the haymow had velvet seats instead of mice-shredded batting, and bells jingled around the neck of the horse that was harnessed to the little sleigh.

And once a whole row of cows must have been milked together, their tails swatting flies, for the machinery—the separator—still stood quietly in place with big cobwebs holding it together. Once they had made butter in the milkhouse, where now only a small silver pail full of warm milk from the black cow hung for us to carry together, and they put the now silent silver cans of milk in the wagon with the wooden wheels and drove to the creamery in Scotch Grove.

Once the big tank in the attic had been filled with water by the finned wheel, for the wind was the only power and an extra store was needed for the large family. Once water must have run from the brass faucet in the sink in the washroom, for still old overalls and coats hung that no one wore, that were for lining the doors and windows when the wind blew in winter.

All this was before we came, my brother and I, but we knew the strange quietness had something to do with us. We did not talk about it but lived instead in the pretend world on a ranch in the Wild West where we were needed to ride our horses and frighten the wolves away. We played the game at night after our mother had turned out the light, and we played the game in the bush cave in the orchard, and we played the game as we waited for the yellow bus together. When we got back off the bus, we would resume the game, but we did not share the game with others.

Once when I was a little girl I took my mother's broom to the barn. I began to sweep the cobwebs down that formed a ceiling for the horse stalls, but soon after I started, my Uncle Jim came. "What are you doing?" he asked. "I am helping us get less behind," I said. He took the broom from me gently. "This is a house broom," he said. "Take it back to the house." I did not try again.

"Why would you even think of going back?" asked the psychiatrist. "You make it sound like the Museum of American Farming." I had dreamed of the house three nights in a row.

"I don't know," I said, for the thought of returning, the thought of becoming my mother completely, terrified me. I had gone to Coe College, I had become a teacher, I had married a profligate spender, and I had been left alone with two babies and no money. "Surely she is living her life over through me. She is trying to get it right through me and validate her own choices."

4

The Scots

We said our farewells for the last time and took our places on the crowded boats. The shore fell away and above our heads the white gulls whirled in confusion and cried querulously. Duncan Mc-Donald filled his bagpipes, and "Cha till! Cha till! Cha till! mi tuille" came from the chanter with the wail of the Skye in it, and the booming of the angry seas. The wind wafed the plaintive notes shoreward, and the old women on the pier spread their plaids to the sky and cried "Ochanerie" across the widening water.
—*"Men of Kildonan," Scotch Grove Presbyterian Church Centennial Booklet*

Aunt Em's family left early, but Vaneta and I lingered over coffee, sitting by the glass doors she had installed on the north side of the kitchen. The area in which her table stood had housed a latticed back porch in my childhood that had held the "icebox," a leftover term from the early model refrigerator's predecessor.

We looked over the back yard, where chickens used to scratch. The grass was neatly mowed. The sharp black-and-white delineations of a bright red-headed woodpecker were startling against the slanted maple trunk by the garage.

"You've improved it immensely," I said, looking around the kitchen. This was my favorite room as a child, with the Majestic Range stove, the tall natural cupboards, and the swinging door that led to the dining room. Vaneta had stripped the paint from the yellow pine floor and the varnish held the light like a clear jar of honey. The stove still worked. Even the original wooden counter had been sanded down and restored.

Vaneta appreciated my admiration. She knew the community regarded her as rather eccentric for the care and money she had lavished on this house. For the most part, she had remained absolutely true to the original designs. The restoration consumed much of her inheritance, she readily admitted. What she had left was the land, and right now part of that was covered with standing water. She had other land on her mind that morning.

"Paul Ernie Paulsen told me you had a cemetery plot." He was a neighbor and an elder in the church.

"I do. You want to buy it?" I was joking.

"Yes," she said, "I do. I don't know why I've started thinking about that so much lately. Maybe because everybody our age is dropping off with cancer."

"Are you serious? Do you really want it?"

"Yes."

"Why? Are you going to get one for everyone in your family?" I couldn't imagine much enthusiasm from her grown children in Arizona.

"I don't know about them. Actually, I don't think there are any cemetery lots left. I just know about me. And I want one. Would you really sell it? Isn't it important to you to be buried here?"

"No. I mean yes, I'd really sell it, and no, I don't want to be buried here. I feel as if it's taken me thirty years to get beyond all the parochial views I got from living here. I don't want my body trapped in a cemetery with a bunch of Calvinists."

"Your mother's there."

"She was trapped, too."

"Well, I want it, then," Vaneta said emphatically. "How much do you want for it?"

"I don't know. What is it worth?"

"We'll ask Paul Ernie," she decided. We sat for a minute in silence looking out the glass doors. An oriole flew to the young Scotch pines Vaneta had planted to the northwest of the house for a windbreak.

"Can I ask you something, Barb?"

"*Anything*, Vaneta!" We both laughed. For women with infrequent exchanges we know a surprising number of each other's secrets.

"What is your name, *really*?"

"My name is *really* Barbara Scot."

"But your husband's name is Jim Trusky."

"That's right."

"So you were never married to a Scot?"

"No. Why do you ask that?"

"Some people here say that. They knew you as Norris—then as Murphy. And somehow people know you aren't married to a man named Scot. So I've been asked if you were married a third time."

"No," I said dryly, "it only took me twice to get it right." I knew she wanted the story of my name, but I made her ask for it. It annoyed me a little that she insisted on addressing my mail to Barbara Trusky.

"So why Scot? Are you one of those *feminists*?" She arched one eyebrow.

"Yes, I'm one of those *feminists*, but the name Scot didn't start as a feminist issue. It started because I needed a phone. When my first husband departed, he left a long-distance phone bill of $90. I couldn't pay it, so they cut off the phone. I did without it for a month, but I had two babies and I needed a phone. When I called the phone company and gave my name as Barbara Murphy, they wouldn't install a phone until I paid the bill. My credit had gone bad with his. It was obvious I would either have to lie about my name or get a new one. So I decided to change my name."

"Why didn't you go back to Norris?"

"It was the name of a man I never knew."

"Hughes, then. Your mother was named that."

"Not when I knew her. She kept her married name until she died and we kept it with her." For the first time I focused on my resentment at having a name that immediately identified us as abandoned. No one else in the community had shared the Norris name. "I'd heard too many laments from Grandma about the end of the Hughes name with your dad because his infant sons had died."

"*You* heard it—my God, those dead babies had birthdays my folks observed every year. I felt guilty even being alive as a girl."

"Well, *see*. No, I could never have used the Hughes name."

"But why Scot?"

"I sat up that whole night making a list of names I liked—some of them were family names, even, like Clark." Not quite a family name. The side of the family we could never claim. "I especially liked Clark. But people own names. To assume a name that people own is rather presumptuous. I started thinking about other possibilities with historical precedence like occupations and places. Barbara Scotch Grove was obviously awkward. But Barbara Scot sounded perfectly normal. And by using one *t* I wouldn't be taking my name from all the Scotts of the world. I filled a paper with it. Barbara Scot. I liked it. I couldn't wait for the phone company to open."

"So did you lie?"

"It wasn't a lie. By morning it *was* my name. And the phone company came right in and installed a phone for Barbara Scot. I've gone by Barbara Scot ever since. I resented having to get the court's permission, but I did it, rather than face a hassle."

Vaneta stared at me silently. Then she said, "You shouldn't have any trouble understanding why I want to be buried here."

"What do you mean?"

"You're doing the same thing. Only you took it with you and I want to come back to it." She was right, of course. We smiled at each other across the table.

"Barb," she said, "I don't have any money to pay you for the lot now."

"Vaneta," I answered, "the lot means something to you. It means nothing to me. If you'll address my mail to Barbara Scot, you can have the damn cemetery lot."

"Do you mean it?"

"Yes!" We smiled again. The woodpecker was back on the maple and I fastened the binoculars on it.

Vaneta spoke again: "One more question."

"What?"

"Now that you're remarried, isn't your *real* name Barbara Scot Trusky?"

I sighed. I set the binoculars on the table. Much more than the seven-year span in our birth dates separated us on this issue. "Vaneta," I said firmly, "my *real* name is Barbara Scot."

•   •   •

My name was Barbara June. June was when the peony bushes in front of the house dropped their petals. One bush had blossoms as red as the velvet dress on the china-faced doll that was in the bureau in the hired man's room. But there was no hired man. The hired man was a long time ago. I must not play with that doll, because it belonged to Aunt Em. "What is so rare as a day in June?" quoted my mama. "Then, if ever, come perfect days." But I was not a day in June. I was a little girl.

"Your mother wanted to name you June," said my grandma. "But your father wanted to name you Barbara after a silly movie star." But I was not silly. Was I silly? "No," said my grandma, who was peeling potatoes in the gray washbasin with the white flecks. "You are a good girl."

In my mama's old book her name was Katie May Hughes. May was when the jack-in-the-pulpit stood in its little cone under the trees. "See how the cottonwood leaves go from folded birds' feet to round green coins," said my mama. But now her name was Kathleen. Kathleen Hughes Norris. But my grandma said her name was Kate.

We sat on the porch in the evening in our flannel shirts. "I don't know what's going to become of us, Kate," said my grandma. My head was in my mama's lap. Her apron was damp from the dishes. My Uncle Jim came up the slanted sidewalk, which had lines of grass in between the squares of cement.

"Kate," my Uncle Jim said, "have you heard that Pauline had a baby girl?"

"Oh, that's too bad," my grandma said.

"Why do you always say that?" said my mother in a hard voice.

"I just meant it's better to have a son first to have the name secured," my grandma said.

It was too bad about Bert Clark, because he did not have any sons and the Clark name would end with him. And it was too bad about Frank Sutherland, because he had only Eloise and the name would end with her. And it was too bad about Esther Sinclair, because the name would end with her. And Bill and Fannie had only June, so the name would end with them. But the worst of all was Uncle Jim, because his sons had died, so the Hughes name would end with him. "But Bobbie's name is Robert Hughes Norris," I said. "That is not good enough," said my grandma, shaking her head.

We walked to get a little sheet of candy for a penny while we waited for the big kids to get out of school. Then the buses would come. "Now what is your name?" said the man in the store.

"My name is Linda Guyan," said the girl with the blond hair.

"And what is your daddy's name?"

"My daddy's name is Harry Guyan."

"Now what is your name?" said the man in the store to me.

"My name is Barbara June Norris," I said to the man. The hot flush began.

"And what is your daddy's name?"

After my daddy was dead, my Grandma Norris asked my mother to bring us to Minnesota to visit. She was very tall. Her name was Kitsy, but her real name was Mary. "For any sake," she said, "oh, for any sake." And Grandpa Norris had a funny name. It was A.B. The A. was for Arthur.

"What is the B. for?" I asked.

"The B. is for Bumblebee," he said.

We went to the cabin on Green Lake. When we were at the cabin the neighbors came.

"Which Norris are you?" asked the woman in the flowered dress. I did not know what to say, so she said again, "To which Norris do you belong?"

"I don't know," I said.

•   •   •

So my name was Scot, even though I was not descended biologically from the Scottish immigrants who came to the area and established the Scotch Grove Presbyterian Church. But Eloise was. Eloise was my father's first cousin and had actually known my father from childhood. I went to see her as soon as she and her husband, Edwin, returned to Scotch Grove for the summer. Eloise could be counted on for the truth.

The first thing Eloise did was to straighten me out about the Clarks, the lineage she shared with my father. "Well now . . . we have lots of romantic stories about religion and freedom, but it was mostly land that made them move. Or gold. Some of them went on to California looking for gold, but I don't think they found much. Most of them came back here. The first ones had to pay the government $1.25 an acre. The settlers got here before the land office was even set up. Relatives would send for others to come. The Clarks came in successive waves from a Calvinist settlement in Mercer County, Pennsylvania, only a few years after the first Scots came from Canada. So all the Clarks around Scotch Grove are probably related some way or another; certainly the early ones in our church were."

"I'm trying to track a William Clark," I said. John Newton Hughes's memoirs had mentioned a particularly interesting church trial.

"Well now . . . we have Williams and more Williams. Both saints and sinners, no doubt. You know Bert Clark, of course— one of the saints!" We both laughed. He was a beloved white-haired neighbor of my childhood and an uncle of both Eloise and my father. "Bert was W. B. Clark, you know. And the W. was for William. The name William goes back to Pennsylvania. If you find a William Clark in Scotch Grove, he's probably ours one way or another."

Eloise spoke with the distinctive drawl I remembered from childhood. She would start a sentence, pause on the second word, and let it slide along as if she were thinking aloud. Her voice was musical, like a gentle waterfall with silver in it. I had always loved Eloise, even though I never thought of her as a relative because she was on my father's side. No one could be purer Scotch Grove Presbyterian Church than Eloise. Her father was Frank Sutherland, a direct-line descendant of John Sutherland, the leader of the first Scots who arrived in the wooden carts with his wife, Margaret McBeth, and their ten children in 1837.

"Eight boys, would you believe it! The littlest girl, Christi, died the night they arrived at the Maquoketa River. It's all written down right here." Eloise opened one of the pamphlets written for the centennial celebration in 1937. She read aloud, " 'The same night, frightened by a prairie fire, the family fled, the mother carrying the dead baby in her arms.' "

"What a sad beginning."

"It was," Eloise agreed. Then she laughed. "I'll tell you, though, Barbara, my Aunt Josie was the one who gathered the information for this and she was given to drama. She marched those old Scots through snow with the bagpipes playing. I suppose they really did it, though. I've gone back up to Canada. In the Manitoba museum you can see a model of the oxcarts they used to come down here. All wood they were, not a bit of metal, so that they could do all the repairs themselves, as they were four months on the trail. I guess that wood rubbing on wood made an awful screech. I have a whole box of material on church history you can take to Vaneta's with you, although you need to go to Paul Ernie for the manuscripts. Ask him to show you the big map he made for the church." We joined her husband, Edwin, in the living room.

In 1955 Eloise was the first woman elder ordained in the history of the Scotch Grove Presbyterian Church. She was still an elder in the church, although on inactive status because she and her husband spend most of the year in a retirement community in Arizona. They had been going there for thirty years. "We were one of the first families in the retirement community," Edwin told me. "We were there when it was incorporated. Pioneers, that's what we were." He was showing me the videotape of their circuitous trip from Arizona to Iowa this summer. We were up to the part where they visited Lawrence Welk's home. I was more interested in my father's brother Howard, whom they had visited in Montana. Edwin backed up the tape for me.

"You'd love Howard," Eloise said. "Well now"—her voice slid in a musical glissade—"I shared your letter with him." I'd written her earlier to tell her I hoped to be able to see her when I came to Iowa. "We talked a long time about your dad, and I know your Uncle Howard would like to hear from you, Barbara." I'd met him only a few times a very long time ago. He came for my father's funeral. He was tall with black hair. My brother had run to the car. "Are you my daddy?" he had asked. Doesn't he know? I thought. Doesn't he know our daddy's dead?

On the videotape Howard, bald, with a white fringe, played the piano, even though he was now blind. He and Eloise were singing "Faith of Our Fathers." "Oh, how our har-arts beat high-eye with joy." That line evoked unexpected nostalgia for me. I knew I should try to talk with Howard even though he'd been twelve years younger than my father. But I didn't know him well enough to imagine how he'd feel about sharing family information.

"Call him, Barbara," Eloise said again. "You'll be pleasantly surprised. He can tell you some of the good things about your dad, like I'm going to." I resolved to get in touch with him.

"I know my father had good qualities," I said a little defensively. "My mother wouldn't have loved him so much if he'd been rotten to the core."

"He wasn't. And every time I hear about another of your wild adventures like climbing mountains or traveling to some little-known country, I think to myself, 'That's her dad in her.'"

"He never climbed a mountain." I was surprised at the warmth she felt toward him.

"He would have loved to."

"Well, why didn't he, then, instead of screwing up so many lives?" Eloise was right. I wasn't looking for his good qualities.

"You don't have any idea how we were raised. Climbing mountains never would have been a choice for Robert. We always called him Robert in the family, you know. He was named after our grandfather Robert Clark. He was supposed to be a farmer." Eloise was two years younger than my father. Their mothers were sisters. "I was scared to death of my grandfather—that's your great-grandfather Clark. He was a tall, white-haired, long-bearded scarecrow who was blind, and we children had to lead him around. I was only five when he died."

It occurred to me to start worrying about my eyesight. "Tell me anything," I said. "I just want to believe my father was real and human."

"Barbara," Eloise said firmly, "he was one of the most real and human people you'd ever want to meet. Now, they lived in Minnesota, you know, so I have to honestly say I didn't know him that well as a child. For that matter, while he was married to your mother I was in the service, so I don't know a lot of specifics about that, either. All the boy cousins were up in Minnesota and down here it was all girls. He had a terrible birth. My mother stayed with Aunt Kitsy the whole time—two days of hard labor. They thought they were going to lose both Aunt Kitsy and Robert. By the time he was born he had the most awful misshapen head. For a long time the pictures show him wearing a little cap." She paused, honestly trying to think of pertinent information. "Do you know the story about the $1,000?"

"No."

"Well now . . . Robert was given $1,000 when he was born by Grandfather Clark because he was the first grandchild. In 1912 that would have been a lot of money. My mother always thought he never saw a cent of it—although Howard thinks he may have been given some. We all knew about it, so I'm sure Robert did, too. I always wondered if that didn't have something to do with his irresponsible attitude toward money."

I'd never heard anything about this. "Why wasn't he given the money?"

Eloise hesitated. She was reluctant to relay negative information, so she couched it in vague secondhand terms. "They say your grandfather A. B. Norris was a rather hard man, Barbara. My mother certainly thought he was severe with Kitsy and had a story she repeated about him and Kitsy's graduation watch. According to my mother—who may have exaggerated things, of course, in support of a favorite sister—Aunt Kitsy had been given that watch by her father, but A.B. made her sell it to a neighbor when they moved to Minnesota. All her adult life she saw that watch on the neighbor's wrist."

"How strange. Why would he make her sell it?"

"They went through some pretty hard times, you know."

"Is that why my father didn't get the $1,000?"

"No, I don't think so. Howard says he doesn't remember a time when his father wasn't mad at Robert. My mother said she heard A.B. say once that Robert had given him so much trouble that he'd never give him a cent."

"What did he do, for God's sake?" I asked. Eloise shook her head. I told her the story I'd heard about jail.

"I don't think so—at least not that I ever heard. He went to agricultural college for a year—not even a year, really. Once he was away from the iron hand of his father he sort of went wild. He was in the CCC—you know, that New Deal agency—for a while." That was the first and only time I heard that. "Then he was out in California—I remember because an uncle out there wrote my mother and asked why Robert needed money. I know he'd asked my folks for money when he was down here."

"He was apparently good at that." Eloise wasn't helping my opinion of him as much as she had wanted to. "Tell me something good, Eloise, something warm and human that you remember about him."

She thought a moment. "He was always extremely considerate and polite. He told funny stories. It was great fun to listen to him. I know his parents considered it lying, but he was really a very creative dreamer. He was punished severely for lying." She paused again, searching her memory. "As the oldest cousin he was always organizing some game for us when we were together. Once we all went to Yellowstone Park, and I remember him worrying about whether the little ones could see when we were watching the rangers feed the bears the garbage."

"They *fed* the bears garbage?"

"Yes." Eloise could tell I was rather disappointed, but she was too honest to fabricate stories. She tried another tack. "I think your mother fell in love with him because he was so creative and so much fun. You know, her father, Gid Hughes, was a severe man, too. I'll never forget when your folks were on their way to Colorado in that trailer. I just happened to be home from the service—it was during the war, you know, and they stopped in to say goodbye. None of us had ever seen a house trailer that you could pull behind a car before. They showed us the inside. Your mother was excited—and happy in a giddy sort of way—very unlike the quiet woman I knew later."

I just looked at Eloise. This was certainly a new slant for me. Throughout my childhood Grandma had referred in vague terms to an episode in Colorado that involved a trailer and social disgrace. Her ominous innuendos were borne out by the record of the adventure in my box of letters. And my mother had told me something of it the one time we had honestly talked of her marriage when I was in graduate school. "Oh, Barbie, I was so humiliated when I came home," she had said.

"Eloise, if he wanted a life of adventure, why did he marry my mother and try to farm? People went West all the time—even then. Why didn't he just do that?"

"I think he was probably trying to live the life that was expected of him. And the chance for farming fell in his lap with the situation with your mother. He wasn't cut out for it. He wasn't the kind who could wait for crops to grow. He liked new things and changes. He always had a crazy scheme—I will say he exaggerated. And he did seem to feel that money was there for the taking."

He certainly took my mother's, I almost said, but didn't. Eloise was succeeding, in spite of her lack of specific details, in broadening my view. I had to think about what she had said. But I still wanted to get one story straight.

"About when he died," I started. Eloise looked out the window. She didn't want to talk about this very much.

"Barbara, it was the saddest funeral I have ever attended. And by now I've been to more than a few. I just kept thinking, What a wasted life. Your mother sat alone in the back."

I remember the day. I pretended to have a headache and stayed home from school and Grandma stayed with me. It was still cold enough that we had the pocket doors into the parlor closed, with the davenport in the dining room. I curled up there all day while Grandma put the cool washrag on my head.

"I know it was in Luzerne," I said slowly, because I wanted Eloise to confirm a story. "But that seems odd to me, because I'm sure my mother said that he left Edith, too."

"Well, I don't know," Eloise said. But she did.

"There was something about yet another marriage." I wanted her to tell me her version of the events. She was reluctant, because it wasn't going to bolster the more positive view of him she was trying to give me.

"Well . . . I heard that, too." Eloise sighed, and I had an image of her at the church organ she played for so many years. Her sigh was as if she had gently let her finger slide down the keys.

"I don't know if this is true." The usual preface to everything I learned about my father. "Here's what Len Campbell told Uncle Bert Clark, who told my mother. It was said that the car he used when he killed himself belonged to a woman in Colorado. And on the seat was the marriage license. He'd been married again and would have been arrested for bigamy."

It was my turn to sigh. "How did he always get himself into such a jam?" She'd confirmed the story for me. I'd heard it first from my grandmother. "What he did to your mother was terrible, just terrible," she would say when my mother wasn't there. "He never sent her a cent, not a cent. And she wasn't the only one he left with children to support."

"Why didn't he just have affairs instead of getting married?"

Eloise's eyes brimmed with honest tears for a cousin she had truly loved. "Because, Barbara, in his heart he believed all the same things as the rest of us. You don't kill yourself at such a young age because you're irresponsible. You kill yourself because you have a moral core you have violated—or a strict vision of what your life should be and you think you can never attain it."

Well, yes. I can vouch for that.

"And your father wanted so desperately to get it right."

•   •   •

Before my daddy killed himself I used to put a blanket on the short piece of railing on the front porch. This piece of railing by the side steps had a round ball right at the top of the short end pillar so I could pretend I was riding a horse. I did not have cowboy boots, but I had brown rubber boots with a picture of Roy Rogers and Dale Evans on the side. My jump rope was tied around the ball which was the horse's head. Then I would pretend that the man who was coming up the cement walk was my daddy, and when he came to the porch he was going to say, How is my little girl today? But it was really Uncle Jim, and what he said to my mother was She is going to make that post all wobbly if she pulls on it, Kate. But after my daddy killed himself I did not pretend that anymore, because I understood then that he would never ever come back.

I liked to stay with my cousin Shirley because she had a pony named Dandy and she had a daddy named Uncle Dick. Uncle Dick would say you-see-whad-I-mean-see after everything so fast that it all ran together. Then he would say ya-seee again, making it longer, and then he would take a breath. He called me Barb-ra, saying the name so fast that I thought he was talking to someone else. He talked loud and I was a little afraid of him, but Shirley said he liked me. Once we were painting the corncrib together and I fell off the ladder, spilling my bucket of paint. "Daddy would have killed me if I had done that," Shirley said. But her daddy, who was my Uncle Dick, just laughed when he picked me up.

Jack Naylor from Scotch Grove married Alice Clark, who lived up the road at the old Clark place. He had black hair and laughed a lot. My grandma said he was a good man even if he drove his car too fast and made his tractor race around the field. He picked up his little girls and tossed them in the air. He kissed them right there in church.

"Why do you always talk about the ghost of your mother?" asked the psychiatrist. "She wasn't the one who committed suicide." I had carved triangles up the inside of my right arm, but I was not really going to kill myself. In the summer of 1972 I was trying to earn enough money to survive and feed my children by working at a doctor's office, a job procured by a friend of a friend. In spite of seven years of experience and a master's degree in English, I could not even get an interview for a teaching job. I left my babies with a sitter from 8 to 5:30 while I worked at minimum wage for a doctor. I had not paid the rent for two months because I was paying the psychiatrist.

"The ghost of my father, too," I said bitterly.

But I'd be dammed if I was going to kill myself just to satisfy my father's ghost, so I sold my part of the Farm. I sold the Farm so I could quit that worthless job at the doctor's office and go back not to my grandmother's house but to graduate school in history at night when my children slept. So I could pay for the therapy.

I sold the Farm to my brother. I was so deep in personal pain I could not see that he was tottering on his own abyss of alcohol and financial ruin as he lived in a fantasy world that was some confused cross between the grandiose schemes of my father and the land empire of Gideon Hughes. Within a few years he lost the whole damn thing including family relics in a sheriff's sale and disappeared.

We lost the Farm my mother saved.

And she never bought a single thing for herself.

•　　•　　•

Paul Ernie Paulsen was big and wore bib overalls. He gave me a strong hug. "I hoped you'd show up here." He laughed. He and his wife, Evelyn, had just returned from vacation. "You're the talk of the neighborhood, running around the whole square early in the morning."

"No doubt," I sighed. "Some of you ought to get out there and run with me."

"Not me," he said. "Evelyn's doing some walking. You look pretty skinny to me. If all you health nuts are going to quit eating beef, the farmers will go broke. My theory is you need some of that fat on your joints to keep you from getting arthritis."

For several years when his farming operation was thriving, Paul Ernie had rented my land, but our association went deep into my childhood. By church standards he was a latecomer, for it was only in the 1940s that he moved onto the old Angus Sinclair place, which was directly east of Sweet Memories. But in my life he was a fixture, an elder in the church, a farmer whose form I recognized on his tractor across the field. I wanted to see the map he had made of the journey of the Scots. He also was the somewhat unwilling possessor of the entire archives of the church. "I told the session we've got to put this stuff somewhere so it won't burn up if there's a fire," he complained as he hauled the cardboard boxes from his study.

We had to climb to the attic for the map. "I made it for the young people," he said. "If you don't understand your history, you don't know where you're going."

"Something like that," I agreed. "At least you certainly don't understand where you've been." John Newton Hughes's memoirs credited much of our own family's mental and moral fortitude to the guidance of the Scotch Grove Presbyterian Church. I had to agree. Every single Sunday. We went every single Sunday of my life. I could picture in detail the shift of light and shadows at the front of the sanctuary as the seasons changed. How could I hope to understand my mother without understanding the church?

"Too bad Esther Sinclair has died," Paul Ernie huffed as he climbed the ladder stairs. "She coulda told you an earful—not only about the early Scots, but about your mom as well. And she woulda, too." We both laughed. Esther had lived alone and her penchant for long phone conversations on the party line was legendary. We emerged from the ladder into a large attic that covered the entire house.

Starting in Sutherlandshire in the Highlands of Scotland, where the enclosures for sheep had forced the tenants from the land, the colored lines Paul Ernie used on his large map traced the first short trips north to the Orkneys and then the long voyages to Canada. "Sorta like the Puritans," Paul Ernie said, "except the Scots went to Canada first instead of Holland. And of course, it was later, 1837, by the time the first party made it to the Maquoketa River. The place, according to all the old accounts, where the prairie met the woods. That's the phrase they used."

He stepped closer to the map. The light was dim in the attic. "Actually, it's the *Mayflower* and the Oregon trail all in one." He put his large finger with the blunt nail on the sketch of the first colony layout, the juncture of the Assiniboine and the Red River, the site of present-day Winnipeg. Slowly he traced the thread through Minnesota, beside the Mississippi River to Dubuque, the old Red River Trail. "They stayed on the land except for old Grandma Livingston. She fell off the cart and broke her leg, so one of the grandsons had to float her down on a raft on the Mississippi." Then he moved his finger to the west. "The oxcart part of it was over a thousand miles, mostly on foot. They spent the final night right here at Dales Ford on the Maquoketa. Or at least the first party did, the one led by John Sutherland. You know where I mean, don't you? Where the old bridge washed out in the flood of '51. Down below Millie Kuper's house."

Yes, I knew where he meant. I didn't even have to close my eyes. "Just over there is where they crossed during Black Hawk's time. In 1833 Jefferson Davis and Abraham Lincoln pursued the Indians to the ford. The river was swollen with summer flood and some of the Indians stood guard while the others swam over." Millie Kuper had told me once when I came as a child on the horse.

"Yep," said August Kuper, rocking back on his heels as he talked, his overalls loose and cool over his bare shoulders. "We used to find quite a few arrowheads down toward the water." Indians, I thought with excitement as I threaded my way to the bluff. I pictured myself in a buckskin dress and shaded my eyes as I stood on the smooth rock high above the coiled river.

By the time I went to Dales Ford it was late afternoon. I left Paul Ernie's house in Scotch Grove and followed the straight, well-graded road to the east. As I turned north, I could see the house on the road branching south where Esther Sinclair used to live. Suddenly curious, I brought the camper to a stop at the side of the road. The house had brown siding instead of the peeling white paint I remembered from my weekly piano lessons. I would go that way when I returned to Sweet Memories, I resolved, shifting back into first gear. The last Sinclair. I pictured us sitting together on the doorstep after my piano lesson. Paul Ernie was right. I could have learned a lot from her. I had, in fact, but more about the history of the Scots than about my mother. Esther was my mother's contemporary. They had attended Coe College together and remained friends. Why did I remember her only now that I needed her? I thought with sudden guilt. Surely my mother would have wanted me to keep in touch with Esther.

Reaching the small sign that declared the location of Dales Ford, I parked the camper at the top of the hill. Even the large-wheeled carts of the Scots would have had trouble navigating these deep ruts the recent heavy rains had used as funnels to the river. Apparently the Boy Scout camp that had briefly flourished in my high-school days was no longer here. The wide swale that had once marked the wagon road to the sandy ford was choked with young maples, ash, and poison ivy. Still evident, however, were the steel pilings on either side of the river used for the bridge that had washed out in 1951. One leaned permanently askew in muddy water that had barely abated with a three-day respite from the rains. The sandy bar I remembered was not visible in the middle because of the high water, but on the far side an ecru mound molded smoothly into the river. There we had crossed the bridge for a picnic when I was so small that my mother had carried me down the bank. The picture I used to have, taken with her old Brownie box camera, showed me wearing a little bonnet, so I must have been very young. Perhaps I remember the day so well because of my mother's laughter.

I rode in the back seat singing because I was happy about the picnic. We were in my grandpa's car, but my grandpa was not there. He had never been there. The sun-gold leaves whirled by the window. After my mama carried me down the bank, I was allowed to take off my shoes. The fine sand squeezed through my toes like flour. I slid off the blanket because I wanted to feel it on my legs. In the shade of the bridge the sand was cold like my mama's Sunday dress, but in the sun the sand was warm.

She cut a long stick for my brother and tied a string on it, fastening a safety pin on the end. The leaves were red, and up above, the big birds circled and circled. When she stuck the end of the pole in the sand for him, the silver pin flashed in the shallow water. Again and again we filled the lard bucket and poured water in the hole we had dug with wooden spoons. And my mama knelt beside us, making magic shapes with wet sand.

There would be no wading the river today, as I had thought of doing. The water was simply too deep, even at this sandy ford that in a usual summer's flow would afford passage. I turned to the right on an ill-defined road that followed the riverbank. The linden trees were in bloom and I could hear bees high above me. Across the river a cardinal called from a cottonwood tree that hung above the water. A wren warbled incessantly from the dense shrubbery behind me.

The woods seemed so thick and tangled that I was glad for the indefinite lane. The Scots couldn't cross now, I thought. The water level must be more as it was when Jefferson Davis and Abraham Lincoln watched the natives swim the river. I knelt to pick up small marble-sized green walnuts that had blown off in storms, feeling some comfort from their familiar oily smell.

A little meadow opened on my right. An old car rusting in a gully at the edge of the clearing surprised me. How did it get there? Somewhat disappointed, I turned around and retraced my steps. A hairy woodpecker, black and white with spotted wings, drilled high in a maple between me and the river. I stopped by the pilings again. On the other side of the water five birds, dark and large, circled in the sky. Turkey vultures, probably, I decided, swinging the binoculars in place. I was right. I fastened my sight on the bridge piling across the river that was partially obscured by greenery. A slim dark bird perched on the tilted cylinder. White band on black tail. Eastern kingbird. This time I knew without looking in the book. Perhaps they were quite common, after all.

Suddenly my brother ran up the bank. "A fish, a fish, I have a fish!" he cried, and my mother looked at him in disbelief. "A fish, a fish!" he cried again, and so we ran to the water and there it was, a little silver fish that had come as an offering to the safety pin. It hung like a little Christmas ornament, but when my mother put it in the lard bucket, which she had filled with water, it came alive again. "I caught a fish," my brother said proudly. My mother, who was kneeling by the little bucket, smiled and clapped her hands when the little fish began to swim. And then she laughed, her face framed with the red leaves across the river. And then we all laughed and danced together, making a circle in the sand.

·   ·   ·

The brown-and-white owl lived in the old-barn-where-the-Henrichs-place-had-been. Every time my brother and I rode our bikes to the piano lesson at Esther Sinclair's house we stopped at the barn. If we looked in the hole where the boards were broken out, we could see the owl and the owl could see us. Its big eyes shone like new pennies. The owl was a good bird, said my mother, and we must never throw things or scare it. Sometimes people were mean to owls, but that was because they did not understand their habits. Owls were different from other birds because they came awake at night. If the owl did not live in the barn, the mice would eat all the oats that Uncle Jim put in the barn. So we must be kind to the owl. But we must not be late for the piano lesson.

I sat on the dimpled stones outside the door while my brother sat at the piano. The cats rubbed my legs and the kittens played with my shoestring. Today my brother went first for the lesson. When he played his lesson first, he rode his bike home before my lesson was done. So I could listen to Esther's stories for a long time. "She talks and talks," scolded my grandmother.

That was because she lived alone, my mother explained. She had come home after she finished college to care for her parents, who were old and ill. Honour thy father and thy mother. When they died she was all alone because the young man to whom she had been engaged had grown tired of waiting. He eloped with another woman. "Your grandma thinks everyone should be busy all the time," said my mother.

The stones on which I sat while I waited for my brother to finish made steps to Esther's porch. They were round and older than old. Esther had told me the story. They came from Scotland, brought by someone in her family. They had been carried on the boat and then in a wooden cart for thousands of miles to grind flour. I did not think so. Flour came in a sack that my grandma hemmed for dishtowels. But Esther said it was true.

Esther was the last Sinclair. Laura Sinclair, who had a voice like a beautiful bird, had lived on the other farm, said my grandma. But she got the cancer and died. So now only Esther was a Sinclair, which was a special thing to be, because they had been here in the beginning. In the beginning, God. And the Sinclairs. And the Sutherlands.

Esther knew the stories of the beginning. The Sinclairs had come from a land far, far to the north, almost at the top of the world. Caithness and Sutherlandshire. The boat in which they came across the sea had a huge bin of oatmeal and a bull and cow from Rosshire. "Theirs was a hard life," said Esther, "and they were hard people, too. Even in the Scotch Grove Church they wouldn't allow any musical instrument for years and years. And the young people were not allowed to dance."

Esther was an old maid. She lived with cats in the house. "Think of it," said my grandma. "To live like that." Grandma did not want our cats in the house. I liked Esther's cats. Sometimes the big black cat slept under the piano bench when I played my lesson. The kittens had untied my shoestring. Now my brother was playing his scales.

Esther did not have a beautiful bird voice like Laura Sinclair, who had died. She had a voice that talked on the party line. Seventeen parties were on our line. We heard every ring. Esther's ring was one long and one short. To talk on the telephone was to waste time. That is why my Uncle Jim did not have a telephone. If he had a telephone, Aunt Frances would waste time on the party line. "To talk like that is a disgrace!" said my grandma. My mother sighed but did not say anything.

But the biggest disgrace was that Esther Sinclair, whose great-grandfather had been one of the pioneers who'd founded the Scotch Grove Presbyterian Church, had joined the Catholic Church in Monticello. The Catholic Church! "It's a disgrace," said my grandmother. "I can't think what Donald Sinclair would say."

My mother was making my Sunday dress longer by letting out the hem. "She did it because she was lonely and sad. She felt that the people in our church were mean to her. And because she wanted to play the organ music." Esther had gone to Coe College with my mother. Esther could make her short fingers swoop over the keyboard like swallows in evening.

Now it was my turn for the lesson. My brother ran out the door toward the bikes. A cross with Jesus on it hung above the piano. This Jesus was not the same as Jesus in our church. The Jesus in our church was carrying a lamb. Esther's Jesus had stretched-out arms. That was because Esther was a Catholic. "What's wrong with the Catholics?" I had asked my mother. "Nothing," she had answered. "They just have bigger barns than the Presbyterians."

I did not play my lesson very well. "You must practice more," said Esther. "You should not waste your mother's money." I was ashamed of myself. The black cat was not under the piano bench. But Esther played a duet with me at the end of the lesson. "You should practice more," she said. "You could do well in music." And when I begged, she played the song that made her hands fly like little birds over the keys.

After the lesson we sat on the stones. She could not tell a story today, she said, for she was tired. She had not slept last night.

"Where is the big black cat?" I asked. The kittens were playing with my shoestrings again. "He's dead," said Esther. But then she did not talk. Esther always talked. She talked and talked. But that day she did not talk. Instead, she began to cry. Not big sobs, like I made when I told my mother later. She cried with no sobs at all and just tears running down her face. I put my arms around Esther. She did smell like cats.

"Some boys ran over her big black cat and they threw him up on the grass. And they yelled dirty things about her being an old maid and roared away honking their horn and laughing." That is what I said to my mother later. "Oh dear," said my grandma. "How mean people can be to each other."

My mother was quiet and sad. We cut up the apples for a pie. My mother rolled out the dough on the breadboard. "You'll never know how much it can hurt to have people say things like that. I hope you'll never know." My mother took the pie she had baked to Esther. I felt very bad about the black cat.

And I felt bad about the owl. The next week when we rode to the piano lesson the owl was not in the barn. It was out on the fence. Someone had shot the owl and nailed it to the gate where Uncle Jim had the sign that said NO HUNTING. The head hung sideways and the eyes were no longer bright like new pennies. The wings were stretched out and nailed to the fence. My mother would be sad and my Uncle Jim would be sad. I felt very, very bad about the owl.

5

Faith of Our Fathers

Faith of our fathers! living still
In spite of dungeon, fire, and sword,
O how our hearts beat high with joy!
—Hymnal, Presbyterian Church, 1933

John Newton Hughes first alerted me to the fact that public scandal in our family was not limited to my father by including in his memoirs the church trial of William Clark, Jr., whose crime was "anti nuptial fornication." He used the story, which was taken directly from the Scotch Grove Presbyterian Church records, to illustrate to his progeny the early church's effectiveness in restoring wayward youth to the fold. Less pious than my great-uncle, I was intrigued both by my own genealogical connection to the sinner and by his audacity. I had books and photocopied records spread over the dining table at Sweet Memories.

"I suppose they meant 'ante' as in antebellum," I speculated to Vaneta. "Some well-meaning revisionist scribbled an *e* over the *i* in the manuscripts. But if Uncle John thought it should have been corrected so as not to embarrass the church fathers, he would have changed it in his rendition of the trial."

"Either way she was pregnant when they got married, right?" Vaneta asked. We locked eyes. Both products of the fifties, we mentally reviewed our list of high-school girls who'd been pregnant when they were married.

"How did they ever dare?" I was honestly baffled. "He was the son of an elder!" I had figured it out with the records. We both laughed. But it hadn't been funny to my mother. "I can't bear any more shame, Barbara, I can't even talk about it," she said when I asked what would happen if I came home pregnant.

I read aloud from the Scotch Grove Presbyterian Church session records of 1859.

The session then proceeded to the consideration of charges against Wm Clark Jr now brought by common force and well known to the members of the session, viz: That he is guilty of anti nuptial fornication, his wife having presented him with a male child within less than four months from the time of their marriage in June last, and that he also without making any acknowledgement to the church partook of the communion on the 3rd of July last.

"*Well*," sniffed Vaneta in mock seriousness as she bid me good night, "I'm certainly glad this is coming from the *other* side of your family."

William C. Clark first came under scrutiny from the elders in February 1859 because of rumors of "unchristian conduct." The immediate infraction with which the session dealt was that William had been "engaged in a ball or dancing party." William Clark immediately confessed to the dancing and promised to "carefully avoid such occasion of offence in future." Initially the investigating committee did not report on the "other rumors."

The "other rumors" apparently confirmed themselves by the precipitous arrival of William Clark's son only four months after his marriage in June. That meant that by October the session was ready to act. The elders "proceeded to the consideration of charges" that William Clark was "guilty of anti nuptial fornication." This sin, interestingly enough, was never mentioned in isolation. Of at least equal concern to the session was the fact that William Clark "partook of the communion on the 3rd of July last" without confession of the sexual misconduct. This insistence on complete honesty before God remained part of the Scotch Grove Presbyterian consciousness into my childhood. "You must never lie," said my mother. "The

Catholics have confession," said the minister. "But to be a Presbyterian is to approach God directly. He knows. If you are telling a lie, even by omission, He knows."

He knows. If I squat quickly behind the rosebush, He knows. If I touch myself there in the bath, He knows. He knows, He knows, He knows.

How had they dared? In 1859?

I was also interested in the fact that William Clark's wife was not included in the proceedings. The session minutes indicated strict vigilance of other women's moral behavior. Only after combing marriage and church records was I able to establish that his wife had not been a communicant of the church, and the elders were scrupulous in observing such boundaries.

They were equally scrupulous in pursuing a case to the final resolution. From February 16, 1859, until late in the fall of the same year "Wm Clark Jr" was not far from the elders' minds, as frequent references in the minutes indicate. On November 5, 1859, William Clark was "restored to the communion and Christian fellowship of the church" after he acknowledged his sin to the elders and consented to the reading aloud of the minutes of the trial proceedings to the entire congregation.

This pleased John Newton Hughes.

The duties of the ruling elders as guardians of the flock had been successfully performed . . . Many years after this occurred I saw this same William Clark regularly on Sunday mornings sitting in his pew with his wife and family by his side . . . His heavy shock of hair and his thick beard were snow-white, his limbs were bent and stiff from the effect of hard farm work. We all knew him for a good man and would not have thought that in his youth he could have been a defendant in a Church trial.

I gathered all my sources from the table, stacking them in tidy piles. The case certainly presented an interesting contrast for me. My father's scandalous behavior, which had so imprinted itself on more immediate community memory, had received no such attentive concern from the elders of the Scotch Grove Presbyterian Church, which he had joined when he married my mother. The monthly minutes from the church session meeting following his flamboyant departure in 1943 with another married woman within the community stated, "Little of note has occurred to report to the session." That meeting was held at the home of W. B. Clark.

I felt uncomfortable, almost angry, at my great-uncle's description of William Clark's piety in later life and his use of the story to illustrate the successful process of bringing sinners back to the fold. It implied to me the familiar lesson from my childhood: Play by the rules of the church and your life will turn out all right. Repent and conform. Not only was that an oversimplified approach to life, I thought irritably, John Newton Hughes didn't even have the right William Clark.

The materials I had gathered indicated that the William C. Clark, Jr. (whose wife was Flora), of the trial was not one and the same as the William Clark who had served as an elder during John Newton Hughes's childhood. (Uncle John's William had a wife named Margaret Jane.) Uncle John, a pious man writing private memoirs, had not been aware of the Clark penchant for naming male offspring William.

If my sources were correct, the William C. Clark, Jr., of the church trial transferred to the "Four-Horn" United Presbyterian Church of Wayne Township west of Scotch Grove in 1861. He then enlisted in Company D of the 9th Infantry, part of the loyal citizenry of Scotch Grove who "sprung up from all sides ready to sacrifice their lives" in the Civil War. William C. Clark, Jr., died on April 16, 1862, and is buried in the National Cemetery at Springfield, Missouri. He was honored by his country before he had a chance to be tempted into sin again.

Vaneta was expecting guests at Sweet Memories the next day, so I carried the books and papers to the bedroom in successive loads. Not that it mattered *which* Clark it was, I said to myself as I climbed the stairs with the last load of papers. Eloise was right, they were all related some way. I looked out the window on the stairway landing. Lightning flashed in the distance, portending still another thunderstorm before morning. I felt a momentary anger at them all, Clarks and Hugheses alike. I'd been taught that a particular spiritual order gave definition to life. Rights and wrongs strictly adhered to brought their own concomitant reward. Confess and make peace with God and you died revered with a long white beard. Run away with the neighbor woman and you died by your own hand at thirty-seven. Thou shalt not bear false witness. Thou shalt not commit adultery.

I shut the door to the blue bridal suite—almost too hard—I didn't want to wake Vaneta. Look where that got *you*, I said silently to my mother in her wedding picture. No one followed the rules more faithfully than you. And John Newton Hughes commended you as a "true woman." "Your faith in Bob, and your loyalty to him is no more than a true woman could give under the circumstances . . ." Well, I followed the rules pretty faithfully myself for a long time, I said to her resentfully. Even the ones about sex. And look where that got *me*.

•   •   •

Because tomorrow was church my brother and I took a bath together in the tub with the funny clawed feet. The blue heater had an oily smell and the flame showed through the curved door. Beside the heater the warmth came in wavy lines. My mama had carried the water from the black stove up the back stairs. It hissed when she poured it in the tub. But the water from the spout was cold. When we sat in the tub the water was warm, but our skin had the bumps like when my mama scalded the pinfeathers from the chicken. "Now you must wash down there," she said, giving us each a soapy washrag. When we stood by the heater with the biggest towels she said, "Because boys are different, that's why. And when you get married that's how babies are made." "By boys?" I asked. "By both," she said. My brother and I giggled together. "But you must never, never touch each other there."

The most exciting thing of all was when I stayed overnight with my cousin Shirley. Then we could ride the pony, whose name was Dandy. Someday maybe I would get a pony. One night when I stayed with Shirley we went to the Minstrel Show in Monticello because of the Lions Club. No lions were there. Just people dressed up funny with black faces and red lips. One man who was dressed in a skirt pranced across the stage. He had two coconuts tied on his chest. His face was black but his lips were like a clown's. "I've got a lovely bunch of coconuts," he sang, and bounced the coconuts in his hands. People laughed and laughed. Shirley and I laughed and laughed. "Why are their faces black? What did the coconuts mean?" I asked my mother later. She had not known we were going to the Minstrel Show. She did not laugh. "It means you won't go to such silly shows again," she said.

When I was ten years old I could be in the 4-H. Head, heart, hands, and health. But I must be in girls' 4-H. That was the rule. Sometimes girls were in boys' 4-H, but they had to be in girls' 4-H first. Then they could lead a calf at the Great Jones County Fair. But boys were never in girls' 4-H. We did not have a calf. The calves belonged to Uncle Jim. So my brother could not be in the 4-H. 4-H meetings were on Saturday. I had to give a demonstration. How to sew on a button. First you put the thread through one hole. Then the other hole. Before you tie the knot you wind the thread under the button so it will not be too tight against the shirt. Outside the window the sun was shining and the fall leaves blew by the glass. I did not like to be inside on Saturdays. "You do not have to be in 4-H," said my mother, smiling. I was so happy I ran through the field. When I fell down I rolled and rolled in the tall grass. The long blades of grass made straight lines on my arms.

My brother and I wore T-shirts and jeans. "You must not let her wear overalls all the time," my grandma said to my mother. "She does not act like a girl." One day my chest was sore on the left side. When my mother looked at it, she said, "Soon you will not wear T-shirts anymore." I cried and cried, because I did not want to look like a girl. I wore an elastic belt around my chest at night. But when I was in seventh grade my mother sent for a bra so I could wear it on gym days when we had to undress for the shower.

By the creek stood a large cottonwood tree. One huge limb stretched across the water where we put rocks to make a pool. But the best limb was higher still. If I climbed to the first limb I could reach the big round knot where the branch had broken off. When I stood on the knot I had to press my body hard against the tree and hang on to the bark, which was gnarled in deep crevices. I liked the feel of the bark. I grabbed the small branch, and when I pulled myself up with my arms my body ached. When I reached the next large limb, I sat on it as if it were a horse, leaning my face against the arch and feeling the gnarled ridges of the bark between my thighs.

If I did not get up we would be late. I lay on the carpet at the top of the stairs because my stomach hurt. It was not a pain I had felt before. But I wanted to go swimming with my brother, who impatiently snapped his towel. "Come on," he said. "You're not sick." We were going to the band concert in Monticello. My mother and Esther Sinclair would sit in the car and listen to the band while my brother and I swam in the pool. I did not swim in the pool that night; instead, I sat in the car with my mother and Esther. The stomachache did not go away until the next day when the red finally came. "Now you are a woman," said my mother. "My little girl is now a woman."

In ninth grade the home economics teacher said this to our class of girls: "You are never too thin to wear a girdle. It is a signal to men if you do not wear a girdle. They know what it means. So you must always wear a girdle." The boys were not there. They were in shop class. My mother did not wear a girdle. She wore a garter belt. "I think you are too thin," my mother said. "You don't need a girdle." I was now five foot six and weighed 105 pounds. I repeated what the teacher had said. The other girls had girdles. My mother shook her head, but we got out the catalogue. We ordered the smallest size. It was too big, but I wore it over two pairs of underpants.

My boyfriend and I sat in the car. A pair of foam dice hung over the rearview mirror. "Not there," I said. "You should not touch me there." But I wanted him to. So he did again. My mother turned on the porch light. I was so embarrassed. We sat up straight in the car. We talked about school. My mother flicked the light on and off. I was so embarrassed. We talked about God. He was thinking of becoming a minister.

Then my mother opened the front porch door. "Barbara, it is time to come in." I wanted to die. I stormed into the house.

"We were talking about God," I said to my mother, who was reading at the table. She did not answer. "You embarrassed me," I said loudly. She looked up from her book.

"Don't talk so loud," she said. "You'll wake up Grandma." I said I didn't care. "I've been married, Barbara, it's not as if I don't know what people do."

"Well, I'm not married," I said.

"Don't let that be a problem," she said.

In college I was in love. But I saw the boy only on vacations because he went to another school far away. We wrote every day and our letters were full of desire. His family lived in Chicago and he drove his mother's blue Impala to see me. We went to the farm and he slept in my brother's room. My mother and grandma were very polite, but he was not a farmer. He brought a rosebush for my mother. I could tell she was embarrassed. We had only pink old-fashioned roses by the house. "Where can we go?" he whispered. The moon was very bright and the inside of my arms ached.

"We are going for a drive," I told my mother. She looked at me carefully.

"I love you," she said.

I wanted to and he wanted to. But there was nowhere to go. I did not want a neighbor to come by on the road. So I opened the gate at the old Ebenezer Sutherland place, across from where the number five school had been. We drove down the lane.

But I was afraid. "If you loved me you would," he said. The next year we planned to marry.

"That's not it," I said. It had to do with my mother's shame, but I could not explain that. We sat quietly. He did not want to hurt me, but he was disappointed. He had driven all the way from Chicago. He put his head in my lap. I could see the dark shapes of the feeder calves behind the car. They were curious about the car in the moonlight.

The car began to rock. But we were not making love. The calves had come up to nuzzle the car and it rocked like a boat. My boyfriend sat up in surprise and we began to laugh. But he was afraid of the calves. I got out of the car and shooed them away. We drove home in the moonlight with the lights off. "I thought they were buffalo," he said.

We sat in a bar in Germany. My mother was dead and my grandma was dead, too. I had married a boy from the farm, but he had become a doctor. Now he was becoming a surgeon. The marriage was over, but we were not brave enough to say it aloud. He was explaining to me that he needed to experience more women. Or that he had experienced more women. Or that he needed more experienced women. I could not think because of the blue smoke in the bar. I did not know what to say. I had left the baby with an elderly couple because I thought he wanted to see me. What was I going to do? My mother was dead. Where do you go when there is no one to go home to? "Do you know," he said expansively, for he was explaining sex to me, "that I have never made love to a virgin?"

Virginity. Yes, that is what the home economics teacher had said. The greatest gift a woman can give her husband. That is why we must all wear girdles. "Me," I said. "How about me?"

"But you were my wife," he said.

•   •   •

I let myself out of the house quietly and jogged west on the spongy road. By starting this way I could make an entire loop around the square. I turned left at Vaneta's B&B sign. Sweet Memories Lane. I passed the old Clark place. Only one shed set back from the road remained, and a tree with a CENTURY FARM sign tacked to it, designating that it had been one hundred years since the prairie sod was turned. "I do remember when your father and mother were married, though," my father's cousin Alice Clark Naylor told me. "Your father must have been staying with us, and a few days before the wedding they asked me to take a walk with them from our farm to your mother's place. I could see the love your mother had for your father that day, and I was nervous about them—not really knowing why. I remember the wedding, too. I can still see Laura Sinclair Lacock singing 'Always.' "

Approaching the next corner, I could barely see the outline of the barn from the old Len Campbell place, where Edith, the woman who went to Colorado with my father, had lived. My scorned mother never exhibited fury, only bewilderment. "I didn't believe it was possible for him to do such a thing, but Bob has left me and the children and has gone out west with another woman—the daughter of a man he always said was one of his best friends," she wrote her uncle John Newton Hughes when she asked for legal advice. "It's humiliating to me to think he left me for her. She was married but was not living with her husband. She was denied custody of her three year old girl."

Vaneta and I had discussed this a few nights ago. "I don't get it, either," I had said. "She certainly sounds like a total switch from my mother."

Vaneta had answered, "Of course she was a switch. The guy had screwed up royally. I don't know exactly what that trailer fiasco in Colorado was, but my guess is, he ended up in jail." We had been rereading the pertinent letters. "Don't you think that Hotel Joyce letterhead was probably just stationery he managed to pick up somewhere? He himself mentions being behind in payments and 'unlawful sale of property.' The story here was that he'd been in deep trouble anyway. But one person here knew the truth and that was your mother."

"But she took him back."

"That's what you did then, you took them back. And some of us, my dear, still do. For better or for worse."

"So why did he leave her, then, if she was willing to take him back, lies and all."

"Barb, he was living with a saint. Saint Kathleen. Think of it. Has anyone ever said anything negative about your mother to you?"

"No. Never."

"So here's your dad, who has just put the nicest woman in the world through all sorts of grief, only to be forgiven, and he surely hates himself, right?"

"I hope so."

"So he finds a woman who is at least equally screwed up who tells him he's wonderful. No wonder he runs away with her. As long as your dad was with Aunt Kate, he was trapped into trying to be the kind of person he just couldn't be."

Jogging along, I decided that what Vaneta had said certainly made sense. Unexpectedly, I stepped in a pothole filled with water and almost fell trying to regain my balance. Now I had one totally soaked foot. This road once was Highway 38, but now it was marked with signs that read LEVEL B ENTER AT YOUR OWN RISK. Blackbirds chirped in the cattails along the ditch, not quite awake enough for full song. Puny corn in the field to the east was almost totally flooded out. I turned the corner, heading straight east, away from the Len Campbell place.

Maybe I was being too hard on my father because I was privy to my mother's pain. It's not as if he, with his curious elopement, created as much as an original variation on an old theme—even for the Scotch Grove Presbyterian Church. Consider J. Lewis Corbett and Elizabeth Bently. They had the elders wringing their hands in despair in the yearly report to the Dubuque Presbytery for 1869. "A spirit of worldliness and some intemperance and other vices exist, and the state of vital Godliness is far from being such as we could desire throughout the congregation around."

The "general rumor" of "scandalous conduct" investigated by the church revealed that Elizabeth Bently had engaged in the sin of adultery and "attempted to elope with her own brother in law,

J. Lewis Corbett, and other aggravations." The name of J. Lewis Corbett was ordered "to be stricken from our roll." He and his wife had been called to task before for holding dances in their home.

I wondered where the lovers had been headed when the elopement was aborted. My father's adventure had been threatened with a similar fate. "Len Campbell came and said he would have them arrested," my mother had told me. "He didn't want me to file for divorce because that would release Bob legally. He said he would make him come back. It even went through my mind that maybe somehow it could all be the way I wanted it to be—just for a second it flashed in front of my eyes—but I shook my head because I knew it could never be."

By this time I had rounded the third corner and turned north toward the church. The old homestead site at the road junction remained a working farm of sorts although no livestock was in evidence. A plastic deer stood in the windbreak northwest of the stately old house. Who lived here now? I slowed down and walked as I approached the church.

I wondered as I opened the door how many churches would dare leave the door unlocked today. I left my shoes outside, but my wet socks still made damp prints on the floor. My pen had slipped out of the notebook when I was running. I rummaged around in the small room where I had first had Sunday school and later communicants class. Nothing. On a table in the back of the sanctuary two pencils stood in a cup. I took one. "I'll leave it with Vaneta," I promised aloud.

I went over to the north side of the church and counted up four pews. Or was it five? We sat in the same place for years and years. I stood, baffled, at the end of the row for a minute, placing all the other families. On the south side I could see Frank and Blanche Sutherland. Edwin and Eloise. Bert and Ella Clark. Jack and Alice Clark Naylor with their daughters. Ruth Clark Grom with her three sons. Paul Ernie and Evelyn Paulsen with Sherry and the rest. On our side, Arthur and Mary Wilcox with Jeanette. It must be the fourth row, I decided, and sat down. I was surprised that my feet touched the floor, as I remembered my mother putting her hand gently on my knee when I was swinging my feet during the service.

Each pew had a Bible, a Revised Standard Version. I took the one from the little cradle in front of me. Engraved on the front was *In Memory of Kathleen Norris.* I'd forgotten we did that. I liked the King James version better myself, but my mother thought it was ridiculous that people refused to change. "It's all translation, anyway," she had said when I argued that they were changing the words of God. My vehemence seemed amazing now. Indeed, the whole argument did. I picked up the hymnal. I remembered a green book and this was maroon. Same hymns, though. "Faith of our fathers, living still."

Only my father was not living still, and it wouldn't have done any good to tell me as a little girl that it was a problem of misplaced modifiers in my mind. I thought of it every time. He was dead, most ignominiously. And you must never, never lie. "What does your daddy do?" "He ran away . . . He's dead." The pause. They knew. It was very, very bad.

Here I was again, thinking about him dying.

In Oregon when I felt the dark seductive swirl pull down again I said to the psychiatrist, "I don't get it. Why am I still thinking about it? I thought that was all behind me." "Don't do it," she advised. "Your children will never get over it."

And I never let myself think of suicide again, because the last thing in the world I wanted was for my kids to duck their heads in shame and confusion.

Golden light streamed through the church as the sun hit the yellow pane in the window beside me. In the front of the sanctuary the ray centered on the small baptismal font and made a shadow of the cross on the wall. I wasn't uncomfortable there—a place of such warm memories, really, and such good people. I just didn't find God inside buildings anymore. I wanted to see the sunrise, so I got up and left the sanctuary. After retrieving my shoes from the cement platform, I sat down on the top step to put them on.

I didn't feel like being hard on my father this morning, even though there was no denying my mother's pain. Thirty-seven was awfully young to die. Maybe Vaneta was right, it wasn't just his faults that had made the situation impossible. After all, lots of people got their lives in a mess. Like old J. Lewis Corbett, brother-in-law of Elizabeth Bently. I wondered what had happened to him. Probably lit out for the territories. The foggy hollow in the bean field quivered with light. A burst of breeze strummed through the Scotch pines and a cardinal began its song. I bounced up and down on my soggy shoes a couple of times, trying to get some of the water out. Then I began jogging past the cemetery and turned west toward Sweet Memories.

I was singing aloud in rhythm with my steps. In fact, I was dancing along with my arms up, snapping my fingers at the beginning of each measure. I had to laugh at myself—Vaneta's neighbors would think I was crazy. "Oh, how our har-arts beat high-eye with joy!" The large cottonwood on the old Ebenezer Sutherland place that was now my land shivered its stiff leaves like small tin tambourines in approval of my song as I jogged past.

6

The Historical Society

Her life gave evidence that she lived to make pleasant the lives of those around her. It is the fortune of few to be endowed with those rich qualities of Christian virtue and womanly character so liberally bestowed upon Mrs. Hughes. She was sensible, sympathetic, considerate, kind, loving. When married she became to her husband the source of light and joy. She spared no time, no pains, no care to make their home a paradise of love; always willing and anxious to sacrifice herself if by it, she could see that he was happier made.
—An amalgamation of the obituary notices
for Mabel Krause Hughes, who died May 7, 1896,
Monticello Express and *Onslow News*

I had just returned from my morning run when Vaneta came into the kitchen. We were a study in contrasts, she with her nylons and lipstick and I with my scraggly windblown hair and running shorts. "Whatever happened to the big pile of brick from the old brick house?" I asked her. The memory of the picturesque ruin on the Ebenezer Sutherland place was fresh in my mind, for I had noticed the blankness of the field where the house had stood in my childhood.

"I used some to repair the chimney," Vaneta said. Then she pointed to a distinctive row of bricks behind the black stove. "And

I put some behind the Majestic Range when we built the firewall."
I was intrigued, and I felt a sudden physical connection with the
ghosts in my research. Vaneta liked the idea of ghosts.

"Did you ever hear Mabel's bells?" she asked.

"I don't believe in *real* ghosts," I cautioned Vaneta. "What do
you mean, did I ever hear Mabel's bells?" We both knew about
Mabel Krause, our grandfather Gideon Hughes's first wife, who had
died from an infection contracted during childbirth in 1896. A sad
story, especially as it seemed such an unnecessary death. The Scotch
Grove cemetery with the stones of so many young wives gave mute
testimony to the hazard of being a woman at that time. The child
had died within a few weeks, too.

"When my dad was in the nursing home, he suddenly opened
up and told me all these old stories and one of them was about
Mabel's bells," Vaneta told me. "He said that one of her friends
had died a year or two before Mabel did—I think it was in childbirth,
too. Mabel was staying with her, and right before the friend died,
she sat up and said, 'Do you hear them? Do you hear them? Bells!
The bells!' "

"How did your dad know this? He wasn't even born."

"Grandpa told him once when they were fixing fence. The same
thing happened before Mabel died. Right before she died she sat
up and said, 'Gid, I hear the bells.' "

I don't discount the supernatural, but I don't seek out this kind
of story, either. "Vaneta, I am reading from the obituary." I picked
up the book on family genealogy. "It says, 'Thursday afternoon she
sank into a heavy sleep. She aroused once and placing her arms
around her husband's neck uttered only one word, "darling," 'twas
the last she spoke on earth. She sank back into a peaceful slumber,
and about ten o'clock her spirit took its flight.' " I looked up and
Vaneta was staring at me intently. "With all the flowery superfluous.
comment that they were given to using in newspapers in those days,
the obituary does *not* mention bells."

"They probably wouldn't put that in the paper. But Dad never
would have told me about it if he didn't think it was true."

"Did he hear bells?"

"I wished I'd asked him. I didn't take the story very seriously then myself. But I've heard them."

"You're not dead, are you?" I smiled at her seriousness.

"I'm not kidding, Barb. The first time I didn't know what it was. I thought there might be someone at the door or something outside. Then I remembered what Dad said. I was scared because I thought maybe it meant I was going to die. But I didn't, obviously."

I thought of all the times I'd scared myself in this house as a kid. The worst for me had been when a car would go by on the road in the winter and throw the shadows of tree limbs like skeletons dancing on the wall. "Maybe it was just the wind in the wires. I used to think there were voices moaning outside Mom's room. Or wolves howling." I saw myself as a child in my mother's white iron bed. "The telephone wire used to hook up right next to the window. I was afraid of the wind for years."

"This wasn't the wind." She wasn't kidding at all. "I've heard other things, too. I'm not telling you this because I'm scared. I'm not. I wasn't afraid of the bells after the first time."

I stared at her. "Mabel didn't live here. The house was built after she died."

"I think that's part of the problem."

"Problem?"

"Grandma didn't like this house. I'd tell her I was going to fix up this house someday and she'd say, 'You don't want this old house,' and smile sadly." Vaneta sat back in the chair and hugged her knees.

Some sort of mystery had always lingered around this house. It was lovely late-Victorian architecture. Although not unusually lavish, it had unexpected detail in woodwork with parquet floors, an open staircase, and a mantel above the fireplace. But it had always been furnished with the most utilitarian sparseness. "A home that reflected parsimony, colors of dark brown and green predominating," wrote my mother's astute cousin Lenore. Maybe Vaneta was onto something.

A romantic story could be constructed in retrospect from the old accounts. Gid Hughes, the enterprising, hardworking young farmer, waited until he was financially secure before he married. That wasn't unusual in Scotch Grove. Many of the marriage records reveal men in their thirties—some even in their forties—getting married. Women married younger, but sometimes they taught in country schools for a few years, or, if they were poor, like my grandma, worked as hired girls for more established households. Gid would have been thirty when he sought out the eighteen-year-old Mabel. She wasn't even from the immediate area. She lived near Onslow, a community several miles southeast of Scotch Grove. The obituary described her as a country schoolteacher, "a musician of exquisite skill and an alto singer of exceptional beauty." Grandpa was a tenor. "My father had a wonderful tenor voice, you know," my Uncle Jim had said wistfully, as I played the hymns for him to harmonize.

Gideon and Mabel lived for the three years of their marriage in the "old house" that had been moved across the road when the "new house" was built. The old house became part of the storage buildings in the barnyard. The one picture I have seen of them together in front of the old house does not reveal the exceptional vivaciousness and beauty that *still*—one hundred years after Mabel's marriage—is part of the community lore. "My mother used to talk about her," Eloise said. "You know, the old Clark home place was right up the road and that's where my mother lived. After Gid and Mabel were married, Mabel would walk over in the afternoon— she was probably lonesome and the Clarks had a houseful of young people then. They loved her—she was such a jolly sort, and always singing."

But she died. Unexpectedly, according to the newspaper account, as she seemed to be recovering normally from the birth. A few days later she developed a high fever. "Blood poisoning" was what they called it then.

"Think of what it must have been for him," said Vaneta, "to come back to this house after she died."

"It wasn't this house," I reminded her. "This house wasn't even built yet." I was curious in spite of myself. "What do the bells sound like?"

"A low distinct sound, a sort of chime. Not like the church bell at all. It's not exactly like any bell I've ever heard, but I know it's a bell."

I like mysteries, too. "Okay," I said, "let's assume we have this bereaved young husband. Surely, if you look at the cemeteries with all the young women who died giving birth, it was a familiar enough story in those days. Now what?"

"He waited three years to marry again. That would have been a long time for a man who could have had his pick of the young women. Gid had opened his heart to Mabel. I suspect he didn't want to remarry at all. But he wanted children and he wasn't getting any younger. So when he decided to get married again, he deliberately chose someone totally different—he didn't seek out a soulmate who could sing with him again."

I instantly rose to Grandma's defense, but she interrupted. "I know Grandma was beautiful, but think of it. She was a *hired girl.* She'd quit school at twelve to help send her brother through the seminary. Her family still spoke *German.* They were recent immigrants."

Maybe she was right. Grandma had always spoken of her husband in such a subdued reverential tone. I felt sad. "But wouldn't he grow to love her? How could anyone not love Grandma?"

"He was probably fond of her, but Grandma wore patched brown stockings until the day she died," Vaneta said. "Why would she live in a house like this and have to patch her stockings?"

I had my own opinion about our grandfather and it was much less romantic than Vaneta's. "I'm not discounting Grandpa's grief over Mabel's death. But if he was stingy with Grandma he probably would have been stingy with Mabel in the long run, too. The only inconsistency I see is that he built this big house in the first place."

"That's the very thing that proves my point," Vaneta insisted. "This was the only thing he and Mabel planned together. I think the house was built as a shrine to her. The man had two sides." Vaneta had thought this through and was methodical in her explanation. "One side was ambitious, money-seeking, and severe. That's the side that got him so much land. People who saw only that side considered him greedy and hard. But Uncle John wrote about the other side. That side was kinder, and that was the side his children felt—at least the girls—I think he was harder toward my father. He cared for his daughters and protected them. He gave them each a farm at their marriage." She waited to make sure I was with her.

"Go on," I said, "you're making sense."

"That gentler side I see represented in the music. Mabel was the key that unlocked the door between the two sides of Gid Hughes. By all accounts Grandpa loved Mabel. They sang together at their wedding. That's what the article says, anyway. He married Grandma later because she could bake bread and he wanted children. He probably just wanted a housekeeper that would have kids." I shifted my eyes briefly from Vaneta to the Majestic Range, picturing Grandma stirring oatmeal.

"Are you all right?" Grandma had asked me anxiously when I returned from my own wedding. "I know a man can be almost crazy for a woman." What an odd thing to say, I thought, putting my arms around her, wondering what her wedding night had been like.

Vaneta had actually known our grandfather. She was six years old when he died. "I loved him. Of course, I was just a little girl and probably his pet. I thought he was the most wonderful man in the world." She had a picture of them—she was sitting on his knee, a curly-haired cherub at the age of four.

My mother thought he was wonderful, too. In sort of the same little-girl worshipful way as Vaneta. "In the later years when I was teaching, we were friends. I think," she said almost shyly, "that he was proud of me." Long after my father had left her, she told Ruth Clark, who seems to have been the only person in the community with whom she ever talked about the humiliating situation, a strange story. Shortly before she died my mother repeated the story to me. "I had lain awake for hours," she said, "the shock and sadness was positively physical, as if the sharp edge of a broken windowpane was being dragged across my chest and up and down the insides of my arms. There were so many debts. I had no money or employment. I was so shamed. I prayed and prayed. Then suddenly he was there at the foot of my bed."

"Who?" I asked. Surely she didn't mean God.

"My father"—she was looking out the window as she was telling me this—"my father was there at the foot of the bed, just standing there. He didn't speak, but he didn't have to. I knew because he was there that somehow everything was going to be all right."

"The most wonderful man in the world to you and my mother sure had a stingy streak." I read a passage aloud from Uncle John's memoirs. " 'Still, folks who had been neighbors for a lifetime seemed to resent the ease with which he made money . . . His fault, if he had one, was a failure to inspire the family feeling that we are equal partners in the planning, the winning and the spending of the fruits of the family labors.' " I added, "Lots of people didn't like him."

"They were just jealous of the money," Vaneta said complacently.

Someone once said with glee when we were talking about my dad, "Well, at least he got some money out of old Gid Hughes, anyway," as if that was some sort of triumph. The person—why couldn't I think of who it was?—had said that the young men in the neighborhood had dared my father to try to date my mother, dared him to try to take on old Gid Hughes's money. I had put the whole thought out of my mind because that was worse than anything I wanted to believe about my father. I also had felt a surge of defensive loyalty for my mother to think of men laughing at what had caused her so much pain because of her father's money.

I walked over to the Majestic Range and fingered the row of bricks that had come from a house in which I had romantically imagined ghosts in my childhood. What did I know about ghosts, anyway? Certainly the existence of Mabel with her odd diamond-shaped tombstone had been real enough for me in my childhood. And for my grandmother, too—maybe in ways we didn't know. Every Decoration Day until she died she put flowers on Mabel's grave along with those she placed for the rest of the Hugheses.

"So you think you hear the bells because this is really Mabel's house?" I asked. Vaneta's story actually made a lot of sense as far as personal history went, but I wasn't ready to buy into the bells yet. "When was the last time you heard them?"

"Right after I came this year—I had only been here a couple of weeks. I open the B&B the first of May and I always come the week

before to get things in order. So I'd say it was the end of the first
week in May." The thought occurred to us simultaneously and we
reached for the obituary together.

It read as follows: "The sad and unexpected death of Mrs. G. J.
Hughes occurred at her home in Scotch Grove, Thursday May 7th.
Her sudden departure cast a shadow of sorrow over the whole community in which she lived, and left the bereaved husband, parents,
brother, sister and friends stricken with grief."

•   •   •

I had not thought of the man in the white car for years and years.
The row of bricks which Vaneta had placed in the firewall behind
the Majestic Range prompted the memory. Even in middle age I
felt a vague flash of discomfort, thinking of the episode—as if I had
done something to be ashamed of, when of course I was just a child
and any blame surely was not mine.

My hair still hung in the long braids that reached below my belt.
On Saturdays in late autumn when the false warmth of sun turned
to coolness at the first line of shadow, I often rode the horse east,
sometimes clear to the Maquoketa River. That day I must have
waited until afternoon to ride. I needed to choose a closer destination
than the river, which is why I was at the brick house. Probably my
brother was listening to a football game on the radio. Although we
still played our Wild West game, he had constructed other elaborate
fantasy worlds of imaginary football leagues with several notebooks
of complicated statistics. Already we had entered the solitary internal
sphere of early pubescence and spent much of our time alone.

The brick house in the middle of Ebenezer Sutherland's place,
the land that was now mine, had settled into a romantic ruin by
my childhood. Ebenezer's son-in-law, Mathias Sweezy, who had
no sons of his own, sold the farm (160 acres minus 11 acres for the
Scotch Grove Presbyterian Church and cemetery) to my grandfather
Gideon Hughes in 1908 for $1,388. Old lilac bushes and giant
broken cottonwoods framed the homestead during my childhood,
although successive raids for chimney bricks had left the house

crumbling. The structure still resembled a house—enough that on my forbidden forays (Uncle Jim had declared it unsafe) I could imagine the ghosts of the former occupants.

People lived here, I thought, standing in what must have been the kitchen, imagining children eating oatmeal while sitting on warm oven doors. People died here, people now defined only by white tombstones in the cemetery which bordered the land on the northeast corner. People loved here. I shivered with excitement, for I was only twelve, and a young twelve at that, just beginning to understand my undefined longings.

I emerged from the house into the warm sunshine, feeling the startling change in temperature. Under the trees where cows sought shade in summer, the circle of dust was layered with stiff leaves that crackled like corn flakes. The dusty smell of them rose with each step. My horse stood sleepily in the sun, tied to a branch of a giant limb that had broken away from the tallest cottonwood in last summer's thunderstorms. Stretching full length on the broad limb, I must have fallen asleep myself, for suddenly I was aware of shadows having shifted over me entirely with uncomfortable coolness. When I sat upright, I became aware of the white car.

Not just the car itself, which was stopped on the road that bordered the land to the south, just beyond the small creek bridge, but the man who stood behind it, leaning against the trunk. He was looking at me. The sun had shifted again and created slightly wavy lines in the distance between the tree where I sat and the road, so I shaded my eyes. Yes, he was definitely looking at me, and now that he saw I was looking at him, he waved his arm slowly. I was not afraid, for this was 1954 in rural Iowa. Strangers were not dangerous then, just lost on the endless grid of similar roads. I waved back. Perhaps he needed directions. I untied the horse.

Thirty-nine years later I can feel the exact thread of the horse's mane as it cut slightly into my fingers when I swung up bareback. I can see the specific whorl of hair on the horse's neck behind her left ear. I was a child fascinated by design and detail and especially the sudden shifts in pattern or perception. It took only minutes to canter across the field to the fence. At first I did not dismount.

No, said the man with odd sad eyes. He was not lost. He was on his way home. But he had seen my horse across the field and was a horseman himself. Was my horse for sale? I was pleased. My horse was, in fact, a little too fat from all the grain I smuggled her unnecessarily, but to me she was beautiful. No, she was not for sale. She was actually the property of my Uncle Jim, I confided, but I was sure she was not for sale. A long pause ensued. What did this odd man want? He was thin, very thin, and his eyes seemed close to tears. How many horses did he have? I asked. Many, he said. In fact, he needed help exercising them. He had several pictures of his horses in his car. Would I care to see them? I slid from my horse.

At this point I was still a child. If I had told my mother the strange story immediately, could I have remained a child longer? But I could not speak of the incident because I did not understand my body's place in it. Already that night I felt that my body was no longer beautiful and my own. I felt the shame of what the grownups did not say aloud. And it was not until the next night that my mother told me, somewhat hesitantly, that she had learned that day of a warning that had been issued about a stranger in a white car. She framed the discussion delicately, for she did not want to frighten me about strangers or men. By then I had become an accomplice in the violation—at least in my own mind—because I had not told the story in my confusion and shame.

As I climbed the shallow side of the ditch, the coolness of the shade from the cottonwood trunk moved across the road. Yet we stood far from any trees on the thin golden stripe of gravel in the bright sunlight. The man neither removed his hands from his pockets nor moved toward the car, but I felt a cold flush of confusion. This man's liquid eyes had looked through my shirt, had seen the small bumps that were becoming my breasts, had seen the shallow hollow of my curved buttock, had seen where the soft brown hairs were forming. My breathing changed.

If I would sit in the car, he said softly, he would get the box of pictures from the trunk and we could look at them in the shade. The sun was so warm for late in the fall, he said, and we would be more comfortable in the car. How odd that he would speak of warmth when I felt the coldness so dramatically. So if I would just go ahead and sit down in the front seat, he would get the pictures from the trunk. My eyes slid uncomfortably sideways. The car seemed unnaturally dark. I glanced back toward the horse, who had pulled the reins loose as she reached for grass. Her left front hoof stood on the knotted reins.

Then I was back with the horse, untangling her hoof from the reins. The man stood with his hands in his pockets, his eyes more liquid still. He called for me to wait, that I would like his horses, that my horse was beautiful. But again the hard thread of the horse's mane cut my fingers as I swung upward, the hooves bunched before I had settled my seat firmly on her back, my head felt cold as the air rushed through my hair, and my braids thumped in quick rhythm on my back. Already I was confused by the unfamiliar surges of tingling in my own body, by my inexplicable rudeness, and by the sadness of the man's eyes.

I did not look back until I reached the brick house. There I wheeled the horse so sharply she stumbled, almost sitting back on her haunches as she tried to oblige my command. The figure still leaned against the car, but I could no longer see his eyes.

·　　·　　·

Across the road from the Solid Waste Disposal and right around the curve from the County Care Facility stands the Jones County Historical Museum. The museum grounds contain small replicas of early buildings, some long sheds that house the larger collections of machinery, and the library. Arriving a little before the posted opening time of one o'clock, I assumed I would have to wait for the attendant to unlock the chain. I was able to drive right in, however, as a family had apparently rented the picnic space for a reunion. I was glad for their sake that the showers had at least temporarily subsided, as the dramatic wind and thunder with its accompanying rain of the night before surely would have dampened more than their spirits.

The outer buildings were still locked, but the library doors were ajar, so I started there. A young man with slick hair, dress slacks, and a knit shirt manned the table that served as a reception desk. "You're open a bit early today," I said conversationally.

He tilted his head to one side. "Well, I don't know," he said.

I hadn't thought of it as a question that required perusal, so I moved over to browse through the books. He watched me with unabashed interest. Some initial grouping of similar subject matter broke down after a couple of rows. Probably no one had had time to index and sort out all the material that well-meaning citizens had cleaned from their attics. Old schoolbooks were interspersed with contemporary volumes which I had just seen in bookstores. I turned back to the young man. "Is there any catalogue or listing of what you have on the shelves?" He shook his head.

"I'm looking for material about the Native American population that was in the area when the whites came, the Mesquakies specifically." He stared at me. "The Indians," I said.

"Oh, the Indians," he repeated. "Well, I don't know," he added.

I moved back to the shelves and leafed through a few volumes. Anything I found was going to be a matter of luck. Then a stack of pamphlets laid out on a table caught my eye. It was a series of *Jones County Historical Reviews* done up in little newsletter formats. Each one had multiple copies, and the price indicated they might be for sale. "Excuse me," I said to the young man, who was staring out the door, "as there are multiple copies of these pamphlets, do you know whether I could buy one of the extras?" He came over and stood by the table. He inspected the copies in question.

"Well, I don't know," he answered.

"Could you find out?" I persisted. "It would be a convenience to be able to take them with me." He stared at them as if they might give him some information.

He shook his head. "Well, I—"

"It's okay," I interrupted, picking them up and moving to the larger table, "I'll read them here." He moved back by the door and looked out at the grey sky.

The *Historical Reviews* were much more interesting than this singularly uninformed young man. One article without a listed author detailed the arrival of the first Scots. It recounted the familiar story for me with even more hyperbole than the other versions:

"Burning sun, violent hailstorms, wind and rain beat upon them in turn as they plodded on; mosquitoes and flies tormented them." I compared this with another account I had located in one of the volumes on the shelves. Both listed John Sutherland as the first party, but the dates differed. "One long log house was built, this being covered with sod and dirt and here the whole company made their abode during the winter. In the spring [John Sutherland] made a plow from a tree and with this they cultivated their gardens, over which they had to keep a close watch as deer roamed at will over the prairies." That was a nice touch, I decided, picturing the sturdy Scots armed with wooden plows against the marauding deer. I copied the phrase into my notebook.

Another article contained an interesting account of the bad luck of the Livingstons. Apparently when old Grandmother Livingston fell out of the oxcart and broke her leg, it was the start of a string of unhappy incidents—the two most notable involved death by freezing. In the winter of 1840, which was unusually severe, two Livingstons, Hugh and James, were returning from a trip to the gristmill when a sudden blizzard hit. James became separated from the wagon and froze to death before they found him. Five years later, Hugh Livingston, who had escaped unharmed the first time, made the same trip with a nephew on Christmas Day. "They were caught on the open prairie by a severe storm . . . the tongue on the long sleigh broke and the team got away. The young man ran after the team while Hugh remained with the sleigh. By the time help was obtained and they returned to the sleigh, Hugh Livingston had perished from the severe cold weather."

As I was clucking sympathetically to myself over this ill-starred family, an elderly woman entered the room with a younger man, whom I surmised to be her son. She surveyed the library with a little dismay. "Oh my," she sighed, "I think I'll just sit here." She addressed the young man. "Is it all right if I use this chair?" I winced in anticipation.

"Well, I don't know," he replied.

She sat down anyway. "If it clears off, it's going to get hot," she volunteered.

He said it again. I stood up to avoid the irrational degree of irritation I felt toward this laconic young man and began looking at exhibits in the other part of the building. The displays of clothing, which included the names of the donors, were quite interesting. I especially liked all the old button shoes.

When I was nine Stuhler's Shoe Store in Monticello sponsored a contest for a bike. The person who turned in the most pairs of used shoes won the bicycle. I had turned in 110 pairs by collecting from everyone in the neighborhood and asking people to look in their attics. I had lots of button shoes and I was far ahead of the next contestant on the chart in the store window. But the night before the contest was to end, someone else brought in a whole truckload of shoes his father had found somewhere. I cried and cried. "We don't always get what we want just because we want it," said my mother, but she was sorry, too, and let me read a new Black Stallion book she had been saving for Christmas.

The next room caught me totally off guard. It was filled with dead animals. Only one—a coyote, which was identified as having been killed near Dubuque by Gus Norlin—was native to the area. A sign informed me that this collection was PASKER'S WILDLIFE MENAGERIE. A newspaper article dated September 12 was clipped to the sign, but the year was not given. Accompanying pictures indicated clothes of the late 1930s or early '40s vintage.

A Monticello couple, Mr. and Mrs. Gerald Pasker, had left Monticello on January 6 for a three-week hunting safari on the "plains of primitive East Africa" and they returned with eleven trophies, according to the article. Two areas of the East African plains were specifically identified, Karamoja and Bungungu. In Karamoja Mr. Pasker killed a zebra, a waterbuck, a topi, a kongoni, a giant eland, an orabi, and a leopard. The article implied that the killing of the leopard had heroically saved a village as "the natives [were] not allowed to have guns." In Bungungu Mr. Pasker killed a water buffalo, a warthog, a Uganda kob, and an elephant. The remains of most of the animals, including two elephant feet made into wastebaskets, now graced the Historical Museum of Jones County, Iowa. This was an exhausting trip. I didn't recognize some of the place-names and the fauna and couldn't follow the sequence

of the itinerary. I presume in the geographical locations outside
Africa the wildlife was spared. The Paskers returned to Monticello
on February 17.

I went back into the main room, and as the elderly lady was still
chatting with the young man, who greeted each comment with his
four-word refrain, I gathered up my notebooks. The surrounding
buildings offered much more promise. First I went into the large
shed, which housed a collection of antique machinery. Unmarked
in a collection of odds and ends I recognized the old quern stones
from Esther Sinclair's doorstep. I rubbed my hand over the dimpled
surfaces. It would be a hard way to make flour.

Next I went into the blacksmith shop. I especially liked the anvil.
It was exactly like the one in the shanty north of the windmill at
Grandma's place. I had never seen the anvil used, but the pockmarks
on it bore testimony to prior times. The log cabin was unfamiliar
to me except for the sunbonnet hanging on the hook. My grandmother had always worn a bonnet which she made herself. The
reconstruction of the church was like a miniature version of the
Scotch Grove Presbyterian Church. The pews and songbooks were
from congregations that had folded or replaced furnishings with
newer models. The old minister's chair from the Scotch Grove
Church that I had thought was a throne as a child was there behind
the pulpit. I inspected the organ, but it was not the one that used
to be stored in the balcony of our church. I was disappointed. That
organ and I shared secrets. On summer afternoons, with my horse
tied to the fence that surrounded the churchyard, I would slip
through the unlocked door. Pumping furiously on the pedals, I
would pull all the various stops until the organ shuddered with
discordant sounds.

The little courthouse replica had a sign saying LUMBER DO-
NATED BY L. JAMES HUGHES. I laughed aloud. Somebody
must have talked pretty fast to get that. Uncle Jim wanted to give
things away, but always backed out when it actually came to letting
go. I decided to save the school until last. There was still one shed
with assorted overflow in it that looked interesting.

Here I found the only indication of habitation predating the coming of the Europeans. Along with bins of unmarked fossils were two large collections of native artifacts. Walter Eby's arrowhead collection contained forty-four points graced with the sign FOUND NEAR EBY'S MILL. Most were small, probably for birds or little mammals, but a few were long and slender, large enough to bring down a deer. The collection contained two impressive spear points. Maybe buffalo or bear, I speculated. Certainly they were substantial enough to do damage. Henry Heiken's collection was even larger. His farm had been down in the timber with a long lane. Most of his points were white and pink, pretty and finely flaked. He must have kept only the nice ones.

The schoolhouse was an actual school, moved to the site. My mother had taught at several schools in the county, maybe even this one. I rounded the little cloakroom wall and stopped suddenly in surprise. A mannequin stood on the platform at the front of the room and for an absurd second I thought it was my mother. I'd never known her in that brief stage of independence. Although she taught one year after we were back with Grandma, she became more reluctant to leave the farm. Then the country schools began to close and the children rode in the yellow bus to Monticello.

The room looked so authentic that I expected to see girls in long stockings and little boys in overalls. Except for an organ against one wall—schools didn't have organs. A little notecard identified it. Here it was, the church organ! I lightly stroked the keys. My fascination with the old instrument increased now that I knew its purchase had occasioned an inordinate amount of discord in the church. In 1874 Elder William Clark (Uncle John's William Clark, that is), who was then Sabbath-school superintendent, had an excellent tenor voice. Alarmed, no doubt, at the appeal of the lusty singing of the Methodists, whose church briefly flourished a mile to the north, he requested the purchase of an organ. Such frivolity was sternly opposed by elders John and Ebenezer Sutherland, but William Clark secured the majority vote of the congregation by promising to limit the organ's use to the Sabbath school. Elder John Sutherland softened after perceiving no ill effects on the general congregation and, when the subject came up for review, is reported to have said, "I did not put it in here and I will not put it out. Do as you please." Ebenezer was not so malleable. "It was some months before Uncle Ebby became sufficiently reconciled to the organ to attend services after it was used," according to the 1911 Jubilee booklet.

As no one was in the school but myself, I sat down at one of the larger desks. I again imagined the mannequin as my mother. She drove a green Chevrolet, bought with her teaching money. She changed her name legally from Katie May to Kathleen. Arriving at school early, she built the fire so that when the children came, there would be at least a hint of warmth in the building. At night she worked through lesson plans and graded papers. Why had she given it all up?

For one thing, the laws against married women teaching didn't change until World War II. Marriage would not have left a choice. But I am also sure it did not occur to her to continue teaching after her marriage. "Work," my grandmother snorted disdainfully when Aunt Frances took a job at the button factory so she wouldn't have to ask Uncle Jim for every penny. "She calls it *work* just because it's in town. As if taking care of a husband and children isn't work! Who's going to fix dinner for Jim?" I sighed. No doubt my mother abandoned her independence willingly, wholeheartedly embracing the role for which she had been trained all her life. I smiled at the pert little mannequin. "Don't give it up," I advised.

On a side table various memorabilia were arranged and I stopped on the way to the door. A yellowed book had the title *Course of Study for Common Schools*—1921. "Sadie Campbell," read the inscription at the top of the first page. *Sadie Campbell!* That was Len Campbell's wife, mother of Edith, who had eloped to Colorado with my father. I never knew she was a teacher. The only thing I knew about her was that she had something called "nervous breakdowns." I remembered a thin, wiry, tired-looking woman. I opened the book. "Donated by Edith (Campbell) Shaw." I didn't want to think about Edith right now when I was enjoying my mother's brief independence. It actually went through my mind to take the book with me and throw it away. Thinking of a little article I had found in the box of letters, I suddenly remembered the story.

EDITH NORRIS, SAMUEL SHAW

TO BE WED IN JULY

Invitations are being issued for the wedding of Mrs.
Edith Norris of Luzerne, Iowa, daughter of Mr. and
Mrs. Len Campbell, to Samuel Shaw of Frankfort,
Illinois, son of Mr. and Mrs. Lewis Shaw of Sioux
City, Iowa. The wedding will take place at St. Paul's
Lutheran church at Luzerne, July 20th.

We were finishing supper, the usual supper of fried eggs and fried
potatoes at the table with the oilcloth covering that had cherries in
the pattern. I was staring at the webbed backing that was breaking
through the cherries in the oilcloth where the leaf of the table
attached. My mother, who often read the newspaper while she drank
a cup of green tea after dinner, came back into the kitchen carrying
the paper which had the above article. "Who did this?" she asked,
not angry, but with genuine puzzlement. The word "Norris" in the
headline had been scratched through both times with pencil, so
hard that the paper was ripped. She looked at me. I shook my head.
I really didn't do it. She looked at my brother. He stared back at
her defiantly and didn't answer. He and I never once in all of our
childhood talked of our father.

I looked at the mannequin. She was still smiling. That gave me
pause. Edith was just a real person with a mother, too. And she
wanted to leave something of her mother, who had given up teaching
for marriage and nervous breakdowns, in the museum. I put the
book back on the table. Then I went out and sat down in the car,
feeling a little confused and lightheaded.

I idly flipped through my notes. Well, Jones County, I thought,
you're a nice microcosm of the white American experience. Hazy
on anything before the Europeans, heroic version of your own
coming, slaughter of the animals—but your brief slice of history
has it all—arrowheads, oxcarts, and anvils. Love and death. I wished
I had the date on Pasker's Wildlife Menagerie. I could go in and
look more carefully through the article. Or ask the attendant. Right!

Then I felt ashamed. Why was I being so hard on this young man? This was a well-done museum that had essentially captured the essence of a brief period of time. And there wasn't any money here for a professional staff. The museum had been established by people who had actually lived this history and wanted to give more permanence to themselves and their ancestors by leaving a record of their lives.

I sighed self-righteously. I'd just shed a heavy sin. For forty-five years I'd carried a secret hatred in my heart for a woman I'd never met. And I hadn't even known it was there; but now that it was gone, I could feel my heart beat a little higher in my chest. I was momentarily pure enough to qualify for even an old-fashioned Presbyterian heaven. I could afford to be magnanimous to some hapless kid who probably just got stuck in the library on a Sunday afternoon because an uncle was a member of the historical society. But I laughed anyway. I pictured myself asking the question.

"Excuse me, sir. Can you tell me the year that the heroic fury of Mr. Pasker was unleashed on the unsuspecting wildlife of the 'plains of primitive East Africa'?"

I knew what he would say.

•   •   •

The metal railings of the old Eby's Mill Bridge which arc in long parentheses above the Maquoketa River are exactly eight and a quarter inches wide. I measured by placing my hands on a ruler at Sweet Memories in the same manner that I once placed them on the bridge span. That had been when I was home from college and the exact width of the beam seemed suddenly important as I relived a childhood experience. Without an instrument to measure, I used my hands, placing the left hand with the fingers pointing along the span and the right palm crossways, as if to form a T. The width of the steel band was the distance across all of the knuckles including the thumb of the left hand plus the distance from the tip of the middle finger on my right hand to the wrist. Eight and a quarter inches: not very much purchase for a little girl standing at the very highest point of the curved span, when thirty feet below the water swirled in seductive circles.

Although this picturesque bridge, built in 1870, was a favorite destination after I had the horse to ride, my first association with it was one of terror and tragedy. Stretched across my grandmother's bed as she rocked in her little chair by the window, I watched the yellow light fade behind the trees of the orchard windbreak while she told the story. She conveyed the sad tenderness and the simple images and my mind supplied the rest.

Two boys, the Leesekamp brothers, were playing in the water. It must have been long ago, because the dam that serviced the gristmill—once one of the busiest places in Jones County—had still been there. One boy was caught in a deceptive current that whirled beneath the placid surface, and when he disappeared, the older brother dived after him, only to be sucked into the same vortex. By the time it released them, they could not be revived. And by the time my grandmother finished the story, I was whirling myself, as if I had spun on the merry-go-round too long during recess. As I lay on the bed, I felt the heavy pull of the water, saw the funneled blackness and the white limbs twirling, and ached with the helpless terror of those who watched. Never in my life have I entered even the most placid pool without that story flashing through my mind.

Eby's Mill Bridge, however, was also the scene of much happier times. Until very recent decades, when the cottonwoods, sumac, and blackberries took over—forming an almost impenetrable tangle—a long smooth sandbar curved on the north side of the river and was the picnic ground of the entire community. Under the heading "The Harvest Home Picnic Society" in the 1910 *History of Jones County* is the following:

An organization has been effected by the people of Scotch Grove having in view the holding of a harvest home picnic annually. G. J. Hughes is president; Miss Blanche Clark is secretary and Donald Sinclair is treasurer. The picnic of 1909 was the sixth annual affair, and was held in Eby's grove near the mill.

My mother would have been four years old in 1909. Most certainly she would have attended with her family.

Eloise had told me that during the Depression this sandbar was the hangout of all the young folk. "Well now . . . everybody came!" Her musical glissade rippled with the happy memory. "All summer long, every night. Sinclairs had a cottage; so did the Clarks. I don't even know who owned the land. Happy Himebaugh would load up all the girls from Scotch Grove in one Model T. Everybody, just everybody, came!" But I'll bet my mother didn't come then. By the time of the Depression she was a schoolteacher and, by my Aunt Em's account, too shy to join in mixed events.

Although the mill was gone and the sandbar infiltrated with trees when I was a child, during my junior year of high school Eby's Mill Bridge provided a lasting memory, not in the summer but in the winter. As the construction began for the new bridge, the water was dammed behind artificial islands formed for the base of the pilings. The quiet water pooled before it swirled around one edge to the north. The winter was an extremely cold one, with late snow. The ice froze smooth and deep. My brother and I discovered it early in December. With neighborhood teenagers we spent a glorious winter vacation ice-skating during the day and by moonlight as well, building bonfires to ward off the sub-zero cold. I can still draw a diagram of where the current scrolled under silent ice and where tree limbs made jagged cracks across the moon. The old bridge stood sentinel to our laughter. If the whirlpool that claimed the Leesekamp boys still lurked in the water, the placid surface layer had frozen like a smooth black window, keeping back the dangers of the depths.

I suspect it was there and will always be there for me, even though my mother's cousin Les Rickels says the actual site of the drowning may have been farther upstream. But the reality created for me with my grandmother's stories and my own experience on the bridge span have a life of their own.

I was less than ten years old, for I had trouble keeping pace with Uncle Jim's brisk stride. I can't think where we would have parked the car to emerge from the timber at Eby's Mill Bridge, but I was quite hot and tired, so we must have come a long way. Not that I would have whined or even asked for a drink—for ours was not that kind of relationship and I didn't want to be told I couldn't come along. I remember nothing of any conversation.

When I looked up from the water that was moving in tilted fluid slabs under the bridge, Uncle Jim had started up the curved metal beam, walking with his hands held slightly away from his sides.

When he reached the crest of the arc, I was on the beam, too, drawn by some invisible cord between us. I followed him on the narrow metal path, not looking down at the protruding bolts but only at his back above me, until it disappeared over the arch as he began the descent. When I reached the crest he became aware that I was behind him and I felt his fear for my safety pass along the invisible cord in waves that reached me with a jolt—like when a rope is snapped sharply at one end and the motion undulates along it. I looked down.

And I saw it. The whirlpool. It was under the shifting slabs, which presented a deceptive calm. And in the swirling blackness I could see the white limbs twirling, twirling, the boys whose plight provoked such terror in those who watched. I felt the heavy pull of the water. I longed to jump after them, to join the eternal fluid dance that commanded such tenderness in the voices of those who told their story.

He called my name. My uncle called my name gently. I do not remember any other time in my childhood he addressed me by name. I looked at him standing at the end of the arc. Again I began to move toward him. I did not look at the beam, but only at his face, which glistened with beads of moisture in the sun.

7

Women's Work

A woman who would indulge in indecent and lewd conversation, who would knowingly associate with the abandoned and licentious . . . is not of the chaste character contemplated by the statute . . . In order to constitute the crime, the woman seduced must be unmarried and of previously chaste character . . . If she were unchaste, there was no crime. *The injury* [constituting payment of damages] *to the plaintiff, the husband or father,* is dependent upon the chastity of the wife or daughter. . . ."
—Iowa Supreme Court, December Term, 1870,
The State v. Sutherland

Grandma was full of advice. "You watch your mother. No one bakes a better pie. And she even sewed dresses for Besse and Emmy. It's such a shame, such a shame." What's a shame? I thought. I was supposed to be ironing my brother's shirts with the heavy black iron she had heated on the Majestic Range. I hated it and was doing a poor job on purpose. "If you don't learn to iron better, no man is going to want you, Barbie." Oh. That.

On Saturdays my grandmother gathered up the shoes. "We must polish the shoes," she said. "Go and get your brother's shoes." He was the Boy. I was a girl. I did not want to polish his shoes. "I always did my brother's shoes," she said. I told my mother I would not polish his shoes. "It is a little thing she is asking. Don't make your grandmother unhappy, Barbie. We are in her house."

"Well, Ma, exactly what is it you would like me to do?" my

mother said patiently, as she fit another piece in the jigsaw puzzle. Grandma had been complaining about the puzzle. "You'll ruin your eyes, Kate," she said. "Why does she care that you do the puzzle?" I asked when she was out of earshot. The snow had carved large dunes across the driveway and the car battery was dead. What could we do, anyway? "We could be working on the quilt," said my mother quietly.

The year I was in 4-H I had to bake chocolate-chip cookies and banana nut bread for the Great Jones County Fair. My mother would not help me. "This is for daughters to do by themselves," she said. The banana nut bread, which had a crooked crack, won a blue ribbon. My mother laughed. "What a nice surprise," she said. On the way out of the hall we saw old Bill Wright, who lived in a shack with his coon dogs on the hill above Dales Ford. "My," he said. "No lady ever baked me any blue-ribbon bread." So I gave it to him.

When we were in sixth grade we played a running game during lunch hour. Linda Guyan and I could run faster than the boys. The teacher who was standing by the tennis-court fence smiled at us. "Boys do not like girls who can run faster than they can." I began to watch and she was right.

I did not like to sew and got a C in Home Economics in high school. "How can anyone get a C in that?" said my exasperated mother, who knew my only chance for college was to win a scholarship. But I won a Farm Bureau scholarship and another scholarship besides. "Don't talk about it around your brother," said my grandma. "You mustn't make him feel sad." But my mother told Esther Sinclair on the phone, "She is my pride and joy." I heard her say that to Esther.

"Why do you blame your mother, then?" asked the psychiatrist. "It sounds as if your grandmother did much of the teaching."

"No, my mother, too," I insisted. I was appalled now that I had stayed in the marriage until he left me, two years after I knew I should leave. "By the way she lived her life. I was taught this by the women."

"And the men," said the psychiatrist gently. "The men who were already dead."

·   ·   ·

"Do you remember how to call hogs?" I asked Vaneta, who had just walked into the kitchen with flashlights. The thunder was getting more insistent. We had lost the electricity twice in the last week. She stared at me blankly.

"Hogs?"

"Yes, you know—pigs. Do you remember how your dad called hogs?"

"Something about pig-pig-pig at the end." She looked at me a little suspiciously. "Why?"

"I'm just trying to remember exactly how it went. Do you remember the first part?"

"Barbara, you ask the strangest questions." Vaneta sighed. She sat down with the flashlights. "I brought these down in case the lights go out. I also have Grandma's old kerosene lamp on the dining-room table so we can move in there if we have to. Now, why do you want to know about the hogs?"

"I'm reading an article by Lenore." Lenore Rickels Salvaneschi came from Grandma's side of the family, a scholar who had done some articles for the Iowa State Historical Society magazine. "She's describing a hog-calling contest at a Fourth of July celebration and I think we did it differently than the German-Lutheran community where she grew up."

"I didn't know this was an ethnic question. How did the Germans do it?"

"I don't want to tell you yet because that'll stack the deck. I want to see if your memory is the same as mine."

She thought for a minute. "All I can remember is the pig-pig-pig at the end."

"Did you ever do it—feed the pigs, I mean?"

"Not much. Dad never seemed to want me at the barn. He was

always afraid I'd get hurt. I mostly stayed inside and helped Mother.
Did you?"

"I did," I said, "but it was a strange situation. I wanted to do
chores—I suppose to feel needed in some way—but often there
wasn't much to do. But I did feed the pigs. I even called them
myself when they were out in the pasture. I just want to see how
you remember it." We were both silent for a minute, listening to
a faraway sound from our childhood. The glass doors flashed with
the lightning, but we didn't pay much attention, because it was
such a common occurrence. The thunder didn't sound too close.

"I think I've got it," Vaneta said. And she giggled. "I can't say
it, though, because it doesn't make sense."

"Well, *do* it, then."

"What do you mean?"

"Give the hog call like your dad did."

She laughed. "I can't, it sounds silly."

"Oh come on, there's no one here but us." Vaneta was having
a slow summer with the B&B.

She cleared her throat. She began softly. "Here . . . ere . . . pig-
pig-pig-pig-pig," she sang on a one-and-a-half-note interval. She
went from about an F sharp on the "here" to an E flat on the "ere
. . . pig-pig-pig-pig-pig."

"Good," I said, "now do the first part." The first segment was
my point of confusion.

She hummed to herself a minute. Then she sang softly on the
same interval. "Sou . . . ee . . . Sou . . . ee . . . Souuou . . .
eeeeeeee." I grinned at her, because that was the way I remembered
it, too. "Here . . . ere . . . pig-pig-pig-pig." She looked at me and
we both laughed.

"That's right!" I said excitedly. "That's the way I remember it,
too. Lenore has a picture here of somebody calling hogs." I read
from the article: "To anyone not raised on a farm, or at least within
hailing distance of one, the sight and sound of a portly, sun-dyed
farmer standing on a bench and delivering himself of a mighty
'Poo-ee, Pooee, Pooee, POOee' would have seemed absurd, but the
crowd understood and loved it when the stentorian performance of
Henry Schminke won the prize.' "

"Poo-ee," said Vaneta, "those Germans don't know how to call hogs. It's *sou-ee.*"

"But of course," I said, getting into the humor of the situation. I stood up and threw my head back like the rotund Henry Schminke in the picture.

"Sooouuu . . . eeeeeeeee . . . Sooooouuuuu . . . eeeeeeeeeeee . . . Sooooooooouuuuu . . . eeeeeeeee . . . Here . . . ere . . . pig-pig-pig-pig-pig-pig-pig-pig-pigggggggg!"

The lightning suddenly lit up the entire house, the thunder crashed so hard the plaster rattled, and the electricity went off. We jumped for each other, laughing wildly.

"We've got to stop calling up old ghosts." Vaneta giggled as we fumbled for the flashlights. The lightning flashed again and made it easy to see the table. I moved my work into the dining room and she lit the kerosene lamp.

"Wow! I remember *this*," I said of the soft glow. Grandma had always kept the lamp on her bureau for just such occasions—which were fairly frequent when I was small, less frequent in high school as the power systems improved. I'd fancied myself Abe Lincoln, finishing my homework by lamplight. "I guess we got it right with the hog call."

"Don't do it again," Vaneta advised. "You'll blow out the TV circuits!" We laughed.

"Does anybody still call hogs?" I asked.

"I don't suppose so. The pigs don't go anywhere to call them back from."

I felt a certain nostalgia. Maybe it had been a better time. At least animals had some semblance of a real life before they got slaughtered and eaten.

"You ought to let your hair go natural," I observed. "You look like Grandma, you know. I bet you'd have her same snow-white hair." Grandma had beautiful hair, gracefully swept up from her face in soft natural waves and pinned in a bun with horn hairpins.

"I haven't seen my natural hair since I was twenty-two," said Vaneta. "I'll be a redhead till I die, now. If I knew for sure it'd be like Grandma's I'd let it go, but it would probably turn all mousy."

In the lamplight Vaneta did look a lot like Grandma, small with dainty features and bright eyes. But Grandma had always had snow-white fluffy hair, even when I was small. I figured in my mind. When I was six, Grandma would have been . . . she was born in 1878 . . . seventy. Well, I had been totally grey for almost ten years and I was only fifty-one. No wonder she had snow-white hair. Mine was getting there. But I was tall and lanky. I towered over Grandma, and Vaneta as well. Vaneta suddenly got up from the table and disappeared in the bedroom with the flashlight. She came out carrying a small round mauve-colored jar with a silver top. I knew what it was immediately.

"Is there hair in it?" I clapped my hands together. My mind was full of the picture of Grandma combing her hair, twisting it up in a bun, and pushing the horn hairpins through it to hold it in place.

"It's got to be hers," Vaneta said, and she was right. Part of Grandma's ritual had been twisting the combings in coils and stuffing them in the mauve-colored jar. We looked at the little white bird's nest of hair and then at each other, both on the verge of tears. Then the lights came back on suddenly and rescued us. Vaneta blew out the kerosene lamp.

"Well heck," I said, "I liked it better with the lamp."

"Do you want me to light it up again?" Vaneta didn't care; she liked playing old games, too. But I needed to get up early and head back to the State Historical Society library, so I decided to go to bed. My mind was full of images of Grandma as I went to sleep. And that ridiculous hog call. I hummed it softly under my breath as I lay in bed. I knew what I would do in the morning—which seemed a long time in coming, as I was awakened twice by lightning and thunder. Neither time was as dramatic as the crash that had put out the lights earlier in the evening, but I closed my eyes against the startling flashes that made the shade of darkness on my eyelids change. I'd forgotten that in Oregon, where thunderstorms are infrequent and subdued.

As soon as it was light, I jogged to the east. At least this soggy summer was affording beautiful sunrises. I went past the actual hog pasture east of the barnyard where the pigs had run when I was a kid. I didn't give the call there because I didn't want to wake up Vaneta. A sizable pond from all the rain had flooded the lower part of the pasture. It sure would make a mighty good hog wallow as it dried up later in the summer. "What a waste," I said aloud. A sudden movement startled me.

A doe and her fawn had raised their heads and stood poised for flight. They had been drinking at the southern edge of the little lake. Bounding away across the field, they leaped in unison, the doe holding her pace to what the fawn could match. Their tails were white flags. Never had I seen deer this close to the house; indeed, in my childhood I had never seen them at all. Why was I wasting my time mourning the loss of free-range pigs when deer were coming back! I stood watching until they disappeared into the willow brush that lined the straightened course of the drainage ditch creek.

Trotting over the second hill, I topped the rise where the old Henrichs barn used to stand. Little indicated this had once been a farm with barns and a house. Just scrub willow brush where the windmill had been and one crumbling foundation wall from the old barn. I stopped at the top of the hill and turned back toward Sweet Memories. I took a deep breath and sang the familiar two-note song to all the ghosts of pigs in my past.

"Soooouuu . . . eeeeeee . . . Soooouuuu . . . eeeeeeeee . . . Soooooooouuuuuu . . . eeeeeeee. Here . . . ere . . . pig-pig-pig-pig-pig-pig-pig-pig-pigggggg!" No pigs came. The momentary silence was profound. Then the startled Eastern phoebe in the willow bush picked up the same interval I had used. With piercing, clear notes, it threw an echo to the golden flaked clouds which feathered the eastern sky for the sunrise. "Feee . . . beee, feee . . . beee, feee . . . beee, feee . . . beee."

•   •   •

"See how the lightning splits the sky in broken eggshell pieces," my mama said, holding me to the window. That was good lightning, which drew thin lines through the sky that looked like the cracks in the slim blue vase on the mantel. Long ago the blue vase had fallen to the floor, which made the lines spread like a complicated net over the surface. We must dust the vase gently or it would break apart. But sometimes the lightning was bad, like when it traveled down the cottonwood to burn a big hole in the center. Sometimes the lightning even killed people, like the man on the tractor who did not come in before the rain. I must come in before the rain.

Once when my mama still taught at the number five school, the lightning came. My brother and I waited at the end of the walk, but clouds curled, dark as purple plums, and the smell of the wind changed. My grandma made us come in the house, but my mama was walking over the first hill. Oh, Mama, you must come in before the rain. Hurry, Mama, hurry. The purple sky turned black and the lightning tore a ragged hole. Mama, Mama! We pressed against the black window, but the rain came. Our mama disappeared. When the lightning flashed, we could see her walking. We cried and she held us against her coat, which dripped with rain.

The piano bench stuck to the back of my legs where the shorts stopped. If I shifted my leg, the skin peeled away from the bench like tape. How could he want to sing when it was so hot? "It will rain tonight," Uncle Jim had said to Grandma when we sat on the front porch. Heat lightning flashed in the southern sky. "Every time I have hay down it rains." It was true. "I was wondering if she would like to play the piano," my uncle said. He did not say it to me.

The same songs. Each time the same songs. First he would sing the tenor. I would sing the melody. Then he would sing the melody and I would sing the alto line. "The Old Rugged Cross." "I will cling to the old rug—ged cross, rug—ged cross . . ." "Leaning on the Everlasting Arms." "What a fellowship, what a joy divine./ Leaning on the Everlasting arms." "Honey in the Rock." "There's honey in the rock, my brother . . ." Then I would chord and he would yodel. "Yo—o—lay—tee—o. / Yo—dle—o—a—lay— tee—o. / Yo—dle—o—a—lay—tee—o— / O—la—lay—tee—o. / O—la—lay—tee—o. / Yo—dle—o—a—lay—tee—o."

My back hurt from sitting. Salt ran into the corner of my eye. Why didn't my mother come? She sometimes rescued me with a made-up task. The thick air sat on my arms so I could barely move my fingers over the sticky keys. The thunder rumbled in the distance. My legs melted into the piano bench. He opened the other book. The big windowpane rattled in its frame as the thunder moved before the wind. My mother should help me, I thought defiantly. He always sings too long. Let lightning strike the house, I prayed.

The room turned bright white and a ball of fire came down the lightning rod outside the parlor window. Then everything was black and the thunder clapped the very walls of the house together in the total darkness. Rain fell all at once like the Flood itself.

We were dead and I had made it happen.

No, God, no! I'm sorry, I'm sorry, I'm sorry.

I ran for the horse, who stood in the far, far end of the field. I wanted her in the barn where the metal rods drew the lightning safely to the ground. She reared to meet the thunder as I swung on her back, the mane cutting my fingers. I crouched over her neck as we outran the blue lines moving from the southwest, we outran the wind bending the corn sideways, we outran the black curtain tearing with ragged golden lines. From the safety of the barn I stood in the haymow and watched the storm, my stomach tight with fear, knowing even then that it would someday strike, enter the horse's eye, burn a line along her back, and leave her crumpled body on the ground.

•   •   •

"If I die," my grandmother reminded me every night, "my new underwear is in the second drawer."

"Okay, Grandma," I said automatically. I did not think it morbid, merely prudent to have such contingencies in mind. We bathed only once a week in the winter, in water that my mother heated on the Majestic Range and carried upstairs to the bathroom, where the kerosene heater put out a throbbing ring of warmth.

That conversation did not take place, however, until after the story.

"Why don't you go and talk with your grandma just a bit," my mother prodded gently if I dawdled too long after the dishes were done and Grandma was already sitting in her rocker by the bedroom window. I meant to anyway, but I was a child and liked the attention of being reminded of what I knew I should do. Flopping crosswise on her bed, I snuggled into the sour-sweet old quilt.

Even though she protested each time that I already knew the old stories by heart, and even though I did, I loved to hear her tell them. What can be better when you are young than knowing exactly what will come next? I lay there, and she rocked, while the heat lightning flashed, or in August sometimes the northern lights streaked long fingers into the sky.

"Tell the one about the spring." When she was eight years old, her father had bought his own land—after years of working for the more affluent farmers—a forty-acre piece one mile north and a little east of Scotch Grove, close to the spring on the Henry Ahrnken place. They were lucky, she said. When the first settlers came, according to the old folk, the water table was high and anyone could dig six feet and find water. By the 1880s so much of the slough land had been drained that the men would have to dig at least forty feet for a well. But her family had the spring, and one of her tasks as a child had been to carry the buckets up the hill. I knew from her description how the roof of the open shed on the hillside sloped over the mossy wall. The sweet water was cold against my teeth. I smelled the damp greenness and saw the silver flash of the clear cascade as it brimmed over the side of the wooden holding tank to tumble down the hill.

Toward the Maquoketa River. For her family lived at the rim of the timber where the woods and the prairie met. "Timber roogians, that's what we were." She laughed. "Timber roogians and prairie hoogians." Or was it the other way around? There is no one to ask, but a distinct division existed and the Rickels were the timber ones, drawn down the hill by the sandy hollows to the river. "Tell the Sand Hollow one," I said.

So we strolled together down the sandy gulch, lined with gnarly bluffs and wildflowers, with her brothers and sisters. "Say their names," I commanded. "They weren't all there, then," she protested, for she was the third and some were so much younger. She had been farmed out as a hired girl at twelve and came home only on Sundays, if she was lucky. "Say them anyway," I begged. The German names were a magic language to me—German had been forbidden in the schools since World War I. Even in Monticello a straw-filled effigy of the Kaiser had been dragged through the streets and burned.

She started with her parents and listed the siblings in order. Their names reflected the Ostfriesland, Germany, home of the parents' origin. Gerd Rickels and his wife, Gesche Margaretha Bohlken. Gerdjanssen (John), Gesine Margaretha (Zena), Gerdine Hermine (Deanee, that was my grandma), Johann Karl (Karl), Angella Ellenora (Aungel), Heinrich George (Hank), and Wilhelm Friedrich (Willie). Then the babies, as she called them. Emma Auguste (Emmy), Bertha Charlotte (Lottie), and Laura Adele (Daley). And they all came with us, picking wildflowers and gathering fossils, carrying sticks in case unexpected rattlesnakes appeared. And they all spoke German. But she did not anymore. "Only in my dreams," she would say wistfully when I asked her to. But she would sing "Stille Nacht" in the bedroom at Christmas when we had put up the colored lights.

"Tell about school," I said, for the benches with their stained inkwells and the children chanting in unison sounded so romantic to my Dick and Jane ears. The year had been much shorter, Grandma said, at Timber School and Rocky Ridge. Winter term was November through March. Then it was so cold that the children wore their coats all day, taking turns by the stove, with the littlest ones closest. I smelled the steaming wool and the wet mittens, felt the sharp division between the heat on my face and the frigid air on my back. And in the short summer term of May and June, I longed with her to skip down Sand Hollow while the wildflowers were at their best, to gather the white and blue violets, to peek under the canopy of the jack-in-the-pulpits, and to see the stands of nodding mayapple in bloom. She could recite all the counties of Iowa by geographical location, as well as the townships of Jones County, and she knew the exact lay of the rivers. Never was there a question of her going away to high school. Her eldest brother was the scholar for them all. Noticed early for his intellectual promise by the elders of the Sandhill German Lutheran Church, he had been sent after country school to pre-seminary training in Milwaukee, Wisconsin, then afterward to Concordia Seminary in St. Louis, Missouri. So the Rickelses devoted what money they had not to amass farmland but to educate a son to the work of God. "I was so proud to help send money," my grandmother said, though her wages must have been meager indeed.

"The blind lady" was my signal for the story of Mrs. Hoyt. "A hard old lady she was." Grandma could still shudder talking about her. Lyman Hoyt and his wife, Sarah, had arrived from Pennsylvania in 1862. His energy and leadership talents so impressed the Scotch Grove Presbyterian Church fathers that they took the unusual step of installing such a young man as an elder. For a short time he dominated church records, zealously serving on committees to keep vigilance on members' morals. But tragedy struck with a sudden attack of appendicitis, and on April 12, 1865, "Lyman P. Hoyt . . . in the providence of God [was] suddenly summoned by death to his final abode." His sons took over the farm and turned it into a tree nursery. Lyman Hoyt's widow, Sarah, was the "blind lady" of my grandmother's story, for whom she came to work in 1890.

"I was such a little girl at twelve, but I had to bake all the bread, do the cleaning, carry the wood, and have food ready for any who had come from a distance for trees." Most of the windbreaks in the county, the pine or spruce, the California poplars, the elms, the fruit trees, came from that nursery, according to my grandmother. Wagons came from miles away, for the prairie was "surprised by the trees" and they had to be constantly replaced after hard winters. "I had to wash all the clothes, not only for Mrs. Hoyt, but Ben Hoyt and hired men as well." My back hurt for her. The tips of my fingers were numb from the washboard and my hands felt the shriveled softness of too much time in the water. "She was a hard old lady and handy with the cane. Only on Sundays could I go home, and sometimes people would come and I would not be allowed to leave. I was so very lonesome for my brothers and sisters." She worked there nine years, until she married my grandfather, the same year her brother graduated from the seminary.

Sometimes the stories were tragic, like that of the Leesekamp boys and the whirlpool in which they drowned. Sometimes the stories were stirring, like those about the oldest brother, of whom they were all so proud, home on vacations, practicing his sermons from the limestone bluffs. Always I could feel the current of the river, see the curve of the bluff, or smell the wind in the linden trees. But when she was twenty-one, she became a woman and the stories stopped. I could ask for information from that time, but never did the stories come spontaneously with a life of their own. For Gerdine Hermine Rickels, who was of the woods, had married the prairie irrevocably. And Gideon Hughes was a good man, a godly man, but one for whom the love of the picturesque was a weakness.

While her brothers with their German names remained in the timber, became carpenters to build houses and paddle-wheel boats to play in the river—or sallied forth to failed homesteading in Montana—her husband amassed more and more land. While her sister Lottie lived in a quaint sheepherder's wagon with tiny cupboards and a sense of adventure, my grandmother faithfully cleaned the large house her husband had provided and shined the nickel handles on the stove with ashes. Although she had physically moved only a few miles away, her world had become that of the Scotch Presbyterians, who were, in the words of John Newton Hughes, a "steady, hard-handed folk with a firm grip upon the purse strings." And my Welsh-English grandfather found the firm grip much to his liking and emulated the Scots. But his "failure to inspire the family feeling that we are all partners in the . . . spending of the fruits of the family labors" meant she had nothing of her own. Not that Grandma would have asked for a share, not a woman who had been early trained to self-sacrifice and subordination to men to the point of servitude. Surely she did not ask and so she was not given, except by her husband's death. But by then it was too late and she could not bring herself to spend his money. Painstakingly she would patch her brown stockings and underwear. So at her death she had only one unpatched new pair waiting in the second drawer.

Only once did my grandmother come again to Sand Hollow, where she had played as a child. I had followed Uncle Jim the Sunday before and begged to return for a picnic. At first Grandma said no, claiming she was too old and the walking would be too hard. But my mother must have said something to Uncle Jim, who interceded, for she acquiesced. We walked slowly, even Uncle Jim. My brother and I took turns with the picnic basket, until my mother, dismayed that we continually set it in the sand while we looked for fossils, relieved us of it.

And a strange thing happened. As we walked through the hollow, which my grandma complained was already filling up with saplings, she became younger and younger. When we reached the meadow where the hollow widened into a sudden expanse of wildflowers, she picked some black-eyed Susans. She sat on a fallen log to rest and the sun came through her hair in streaks, turning the white tendrils which had strayed from her bun to gold. She braided the stems of the flowers together.

We reached the water. My brother and I stood silently, knowing this was something we did not understand. Deanee Rickels, child of the woods and cascading springwater, surrendered her wreath to the river. The clear young voice of her German prayer followed the swirls in song.

• • •

When I first heard the term *ad infinitum* I pictured it in fruit jars. The fruit jars that had filled the unlighted northwest corner of my grandmother's attic in my childhood were beyond my ability to count or comprehend. Like light-years, the distance to the sun, and the animals that fit into the ark. I had come up the stairs knowing that the amorphous mass that defied my childhood skills of logical assessment would surely not be there. Yet it was a disappointment when I again reached the attic in Sweet Memories, which Vaneta was clearing for remodeling, to find that the fruit jars were gone and the space in which they had stood was quite finite indeed.

Vaneta was entertaining guests downstairs, so I had come alone with the articles under my arm that had spurred the memory. The light was not quite bright enough for easy reading in the attic, but

I stayed, sitting on the floor under the lamp, enjoying the sound of the rain on the roof, the familiar smell of dead bees by the window. I could narrow my eyes and the fruit jars returned, reflecting the light in pallid hues behind walnuts which had been spread on newspapers to dry.

Not that all the fruit jars of my childhood were empty. Rows of jams and jellies flanked by the taller quarts of beans had stood in orderly ranks on shelves. But always they were haunted by the legions of empty jars from a time when men lived in the house, when threshers had to be fed in big noontime spreads, when local political meetings were held in the parlor, a time before the silent movie frames in which we seemed to exist. What was the use of fixing all the food, my grandma complained, when there were no men to feed, only a couple of finicky kids who ate like birds, and a mother who seemed not to eat at all. So, of course, as a child I did not understand the empty jars.

Even though I had actually been employed in weeding the garden, picking the berries, and snipping the beans, I had merely stood on the fringe of what had been the woman's role for centuries. As I knelt between the long rows of beans in the already sultry heat of June, I thought only of how much easier it would be simply to buy a can of beans at Balster's grocery in Scotch Grove than to pinch the pesky weeds between the plants as the dirt made corrugated patterns on my knees. I needed the assistance of one who had actually lived the meaning of the labor. That assistance came from my mother's cousin, Lenore.

Lenore Rickels Salvaneschi was the daughter of the Reverend G. Rickels, my grandmother's brother, whose seminary education had been the source of family pride. She recorded her childhood in a rural Iowa household with my own great-grandmother Gesche Margaretha Rickels in a series of articles for the Iowa State Historical Society.

"Within a small inner room, perhaps ten by fifteen feet, built against one stone and one concrete wall, the 'fruit cellar' contained the apple bin, the carrot bin, the potato crib, the onion basket . . . and shelves of canned vegetables, fruits, jellies, and marmalades."

Although I had been sitting in the library while first reading Lenore's article, I was transported to the very heart of my grandmother's house, her fruit cellar in the unfinished basement.

I heard muffled sounds from outside, saw the slanted late-afternoon light through the small high west window flickering in dusty rays like candle flames, smelled the cool dirt, fingered the dry yellowed paper of the Katzenjammer Kids comics that lined the shelves curling at the edges like old parchment. I pictured snow apples in the bins, potatoes with their bumpy eyes, brown eggs in orderly files in the wooden crate.

In the way that Pompeii added human depth to the power and glory of Rome by preserving people in the positions of timeless daily tasks, Lenore's descriptions preserved the women of my family and their busy days for me. Step by step Lenore led me through that period in rural Iowa when, for the women, "harvest time was not really a particular season, it was a year-round activity. Harvest time meant providing food throughout the year, and it meant gathering and preserving that food whenever and wherever possible." She started in February with the "spring butchering."

"We women would first fry the meat, then place the chunks in jars." I'd almost forgotten the meat in jars—sweet meat which tasted salty and pulled loose in strings. I pictured the golden grainy cracklings in long black pans on the Majestic Range and the lard cool white and pure in the gallon cans.

"The first big crops of fruit were the strawberries and rhubarb." When my mother picked the strawberries on shares in Bert Clark's big patch, she did not wear her garden pants. She wore a clean housedress and knelt carefully. "Don't short yourself, Kate," Bert said to my mama, who was carefully dividing the berries from the white dishpan. But Bert Clark was not short. He was tall, with white hair. "He looks like old Robert Clark," my grandma said. "Only old Robert Clark had a long white beard."

"After the strawberries and rhubarb came the cherries . . . floating in the dishpans of cold water . . . processed in laundry boilers . . . and ladled, boiling hot, into the scalded jars." Beyond the clothesline was the orchard in which the blackberries had run so wild that only narrow paths wound through them to secret places. But my brother and I were like rabbits with our tunnels through the tangle behind the cherry tree, which my mother climbed with a ladder to pluck the bright spots of color.

"Early apples, especially the Duchess . . . quartered applesauce, or made into jelly, the pulp boiled down and left to drain overnight in a flour bag attached to a pole supported on a pair of chairbacks." Duchess, Whitneys, Jonathans or snow apples, white inside, bright white and small. The apple tree by the chicken house that held my rope swing on one limb. "Such a pretty little girl," said my mama, putting the white blossom with the pink center in my hair. "Such a pretty girl." My grandma wore a bonnet to gather apples that looked like the little Dutch Girl's on the box of soap. Each year she made a new bonnet, sewing the seams on the machine that she pumped with her slippered feet.

"Then came the plums . . ." and Lenore described the garnet jars of jelly. When we gathered the plums, it was late summer, for the lane was dust between my toes, soft like the velvet dress of the china-faced doll, cool in the evening. My mother carried the large dishpan, but my grandma gathered the plums in her apron, holding up the corners. The sun sank behind the trees at the old Hoyt nursery grove, leaving bands of color like Christmas ribbons, and the new moon sat in the hoop with a heavy-sided rim.

By the time I reached Lenore's description of the vegetables— "the salty-acid smell of tomatoes stewing in the big kettle," corn, picked in the early dew-soaked morning and husked later in the shade—the ghostly legions of fruit jars in my grandmother's attic throbbed with vibrant color. For I, too, had carried the buckets of water from the livestock tank to the tomato plants, had felt the corn silk tickling where it caught on my collar.

I gathered my articles and descended the attic stairs. Vaneta's laughter floated musically from the parlor. Setting my notebooks on a chair, I took the flashlight from the bedside table. Not that I needed it. No thunder accompanied the steady rain tonight. But I didn't want electric lights for what I had in mind. Under the new thick carpet I could hear the familiar creaks of the backstairs' boards.

Vaneta's restoration hadn't reached the basement. Excess water pooled in front of the furnace. I stepped gingerly across the puddle. The small room clear to the back was the fruit cellar.

The floor in the fruit cellar was dry. With only the flashlight the room seemed amazingly like what it had been in my childhood. An old steel safe with the door rusted shut sat against the south wall. One apple bin was intact. The shelves for canned goods still hung and one was quite full. Jars of rhubarb, strawberry and raspberry jam. Vaneta made them in the old way without pectin. I sat down on a wooden box.

I had broken the line—the line of women that stretched back beyond time. I dabbled for fun as I made my raspberry jam and baked my bread in what had been an entire way of life for all of them. Only if I had the luxury of leisure hours did I engage in the activities that had consumed their lives. I had a sudden nagging doubt. Were they, with their incessant gathering, actually more self-sufficient, more independent, more vital in their contribution than I, with wages I must relinquish to supply even the most basic necessities?

I felt the thin line between what I had considered liberation and what momentarily seemed loneliness. For the first time I understood why I had felt an almost overwhelming urge to return to the farm when I had been alone with the babies. In 1972 the teaching market had tightened. I didn't have a job. How could I feed my children?

You don't understand.

"Yes, yes, I do. Or at least I'm starting to. I understand that you, when faced with a choice of laboring for wages or laboring in the role which was grounded in the toil of centuries of women before you—taking what the land produced and turning it into immediate and tangible sustenance for your family—chose to embrace the older role for which you had been trained by your mother, Dena, who had been trained by her mother, Gesche."

And I understand why my grandmother took the store-bought jar of plum jelly at whose low price they had marveled and placed it on the windowsill with the gaudy commercial label turned away from her. "I couldn't *make* it for that," my mother had said in an odd voice.

"No." My grandmother had answered with only one word. But she set the jar between her and the window to the west. And she rocked silently. For a long time she rocked, stroking her chin and staring at the garnet jar, whose brilliant color darkened with the sun.

.   .   .

Once Vaneta had opened the possibility of ghosts, I became even more intrigued by the people I encountered in the old records. Like Vaneta, I was not afraid of them, but curious, and more aware than ever that our connection with an earlier time was tangible and real. Ghosts or no ghosts, women in this very *place* had defined much of what we were, and I sought out the conditions of their lives not only to understand my mother but increasingly to understand myself. I began listening for bells as I lay in bed. On this particular night the bright moon was an uncharacteristic distraction from sleep, so familiar was the rain in this wet summer that was pushing the farmers to the brink of disaster.

Suddenly I remembered the figure in the mirror on the Fourth of July. For years I had relegated her to the realm of childlike imagination. The very night I decided to believe in ghosts, not only did I realize the figure was real, I knew who she was, now that I knew some history of the area.

This ghost, like Mabel, wasn't a relative, but she was connected to me by way of place. First, the place of her own childhood, which was later owned by my father's people. Second, the place of her seducer's childhood. That land, the Ebenezer Sutherland place, was later owned by my mother's people and finally, in these present times, by me.

The Norris side of my father's family came to this continent from Ireland before the Revolutionary War and settled in Maryland. Not until the 1870s did descendants come to Scotch Grove township. Part of the land that the Norrises bought was the old William McIntyre place south of the Scotch Grove Presbyterian Church. The McIntyres were among the first Scots who had come in the wooden oxcarts. My grandfather was living at the old McIntyre place with his widowed mother, Eliza, at the time he met my grandmother. And *on that land* is where I saw the ghost in approximately 1948.

My grandfather Arthur B. (A. B.) Norris, according to the 1909 ledger, gave 25 cents to the Sabbath school collection eight consecutive times. Perhaps he was trying to impress Mary (Kitsy) Clark, daughter of Robert Clark. After joining the church in 1910, Arthur B. Norris married Kitsy Clark in 1911, and they subsequently moved to Minnesota, where my father was born.

The Norris homesite south of the church filtered down through the family by the time of my childhood to Mary Wilcox, my father's cousin. She was obviously embarrassed by her irresponsible relative—my father, that is—and treated us kindly, giving me boxes of her daughter Jeanette's clothes and inviting us each Fourth of July for firecrackers.

Jeanette's father set off all of the firecrackers while we sat on the front porch. Allowed a sparkler each, we ran around screaming wildly as they quickly fizzled and gave the front yard back to the fireflies. Mary served ice cream and angel-food cake. While the grownups sat on the front porch and talked, Jeanette, my brother, and I played hide-and-seek. I was hiding in the carriage shed, then used as a garage, when the strange apparition appeared.

I cannot imagine that my mother let us use the flashlight from the car, since she was so careful about conserving batteries, so perhaps Mary had flashlights for all of us. My brother searched for Jeanette and me. The shed where I was hiding was narrow, and various items were stored there, including a car with running boards. As I crouched beside a running board, which felt like corduroy to the hand I was using to keep my balance, I could distinguish between the oily hard-packed dirt smell of the floor and the dry, trapped-dust smell from the slightly fuzzy upholstery of the car. My brother, who was "it," passed by the garage, and when he did I had the sensation of having to go to the bathroom because of the suspense. When I could no longer hear him, I started to stand up, and that is when I saw her.

The ghost of Catherine McIntyre—a woman who had been sus-

pended by the church in 1869 for bearing an illegitimate child—
the complainant in the extended legal case of *State of Iowa vs.
Donald Sutherland.*

At first I couldn't imagine where the light had come from, but
I must have pushed against the switch of the flashlight in my
crouched position. The light shone into a full-length mirror leaning
against the wall of the garage. One corner of the mirror was cracked,
but the rest was clear, and a figure with a bonnet looked out.

When I moved forward to look, she momentarily disappeared
and the image became my face. But she returned as I stepped a
little to the side. She wore a bonnet—I think it was blue, but the
light was very dim. I felt no fear whatever; in fact, she was the one
showing fear, almost crying. I wanted to get my mother, not because
I was afraid, but to help this woman who was so obviously fearful.
I stepped to the mirror with the light, but that made her fade back,
and again I could see only my face.

I knew this was magic, good magic, and I should not cry or tell
the others. I could hear my brother and Jeanette far away, and I
knew I should switch off the light or they would see it through the
cracks between the garage boards. But I did not want to leave the
sad-faced woman in the blue bonnet alone. I stood beside the mirror,
not shining the light directly in; she came very far forward, as if she
was trying to see me better. I held the light between us as a candle
so she could see my face. She smiled—as if I was someone of
importance to her, someone she had specifically come to see. I
know she smiled, and then my brother and Jeanette came bursting
in the door. So it was my turn to be "it."

But our mothers called us then. It was too dark, they said, for
us to play, and my mother was ready to take us home to bed. Why
didn't we plan a picnic for next Sunday at the Wapsipinicon State
Park, Mary suggested, and the children could wade in the creek
where it ran over the road. I have a picture of the three of us—my
brother, Jeanette, and I—standing there in the little ford, so my
mother must have said yes. But I did not tell them about the woman
in the mirror.

Later, I told my mother. She was worried. She did not want me
to lie. Twice I retold the story. "Sometimes things seem very true

to us that aren't quite true," she said. "We must never, never lie."
I did not want her to worry, so we must have talked of other things
as we rocked together in the old wicker chair with the weave broken
out on one side.

But of course, that's who it was—Catherine McIntyre. I was
playing hide-and-seek at the old McIntyre *place*. I sat up in the bed
at Sweet Memories and turned on the light. I got out the papers,
both the church records and the photocopy of the Supreme Court
proceedings I had procured just that day.

Catherine McIntyre first came under the scrutiny of the elders
for "promiscuous dancing." The minutes of a series of meetings
followed her moral degeneration from promiscuous dancing to bearing an illegitimate child. No obliging husband came forward with
a confession of "anti-nuptial fornication." In fact, the husband,
when he discovered the existing pregnancy, quit the marriage in
public outrage. "It having come to the knowledge of this session
that Catherine McIntyre has become the mother of an illegitimate
child, and that she married and for a time lived with a husband
whom she deceived in regard to her actual situation as long as it
was possible for her to do so," Catherine McIntyre was suspended
from the Scotch Grove Presbyterian Church on May 29, 1869.

I stumbled accidentally on the criminal court case. On March 2,
1871, in the *Monticello Express*, a letter to the editor stated: "Many
of your readers will recollect the case of the State of Iowa against
one D. Sutherland, for the seduction of Miss Catharine M'Intyre,
a young lady of respectable connections, and good ancestry . . .
The defendant was found guilty by an impartial jury, notwithstand-
ing his four lawyers made a desperate effort to clear him by en-
deavoring to impeach the prosecuting witness, in which they signally
and ignominiously failed."

Days in the musty records of the Jones County Courthouse ren-
dered a brief summary of the trial proceedings and the fee schedule
for the witnesses. All the old names of Scotch Grove were listed.
Donald Sutherland's "four lawyers" had appealed his guilty conviction to the Iowa Supreme Court, and the case was heard in the
December term of 1870.

The specific point of law in the Supreme Court opinion was this:

When Catherine was on the witness stand in the first trial, her lawyer had objected to questions about things she had said and her prior sexual activity. The lower court sustained the objections and Catherine was not forced to answer the questions. This destroyed the suit.

In the opinion of the Supreme Court, Catherine invalidated the presumption of chastity that was inherent in bringing the case because she had not answered questions about her language and virginity. "In order to constitute the crime, the woman seduced must be unmarried and of previously chaste character." Even "indecent and lewd conversation" removed the woman from the chaste category. The only question "decisive of the case" was whether Catherine could establish her chastity by answering questions correctly that proved she was "chaste" at the time the sexual violation took place. If she wasn't chaste, there was no crime, said the Supreme Court, and no damages could be awarded to "the injured, the husband or the father." On that technicality, the decision was reversed.

I put the papers down and shut off the light. The moon was bright, high in the sky, edging distant clouds with a chalky fringe. The good weather wouldn't last. I looked in the direction of the church. The building was hidden in a blue ambiguous lake of fog, as was my land, where Donald Sutherland had spent his childhood.

In my mind, Donald Sutherland was clearly complicit in Catherine's misfortunes. The statute for the crime of seduction required a promise of marriage from the defendant, and the lawyers had not challenged that on appeal. The lower court had been so convinced of his guilt that he was given an unusually severe sentence in comparison to other judgments of seduction on the records of Jones County. Such cases generally were dismissed for lack of decisive testimony. The attempt to have *State v. Sutherland* dismissed was denied, and Donald Sutherland, on the announcement of the guilty verdict, was sentenced to a fine of $600 and ordered to serve ten days' imprisonment. This sentence was not fulfilled because of the reversal by the Supreme Court.

Where had the act occurred with Donald Sutherland that led to such prolonged and public humiliation for Catherine McIntyre?

On his father's land, I wondered, the same land where I had ached for a young man whose promise of marriage was later rescinded? Where I had sat in the blue Impala and thought of my mother's shame? The very land where the man in the white car had ended my childhood innocence about sex? My mind played with fictional possibilities. Perhaps the young Catherine had been a hired girl for the wealthy Ebenezer Sutherland, who could afford four lawyers to defend Donald from the legal consequences of his act.

It did not matter to me that the Supreme Court judge was discussing distinctions in the application of a specific law statute, not what actually did or did not happen to Catherine McIntyre. What mattered was the reality evidenced by the language of the court. A woman's virginity clearly had been considered the property of men: ". . . the injured, the husband or the father."

You must always wear a girdle . . . But you were my wife.

The social effect of such legal definitions went well beyond the esoteric court discussions. The session notes of the church which dealt with this humiliation for Catherine McIntyre never even referred to Donald Sutherland or the criminal case in district court, even though the trials ran concurrently. Even before the reversal on appeal, the church, the repository of the opinion of Catherine's immediate social community, saved only the record of her shame.

It's such a shame, such a shame. I can't bear any more shame.

I picked up the flashlight from the table. I pointed it directly in the mirror. I wanted to see a ghost—to see the ghost of Catherine McIntyre again, because I wanted to apologize for taking so long to recognize her. At that instant I felt entirely certain that Catherine McIntyre had sought me out specifically in 1948. I was a child then, so of course I did not know the story of her life or understand the influence of the past on the present—the threads beyond family boundaries that were interwoven through time and place. No image appeared in the mirror. Maybe if I gave her a little time, I thought, propping the flashlight against a book. All I saw was my own face, ghostly only because of the unusual light, definitely middle-aged, and slightly tired.

Then I noticed a quivering point of light. Could that be Catherine McIntyre? I peered deeper into the mirror. I seemed to be seeing images within images. Then I stood back. I turned my head in an effort to resolve the mystery. What I was seeing was only the glare from the flashlight beam. It was bouncing from the mirror to the glass of my mother's wedding picture on the other side of the room and back again, making odd shimmerings with rings of light.

. . .

In Portland in 1974 I no longer continued with formal therapy once I knew I would not kill myself, but I read Karen Horney's *Self-Analysis* and sought to untangle the knots of my past by recording my thoughts and dreams. That I was not entirely successful in this endeavor can be demonstrated by my choices in graduate school. I continued my penchant for consulting dead men for direction and became intimately involved with the German philosopher G.W.F. Hegel. I could, for a brief time in my life, with only a slight self-conscious twinge, converse fluently with words like "epistemology," "ontology," and "phenomenology." Yes, phenomenology. "With Hegel," I once said at an academic cocktail party, "it is more than the multiple images of tilted mirrors, it is the very space between the images." "Yes!" replied the man next to me with some excitement, and he turned and repeated what I had said. I read the entirety of Hegel's *Phenomenology of Mind*, 808 pages, about as lengthy as the Bible, but not as beautifully written. I related only to interesting phrases: "That was merely the pain and sorrow of spirit wrestling to get itself out into objectivity once more, but not succeeding." I had mostly cerebral relationships with men who thought women should lie perfectly still during sex.

Before my children went to bed at night I told them stories of the farm. Then I would roll up the flokati rug I had bought when we lived in Greece and twirl around the living room with a little blond boy on each hip. Don McLean sang their "favorite song in the whole world," which was "Bye, bye, Miss American Pie/Drove my Chevy to the levee but the levee was dry," and we would sing as loud as we could. They were my pride and joy.

The next year I climbed Mount St. Helens, which had been a

lovely snowcapped cone with a deep blue lake of spirit cupped in its side.

All nature sings/The rocks and trees/The skies and seas. The old Presbyterian hymn rang in a new chorus in my mind.

On that climb I met a man from North Portland, which wasn't exactly Scotch Grove, but he spit like a farmer when he climbed mountains. Then he showed me avalanche lilies, white with yellow centers, trembling above McGee Creek when the snow had just melted on the north slopes of Mt. Hood.

The morning light, the lily white.

"I don't know," said my friend Linda doubtfully. "Seems to me it has a little better chance of making it long term if you like to talk about the same things." (He had barely stayed awake as I recited what I wanted to do with my thesis on Hegel and Greek tragedy. "No offense," he had said, "but do you really *care* about this stuff?")

"How's the sex?" Linda asked.

"Fine," I said. "Just dandy." By then I knew what I had suspected all along: the potential for variation was finite. At long last I'd landed a teaching job. "But sex is sex. And I want to climb mountains."

We had just climbed Mt. Hood. The shadow of the mountain made a long purple triangle across the valley toward Portland as the sun came up over eastern Oregon. The morning light danced on Mt. Jefferson and all the peaks south.

All nature sings and around me rings./The morning light, the lily white. The morning light . . . the morning light . . . "And my boys love him."

After a while, so did I. So I married him. We hiked through a thousand thousand avalanche lilies and we taught the boys to climb mountains.

* * *

Lenore and I finally connected on the phone. Lenore Rickels Salvaneschi was thirteen years younger than my mother, which made her seventy-three years old now. She lived in Kentucky with her Italian Catholic husband. "How did you *ever* dare?" I asked after we had exchanged polite formalities, forgetting momentarily that I was married to a Catholic myself.

She laughed merrily. "Do you know, Barbara," she confided, "the last thing one of my father's sisters said to me was 'Oh, *Lenore*, how could you let your daughter be baptized *Catholic?*'"

Lenore had been kept home from college ten years to tend the parsonage for her father because of her mother's illness. Ten years, before she got her own chance to expand socially and intellectually, to earn her doctorate in medieval literature (going on a Fulbright scholarship to Rome to meet the professor she eventually married), to become a scholar in her own right, to lead discussion groups for women seeking new levels of consciousness.

I had to ask: "Don't you sometimes feel an anger at them, Lenore, a simmering anger underneath?" I was thinking of my own occasional rise of resentment, which still surfaced at unexpected times when I focused on the subordinate role I'd been taught by example, the quiet loyalty to the established order. The price Lenore had paid in her sequestered adolescence was so much higher than mine, yet she was talking only of how much they had loved her, how deep a friendship she had shared with her father, who regarded her as an intellectual companion.

"No," she said simply. "Love is so much deeper than anger that it absorbs it and transforms it as well."

I could feel that truth spread through me while we talked.

"Let me tell you what I remember about your mother," Lenore said. This story I had never heard within the community. "For me, Barbara, your mother was such an exciting, independent person. She had her own car, you know, and was a teacher when I knew her. Women in our family didn't even drive. Even my father, who had to, of course, because of his church duties, worried incessantly about flat tires. But your mother had her own car, a green Chevrolet, I believe it was, and she drove it all by herself to see us in Atkins —clear on the other side of Cedar Rapids. I was so envious. I wanted to be just like her when I grew up."

But that wasn't all. "She took us on adventures, my brother Robert and me. We'd pack up the picnic basket and drive somewhere just for the fun of it. We'd be gone all day. It was so impulsive and exciting that we loved it. Just loved it. She was my favorite cousin. Even though she was thirteen years older and a teacher, she talked to me just like an equal. I loved her."

I was near tears, but I asked for more. "Sometimes she came with her brother, you know, your Uncle Jim. My father seemed especially partial to Kate and Jim. I think he felt that they were repressed in some way, although I have to say honestly he never said that aloud. Not that he didn't respect Gid Hughes—everybody did."

"Go on," I prodded.

"One time Kate had a tremendously animated discussion with my father about evolution. Now, my father was strictly old-line Missouri Synod, with an emphasis on the verbal inspiration of the Bible and the King James version of Genesis. But Kate argued with him for hours."

My mother? Argued with a man? With a *minister*, the Reverend G. Rickels absolutely revered in the family? Was she serious?

"Yes, I'm serious," exclaimed Lenore. "I can still see her blue, blue eyes, bright with confidence as she ticked off scientific evidence. Never disrespectful, you understand. Just confident and solid."

I was astounded. I knew her views on evolution, but I just couldn't imagine this conversation. Not with a man. Yes. Once, when I was in college, I had come home for the weekend with a young man with sandy hair. Jon was his name, and he was a biology major. Rachel Carson's *Silent Spring* had just come out and they spent the whole weekend talking about it. My mother was positively animated, as the book supported her view of DDT and pesticides. She and Jon had talked about it so much I was almost jealous. And surprised. I'd never seen her this way with a man.

"Barbara, there was a whole side of your mother you never knew. I know how that is, my dear, to have different facets, to be more than one person inside."

Lenore must have known. To have grown up in the world described in her articles, trained by my great-grandmother Gesche, by her own mother, who never was comfortable even referring to her husband by name, to have tended the parsonage in her youth for ten years—and later to have led discussion groups to raise women's awareness of their own dignity. I felt ashamed at the smallness of my own resentment.

That night I sat on my mother's bed with the cardboard box she had left in her trunk. I set the little note to one side and spent some time rearranging all the letters in order. The picture with the unfamiliar countenance which Vaneta insisted belonged to my mother had been jostled so it faced away from the bed. I reached over to turn it around and studied it carefully. The eyes were jaunty, almost teasing. They definitely reflected confidence. "And what, young lady," I asked softly, "are your views on evolution?"

I twisted the picture slightly. I could see the tilt of her chin. Yes, the tilt of her chin was the same as the silhouette when she stood by the window. I had forgotten. Thirty years. She had been dead thirty years and I had forgotten. She had faces I had never known. I felt an overwhelming lonesomeness for her. If I could see the hands of this woman in the picture—then I would know. I would never forget my mother's hands, large and capable, blackberry stains in the creases, flour under the nails when she made bread. I wanted to see my mother's hands.

Hers were the hands I called home.

8

Cry Softly, Swallow

> And for all this, nature is never spent;
>> There lies the dearest freshness deep down things;
> And though the last lights off the black West went
>> Oh, morning, at the brown brink eastward, springs—
> Because the Holy Ghost over the bent
>> World broods with warm breast and with ah! bright wings.
> —GERARD MANLEY HOPKINS, *"God's Grandeur"*

I was twenty-one and just entering graduate school at the University of Iowa the only time my mother and I discussed her love for my father and her pain at his desertion. What precipitated her uncharacteristic frankness was that I had been unceremoniously discarded by a young man to whom I had become engaged after a romantic three-year courtship conducted almost entirely by letter and long-distance phone call. He attended a prestigious school on the East Coast and I one of more modest reputation in the middle of Iowa. His subsequent attraction to a young woman from another prestigious school in the East caused him to break the engagement. This action on his part meant, I declared to my mother, the *end* of my life. I would never, *never* marry. So the most intimate details she shared of her life were partially obscured by my own self-pity.

She had cried, my mother said, when she received the letter telling of my broken engagement. How well she remembered the acute pain and disbelief she felt when she first became aware of her own rejection by the man she loved. As she shared her pain in an attempt to absorb some of mine, I began, for the first time, to actively question some of the circumstances she had endured in such dignified silence for twenty years. That night, trying to re-create the reality of her marriage by combining the memory of that conversation with the letters she left for me, I regretted deeply my youthful preoccupation with my own pain.

"I was standing right there," she said, pointing to the slanted window in the sitting room from which one can see the barnyard across the road, "when I saw Bert Clark's car turn in by the windmill." Bert Clark was my father's uncle. "As Bert got out of the car, he looked toward the house, so I knew right away it was about Bob, who had been gone for a week. But Bert Clark didn't come to tell me directly. He went to Jim, who was standing by the windmill. He had something in his hand and he and Jim read it together. I wanted to move away from the window, because they looked toward the house. I didn't want them to see me watching, but I was frozen in place. I can tell you exactly the kind of day it was. It is always so hot in August, you know. Although it was only midmorning, already there was that haze in the air when the outlines of objects are accentuated as if your mind wants to see double. I felt a coldness spread through my chest in spite of the rising heat, for I knew this was something terrible. With the other part of my mind I noticed that the windmill—with the sun behind it—was like a black ink drawing shaded in with pencil. I thought it might be that Bob was dead."

Others knew, but my mother was not told until Bob and Edith called her parents, Len and Sadie Campbell. They also sent them a letter. Len Campbell took the letter to Bert Clark, who took it to my mother's brother Jim. In a first draft of a letter to Kitsy Clark Norris, my paternal grandmother, my mother refers to it.

At first I wouldn't believe, couldn't believe that things were so. Even when I knew they were together I still had faith that there was some explanation. But when I read the letter that he himself wrote to Len Campbell I think something died in me. It was the most terrible thing I ever read. There was no mention of the family he left behind. We were as completely out of his mind as if we didn't exist.

The day she saw the letter was etched in her mind in minute detail. "I kept thinking as I watched Jim walk slowly toward the house that it was odd how I could feel so cold in August. I wanted to turn away and not stare at him coming, but I simply couldn't move or look away."

For my mother the loss of a father for her children was an unspeakable calamity. "It is so much better that he has left you now, Barbara," she said to my tears about the broken engagement, "than after you have committed your life to his course and you have borne his children." I doubt that I was consoled. I was so young and so in love that any amount of suffering with the man seemed preferable to suffering without him. But I asked, at last, for her story.

"I wondered why you never asked," she said. "I knew you must have questions in your heart, but you never, never asked about him, nor did your brother. The one time I wrote to Bob after he left me, I told him his name would never be mentioned to his children until they were old enough to ask and understand. But you never asked and I have been silent so long it is hard to know how to start."

I asked her how she met him. "In 1939 he had come to work for Arend Balster at the hardware store in Scotch Grove. You know, Arend would tell you that he never had a better salesman than Bob. He could talk anyone into buying something. Bob could always get a job when he wanted one, even when he had no experience in the work. He could talk his way into anything. I think it was because however outrageous the lie he was telling, he was so convincing because he believed the lie himself."

"He lied," she said in a letter later, "even when it would have been easier and more convenient to tell the truth.

"To this day I know little of his life before I met him because so much of what he told me I was to find later existed only in his mind. I suspect there are many things no one knew the truth about—certainly not his family." I wonder now what she suspected.

"When he was working at Balster's he was staying at Bert Clark's place. I was teaching at the Slough School that year and I would come home through Scotch Grove because I was staying with my parents. I had my car, you know"—her eyes always brightened a little with pride when she mentioned that car—"and once when I came through I stopped to pick up something at the store just as Bob was leaving work. He asked very politely if he could ride as far as the corner. Of course I said yes—it would have been awkward to turn him down. I knew him by sight anyway, and it was so directly on my way home. After that, he made a point of leaving work at the time I came through. Pretty soon we were sitting in the car at the corner talking for a while before I went home—he said he had been watching me from a distance, waiting to get to know me. Late the next autumn we were married."

"Did you know then it wasn't right?" I asked.

"Oh, Barbara, I was so sure it was right, no one could have told me otherwise. I was so absolutely sure that it was very, very right."

The account of the wedding in the *Monticello Express* is so blurred that I could not make a copy from the microfilm and had to guess at some of the words. The wedding announcement in the November 30, 1939, issue of the *Express* said that on November 25 Kathleen May Hughes had become the bride of Robert G. Norris at the home of her parents in Scotch Grove. Mrs. Marvin Lacock (Laura Sinclair) had sung "Always." The bride had been gowned in blue, and the two flower girls (my cousins Beverly and Vaneta) wore identical dresses. Mrs. Norris, who was a graduate of Coe College, had taught at Monticello Public School and at various country schools in Linn and Jones Counties. Mr. Norris was a graduate of the public high school in Payneville, Minnesota. He had attended Minnesota State Agricultural College and served some years in the U.S. Army in Florida and Honolulu. (I could find no confirmation of the service record.) The newlyweds expected to establish their new home on a farm in Scotch Grove township. (At the Hughes family reunion when I asked her what she remembered, my cousin Beverly said, "I was just a little girl, of course, but the wedding in Grandma's house was beautiful and exciting. You know how that staircase is so lovely set back in the hallway with the parquet floor and the leaded-glass window on the landing.")

My father's parents did not attend the wedding, although a letter from Kitsy Norris dated November 17 acknowledged the invitation had arrived. "We will be looking for you and Kate on Sunday. If the weather is bad just take it slowly and you will get here. Received Hughes invitation yesterday." Then there is a most puzzling line for a mother to write to a twenty-seven-year-old son about to be married: "Now do be careful and do your very best to do your work and all well and be on the square about it all." She concluded: "I am glad you are so happy and hope you always will be." A quick note from Bob's twenty-three-year-old brother Harold, who was on his way down to Iowa to be part of the wedding party—"Come, I will, regardless"—implied they were friendly confidants. "P.S. No girls—I've sworn off!!! (again)"

Bob and Kathleen Norris moved onto the farm in January 1940 with the new year. There must have been trouble from the very beginning. For one thing, even before the move, on December 18, 1939, a loan for $500 was taken at the Monticello State Bank. Although it was paid in full slightly before the due date of June 18, 1940, that was probably because my mother had some teaching money left. "I had been taught to be so careful with money," she said, "and Bob's indifference to it was a source of great nervousness to me from the beginning of our relationship." Right after they were married they traveled to Florida. She hadn't wanted to go and didn't know at first that Bob had managed to borrow the money to finance the trip from the unlikely source of her father.

One letter suggests that, from the beginning, Bob was treated as an outsider to the point of rudeness by some in the Hughes family. Bess, my mother's younger sister, in a letter my cousin included in a family genealogy book, wrote to the other younger sister, Em, of an invitation to a birthday party for my mother which Bob had tried to put together for January 7. Bess comments that her husband, Dick, refused to attend the party. "Dick likes Bob about as well as Jack [Em's husband] does. I believe the folks sense it, too. They never say if they're going to Kate's farm." Besse and Em seem to have shared a genuine camaraderie. They certainly led much freer lives than my mother, who had been the primary helper for my grandmother when the farming operation was at its height. And they seemed to have had their own conspiracy to circumvent the strict control my grandfather had over the older children's lives. Their social escapades, when measured against my mother's puritanical, quiet existence, were positively risqué. But they didn't like my mother's husband, although neither would ever tell me any stories.

My Aunt Bess was evasive when I asked about my father. This must have been the year before she died, the last time I talked with her. "Look at it this way, Barbara," she said. "You children gave meaning to your mother's life. So he gave her something that was worth more than what she lost."

Well, maybe . . . *You'll never know how much.*

One of the first things my father did when he assumed command of the old Livingston homestead, which my grandfather had deeded my mother at her wedding, was to name it The Elms. He painted the name in large white letters on the side of the barn which faced the road and had stationery printed with THE ELMS as a letterhead. That stationery surfaced throughout my childhood as practically the only tangible evidence that he was ever part of our lives. Underneath THE ELMS was Robert G. Norris—Dealer in Dairy Cattle, and underneath that, Center Junction, Iowa. He had big dreams.

"At first," my mother continued, "I was very, very happy. I had wanted to marry, of course." She smiled wanly. "Grandma doesn't like old maids. I can't tell you how many times I heard that." I had heard it, too. "But the nervousness was there from the beginning. I knew Bob made mistakes with money, but I wanted to believe he meant to do the right thing." Whether it was the right thing or not, he was doing it fast. By the time they had been on the farm (which had been given free of debt) a year, he had borrowed $2,700 from my mother's uncle Will Hughes ("Bob lied to him to get it," a later letter said), $750 from my grandfather, and $2,000 from the Monticello State Bank.

My brother, Robert Hughes Norris, was born on September 8, 1940. "Bob was excited when I was pregnant right away," my mother said. "He was good with children, and when Bobbie was born he was so proud." My cousin Beverly said, "He was wonderful as an uncle, Barb. He'd always take the time to throw the ball—or play games with the kids. My own father could never loosen up that way—we were a little afraid of him. But Uncle Bob was so much fun."

Gideon Hughes died on December 25 of that year. His obituary read: "Four children, all happily married, survive." One was listed as Mrs. Robert Norris of Center Junction. Already that was hardly an apt description of my parents' marriage. "I'm so glad my father never knew the full extent of the problems, even at the time of his death," my mother said. She had been married for thirteen months.

On July 13, 1941, my father, Robert George Norris, was accepted into membership in the Scotch Grove Presbyterian Church. My brother, Robert Hughes Norris, had been baptized into the Presbyterian faith a month earlier. My parents lived only a few miles from Center Junction and could have attended the Presbyterian church there, which had been cloned from the congregation at Scotch Grove, but my mother probably preferred to remain in the church where she had been as a child.

In November 1941 the record of problems begins with the letter from John Newton Hughes previously cited in regard to the sanctity of the farm. Vaneta had rescued that letter from Uncle Jim's papers. Hearing of delinquent taxes and a lawsuit brought against my father by a lumber company, Jim had written to his uncle, a prominent lawyer in Des Moines, asking for advice. John Newton Hughes immediately wrote to my mother, who did not reply. He wrote again. After receiving an answer to his second letter of inquiry to my mother, he then wrote to Uncle Jim on November 15, enclosing my mother's reply to demonstrate that, because of my mother's loyalty, the situation was beyond easy solution.

John Newton Hughes's first letter had gone unanswered because my mother was embarrassed. The answer she wrote to his second inquiry was a guilty confessional: "I've known or suspected all along that Bob's business deals didn't always turn out as successful as he let on to me, but he is so good to me otherwise." She detailed the receipt for the first half of the year's taxes but insisted, probably innocently, that the county must have made a mistake to list the rest as delinquent even though she could not recover the receipt. ("I always believed him." She spoke of her faith to me later with a sort of awe in her voice. "I wanted to so much, because I loved him, because he believed himself when he lied. I don't think he knew the difference between what was so and what he wanted to be so.") She had agreed to take out a mortgage on the farm because they needed the $6,000 to pay debts.

Her letter to John Newton Hughes continued: "Even that won't pay all our debts. Uncle Will won't get all his money right now but I'm going to try to see to it that he gets the balance as soon as possible." She defended her husband loyally. "He is good in so many ways and it is hard to admit he has faults, but his weakness seems to be poor judgment in financial affairs. Of course I knew I shouldn't sign notes, but he buys things and gives notes and then the bank won't renew the old note unless the other is included. He means to do the right thing and it always seems as if he should be able to pay at least part of the note before long, but something else always comes up." For the first time my father's failure at farming is mentioned. "Last summer when I refused to sign any more [notes] he sold the cows and machinery. We have rented the farm for next year (not the house and garden). We might as well if we are going to lose money anyway. We can keep chickens and a few cows."

("What did you say when he sold the cows and the machinery?" I asked her when she repeated this story to me.

"I was so stunned I didn't say anything." She had been taught not to challenge men's decisions.)

"I guess I've said too much . . ." she wrote in anguish to her uncle.

The next letter, dated December 2, 1941, two weeks after the correspondence with Uncle John Newton Hughes, is from my father's brother Harold. Initially he chatted about the unusually warm weather and the flu bouts of the family in Minnesota. The family had heard rumors of trouble, probably from Eloise's mother, Blanche Clark Sutherland. Harold referred to her as an aunt "who can't see any good in anyone but her daughter." Harold's letter reflects the family's fear:

I guess I'm writing this more as a pep talk than anything else for I am sleepy from a date last evening, but I do wonder if you'd let us talk a minute.

I don't know everything about what is going on down there. My biggest worry is that in your haste and so on to get that big money you are going to neglect Bobby and Kate— For Heaven Sake don't do that—a fellow can do a lot of things without money but he'll never do much ahead neglecting his family to get it.

Honestly, I used to worry like the very Devil about you, Robert, but I've got some feeling that seems to keep telling me that anyone who has a boy like Bobby and a wife like Kate doesn't need to worry or be worried about—The big thing is to quit trying to do it all alone and let God help. He does if we only give Him a chance.

I'm certainly not doubting but what you're going to make it all come out o.k. in spite of opinions of some certain aunt who can't see any good in anyone but her daughter.

So long, feller—and take care of Bobby and Kate first and the rest is bound to come.

Love,

Harold

P.S. Please give me the straight of it when you do write.

He was from a "good family." They wanted him to do the right thing.

"I can't tell you what it cost me to give up farming," my mother told me. "Not in money, the debts were beyond count at that time. But at least I still had my garden, the chickens, and a few cows."

In December 1941, when my mother was in the advanced stages of pregnancy with me, there was no money to be had. She was alone—except for the baby, my brother Bobbie, in the huge house built by the last Livingston who went bankrupt during the Depression. My father had somehow procured a bulldozer tractor. He went to Chicago, where his plan seems to have been to work with his brother-in-law, who was involved in moving topsoil from farmland outside Chicago to the front yards within the urban area, a practice that became extremely lucrative. His brother-in-law was obviously less than enthusiastic at having him there, and Aunt Em will not talk of that time. "I was too busy with my own babies," she said, and she probably was. She did not reply to my mother's letter, which led my mother to believe there was no future in her husband's work. ("I think Em would have answered my letter if she had felt at all encouraged," my lonely mother wrote in her sadly tender letter of December 3, 1941.)

"Dearest Daddy Bob," the pencil draft began. She started with a reference to a letter she had just received from him, then gave an account of the weather, the washing, and the wages various people had tried to collect which she could not pay: "I gave him $2.00 which just about cleaned me out. . . . George asked for some money this morning but I didn't have any to give him. So please try and send some money." He had apparently worried over their separation. "I don't know why you worry about us being separated. Only you separate us . . . certainly not me." Bob's mother had written and must have been privy to the financial problems. "Your mother doesn't think you should get that expensive equipment, but she thinks I am right in staying here even if you are working away somewhere else."

She proceeded to some bad news about a refused loan and advised him gently to turn the bulldozer back ("even if we do lose money on it"), as there is no way they can make the payments. "Dear Bob, it hurts me so much to have things go against you. Why do you let on that things are different from what they really are to people —including me?" She had just found out he had lied about working the farm himself, about having another job, and about Em's husband's willingness to put up collateral for the tractor in an attempt to have a loan approved. "You must face things," she gently admonished, couching the plea between commentary on the weather and an account of Bobbie in the cupboards pulling out the pots and pans. After a detailed and humorous story of picking pinfeathers from a rooster she has butchered for food, she concluded on a serious note:

"I don't like to write you bad news but I guess it can't be helped. Please be practical about this and see things the way they really are—not just the way you want them to be. And don't blame other people. And dearest, darling Daddy Bob, please take care of yourself. Love always, Kathleen and Bobbie."

This letter did not tell the whole story of the anguish my mother endured that autumn. "It is a wonder Barbara was even born alive," she wrote later in a scribbled draft that appears to be for another letter to her uncle John Newton Hughes. "I won't go into that time. I can only think he must have got started on the wrong track and did the things he did because he was desperate." I was never to know what this meant, but she did tell me, "When you were born [February 16, 1942] I was in the hospital in Monticello. It was such a terrible time. The nurses probably thought I had lost my mind. I simply couldn't stop crying. And you cried, too. You cried and cried and cried. At first you were jaundiced, but that cleared up after a few days. It surely is right what they say about the child feeling the nervousness of the mother, and I felt so guilty for your obvious pain." She put her arms around me, for we were snuggled on the old horsehair couch by then. "Barbara, I never thought I'd tell you this, but one night I honestly thought we would both be better off dead. You had cried for hours—the doctor called it simply the three-month colic. Bob was gone—he was often gone at night, and I didn't know where he was. I had been crying myself and all I could think was that we were both too miserable to live. It was lucky for us that we had Bobbie to think about."

I didn't know how to answer her. It would be another decade before I had any understanding of what she meant.

"If you were so miserable, why didn't you kick him out?" I asked.

"It's not so simple later. That's why I say you're lucky to have this happen now, before you have his children. I was mostly miserable at night when I woke up worrying about the money. He was a tender, affectionate man. He spoke of his love often. I'd never heard that, you know. My own father never spoke of such things. Bob wanted children and he seemed to adore both of you." She amended that, as she was relentlessly truthful. "Bobbie anyway. You were so young when he left that he never really knew you."

She wrote in a letter to her sister Em in May 1942 about my

brother: "He certainly likes his Daddy, especially when Daddy takes him out to the barn or gives him a ride on the tractor. Daddy brought in five baby ducks yesterday morning and he got very excited about them." But she wrote in her only letter to my father after he left: "Bobbie ran and looked inside the barn and he said, 'Is my daddy here?' "

Nineteen forty-two was the year of the trailer. The adventure began shortly after she wrote the letter about the baby ducks, and the entire episode ran from June to the end of December. Vaneta confirmed Eloise's story that my mother was giddy with excitement when they stopped to show her parents the trailer on their way to Colorado. Vaneta said, "I was just a little girl, but I saw that trailer before they left. Mom and I went over to Aunt Kate's farm, probably specifically to see the trailer. I loved it, because it was like a doll house with all the little drawers. Aunt Kate let me open all of them and look in everything. I remember her as being very happy."

By the time my mother recounted the adventure to me, her version reflected not happiness but terror. First, at having left her garden behind. "When I was on the farm I knew I could always feed my children. It is such a feeling of helplessness to not know you will be able to feed your children." I could not have known what she meant when she was telling me the story.

How did he convince her to go?

"He said he was so anxious to keep his family together, that he loved us so much and didn't want to be separated from us again. At first only he was going, because he had a good job and would send money to start paying off the debts. But when he begged me to come, I began to feel I was wrong for not being able to let go of the land. I would have followed him anywhere, really." She followed him to the Ideal Trailer Camp in La Junta, Colorado.

A bank statement from the Citizens Savings Bank in Anamosa, Iowa, shows a flurry of bill paying in July. Surely my father was trying to get off to a good start and square away some of the immediate debts. He missed a few, even little ones. The big ones he simply ignored at this point. A letter written August 6 by Irving Eilers, a neighbor who seemed to be managing the farm in Iowa, refers to an unpaid bill: "Say Robert, Doc. York is getting pretty hot about a bill for $50.25. He is going to tie up the farm account if we don't pay him. I told him that I would not pay it until I got word from you. He gave me two weeks time. He is no friend of mine. So you will have to let me know." York was a veterinarian in Monticello. My father paid the bill on August 11, according to the next statement.

Irving Eilers's letter seemed to be an answer to one my father had written from Colorado bragging about his wages. This lucrative employment, which made "the old cream check look pretty small" to Irving, must have been at the Concrete Material Construction Company in La Junta, because his mother addressed two letters there to "employee no. 495." But the creditor hounds were not kept at bay very long.

Kitsy Norris began her letter in response to a terse note she received from her son on July 28: "Received your note tonight, Robert. I can't see why you said 'if you care to write.' I've been writing right along. And you hadn't written since before the sale and said then you would write the day after so we had looked every day. I saw by the Express you had left Iowa . . . I imagine Bobbie has a time to figure it all out. I do hope you are all well." Then she lapsed into the usual detailing of neighbors' lives and conditions at their little cottage at Green Lake. She referred to a sale which is not mentioned elsewhere and must have been the remaining farm equipment and perhaps some household items, as the cows and larger machinery were already gone. "Your sale certainly did real well for you and we are glad. There have been a few sales in this county caused by men going to the army. I suppose there will be many more before fall." Her younger sons, Harold and Arthur Paul, both eventually ended up in the service. "I see by the paper this evening they think they will defer men from the Dakotas or Minnesota until after harvest. That will help this year's crops but if the war lasts I don't see what people will do . . . I hope you like your work and get along well." She must have been worried.

My mother sent a card to the family in Minnesota in my name, because Kitsy's next letter followed within a week. "Received Barbara June's card and rejoice with her that the tooth is thru . . . Just whisper in her ear that I'd like to know a lot more about her and hope some of you will write soon." She also referred to an article she read in *Country Gentleman* about trailer houses and asked some questions with strained enthusiasm. I think my mother was too miserable to write an honest letter. "Living in a trailer sounds romantic, I know, but it was dirty and confined and there was no place to take you children even for a walk. He was gone to work or somewhere, I never knew where he was. I was there in this little hot tin box without even a window that would open. There was no water hook-up and you were sick all the time."

Then, in a confusing sequence that all took place in August, my father's younger brother Arthur Paul was drafted and my grandfather shut down their farming operation. A green handbill advertised an auction at my Grandfather Norris's farm. "Because I am unable to continue farming due to my son going into the army, I will sell at public Auction at my place . . ." Our unsettled little family apparently made a hurried trip from Colorado to Minnesota to help with the sale of 27 head of cattle, a horse, 125 sheep, 33 pigs, 33 acres of "standing corn in field," and a raft of farm equipment and machinery including a bobsled. Kitsy wrote after my parents returned to Colorado, thanking them for coming. She said, "I can picture you all better now after seeing you." My mother must have put up a brave front, not wanting to trouble them more. "We are getting along all right," Kitsy concluded her letter. She had worries of her own.

In spite of the fantastic wages my father bragged of to Irving Eilers, he continued to draw from the farm account in Anamosa, and by the end of August the balance was down to $100.03. Another letter from Eilers itemized money coming in from the farm operation in cream checks and eggs. "He always collected the money from the farm and made good money in wages besides, but I could never find it. When the bank statements came at the end of the month, there was never any accounting of it," a later letter said. Where did it all go? "Gambling," said my mother's cousin Les Rickels. "I think your dad mighta been in with the high rollers."

In October two interesting and chatty letters arrived from my father's seventeen-year-old brother, Howard. Harold by now was also in the service, the navy, and Howard said he expected to end up there himself before long. He described *Rio Rita* with Abbott and Costello. "Very good, sure laughed," he wrote. My mother was no longer laughing, but we ended up giggling as she told the story.

"Barbara, you had the worst diarrhea of any baby I have ever met before or since. I was frantic to get you to a doctor, but I had no money and Bob had the car. And I was stuck in that trailer with no water. Bobbie was screaming because he was cooped up and cold. The weather had changed by then. You had soiled every single bit of clothing I had for you. I washed what I could in the bucket, but I couldn't get anything dry fast enough. I had used the last dishtowel for a diaper. I needed to run out to the water tap for more water and I set you on the floor because that was the safest place. I dashed out the door for the water. When I came back—you were crawling then and were quicker than a cricket—you had done another job and somehow scooted all around the trailer and I don't know how you did it, but you had poop on everything. I mean everything. I guess it had dribbled down your legs, but somehow you left nothing untouched." I looked at her in horror. Then we started to laugh.

"You shoulda drowned me in the bucket and put me out of my misery," I snuffled, giggling in spite of myself.

"Never, never say that." She held me to her, and we could not tell the laughter from the tears.

"He got in trouble with the law again." She hadn't told me about any other time. "One day in the middle of November he came home in a hurry and bundled us into the car. We drove all day and night to Iowa and he left us at Grandma's. I didn't know what was happening except he was in trouble and I didn't have any of our things with me." I can imagine what my grandmother said to him if she had a chance. Apparently he went right back to Colorado himself on the train.

He was in trouble, all right. Three letters from him followed on stationery from the Hotel Joyce, Colorado Springs, Colorado—"In the Shadow of Pikes Peak." A few lines referred to an obvious fiction of being in the service and "flying"—to start again in a day or so. All were actually postmarked from Colorado Springs. The first, written on November 11, talked about being on a train with servicemen and how there would be no flying because of snow and fog. By the second letter, written December 2, any references to the service were couched in extremely vague terms and he was a little more direct about his "trouble."

"Things are starting to iron out now. I wasn't so sure for a while about anything. I haven't all the details yet as to what caused it all but at least I have been freed of all suspicion and thank God for that."

This had to be fiction. "My flying will start again in a day or so they say. And directly I'll be based somewhere else." This was the last reference to military service.

"It seems Tex made some big mistake on the papers he sent in and the company clamped onto the trailer and charged me with unlawful sale of property. I happened to get a break by having a very fine cop assigned to the case and I wasn't locked up but under oath not to leave town. So I was stuck here but had a fighting chance. The trailer is still in custody but I should receive a clearance on that soon.

"Of course when I was taken up for questions I was out of a job just that quick but when I was freed without guilt I went back for re-assignment and with a little hand shaking managed to make the grade."

So he was in jail and she knew it.

"But believe you me that I found out a lot of things in a hurry. You sure miss a lot by not handling the business, Kate. It's dog eat dog and they will sure bite and bite hard.

"I'm still in the dark so far as a letter from you is concerned. I haven't heard a word from you except that call I made on the telephone."

(I think she really tried to give him up at this time. Beverly said at the reunion that she remembers one episode which could have occurred in 1942, when my mother came to see her mother, "probably for a sister-to-sister talk, you know." She had listened on the stairway.

"Oh, Besse," my mother said. "What am I going to do? I can't live with him and I can't live without him.")

"How are the kids?" my father continued in the letter. "Does

Bobby ever wonder about Daddy? . . . I'm here at the hotel yet so write to me here."

Their letters crossed in the mail. I wish hers had been saved: I doubt that it included much humor or even stories about mischievous children. The surprise for me was how directly he addressed her questions and how much he seemed to care for her. Perhaps he believed in his love himself. I was *not* surprised that he seemed genuinely detached from and baffled by the problems that had developed—and that he had a sense of mysterious negative things having been done to him to cause his bad luck. This letter seems the most tangible communication I have from the person who was my father, but, of course, it was not written to me.

"Dear Kathleen," he began his letter of December 7, using her correct name. She had legally changed it when she was teaching.

"Received your letter today and guess I found out things are in a good jam. And I'm terribly sorry but that doesn't straighten them out very fast I know. So far as I'm concerned I guess I'm done. They have me out of work again. Some of the fellows laid a plot and I was called in and asked to resign which of course there was no use to refuse. And I am out looking for work again now."

She had apparently accused him of taking the registration card for the Chevrolet. That meant she had the car itself but was afraid he would sell it. He didn't have the card and told her where to look for it. Then he addressed her question about the missed payments on the trailer that led to the "unlawful sale of property charge." He explained it was because he was out of a job. He had notified the company he couldn't make the payments, but they were unsympathetic. Somehow it had become the company's fault that he was out of money and without the trailer. "But as it stands I doubt if I ever get a cent from that."

"Now in regards to what I think of the future." That must have been her next question. "All I have to say is just my opinion."

"The farm is in pretty good shape. There is a fair amount of stuff there and Merle is a fair renter. Now as to you handling it, if you don't feel you can then turn it over to some one else to handle. Even the bank but I am sure you can handle it."

"Now as to how to raise money for the note this year." The

perennial question. The note was now up to $10,000. "I'm sure now I can't earn enough now to make up your shortage." Her shortage! "So I suggest you approach Dick and Bess for a loan or sell your interest in the other place or get a loan on it." So Uncle John Newton Hughes was right. That land would have been taken, too, the land I now own. "Or sell the car if you wish.

"Now you'll say what about me? Kate, I owe you a great deal besides a living for you and the kids. As soon as I go to work I will send what money I can to you for that purpose. Now I want you to take whatever else I send and apply it to what I've cost you." The bookkeeping on his payments certainly wasn't a problem. He never sent a cent.

(Right at this point when I work my way chronologically through the letters, I always hate my father. I feel like calling him every nasty name I've ever heard. But with the next paragraph in the same letter, he turns me around every time. And not because he swears eternal love for my mother.)

"Just as the song 'Always' goes I'll be loving you always and working for you but Kate, I'm not going to come back to Jones County to live. Ever. If I ever make enough so you wish to consider it safe to be with me again I'll see to it you can live with me. But even for you and our children I'll never live there."

I didn't stay in Jones County, either. I couldn't wait to get out and see the world, and that's what he wanted, in a way. He was always heading west, always looking for something different, wanting something other than the farm. How can I condemn that? Farming wasn't the most holy of callings, as they said it was, to both of us.

"Your father was an extremely bright man, Barbara," said Les Balster, who worked with him at the implement store. "Once a man came in with a tractor and said he needed it overhauled; it wasn't running right. 'I can do it,' Bob said, 'I've done it a hundred times.' But he had never done it before and I knew it. Your dad had that tractor strung all over the store. But he got it back together and the guy said it ran better than new. And Bob Norris was the nicest man you'd ever want to know. I can't say a bad thing about the guy—except the time he came back and paraded around in cowboy boots with Edith. That must have been hard on your mom."

A year after he had left us my father sent a strange little note addressed to Bobbie and Barbara. He was working on a ranch and had hurt his right hand, so the writing was a childish scrawl: "Daddy works on a big ranch in Wyoming and lives in a log cabin. He rides horse back quite a bit. There is a river and mountains. If they don't take Daddy away to prison he will soon be able to send you folks support money. Bobbie, be a good boy. Maybe someday you will know me again. Say hello to Mommy." The return address was the One Bar Eleven Ranch, Saratoga, Wyoming.

The One Bar Eleven Ranch was later, however. In the letter to my mother from the "Hotel Joyce" he concluded: "I've hurt you so many times and when I do I hurt myself. If you feel that you can I wish you'd send me a snapshot of yourself and the children. Now I have said about all I can, Kate, and I so want you to realize that I'm sorry. Maybe someday you can say 'Thank God it's over and I'm so proud you made it.' Because I do love you, no matter what happens, Kate." And if that wasn't bad enough, he ended with the poignant line "Please teach the kids not to hate Daddy too much."

The man who was never going to return to Jones County to live, ever, came back for Christmas. My mother held out a while, but it was obvious from a letter she sent on December 12 that she would take him back if he showed up. It was full of kid details. She started with "Dear Daddy Bob" and continued in a family tone, telling about Bobbie helping her wrap a package of handkerchiefs she was sending (she had to retrieve them out of pockets and put new embroidered initials on, which shows the state of her finances) and that I was learning to splash water out of the dishpan when she gave me a bath. Both babies insisted on sleeping with her, she said. "I cuddle Bobbie up close to me at night and pretend I'm keeping him warm, but if it wasn't for him I would probably freeze to death." And she closed: "Daddy, we hope things are going better with you and we know you will find a way to make things come out all right." No wonder he came home. He knew she'd take him back. He had started back before the letter even reached him, and the letter was sent on to Eloise's father, Frank Sutherland, whose name he had left as a forwarding address. He might not have been certain my grandmother would let him in the house. Maybe she didn't.

Later my mother was a little less starry-eyed about his return. "I don't think he ever meant to return to Scotch Grove," she told me that day. "He didn't come back because he loved me. He came back because I loved him and he was out of money." He figured there was somehow more for the taking. And he took it. By the time he left for good, he had collected in advance on the cream checks, tried unsuccessfully to sell the hogs, passed hundreds of dollars of checks on insufficient funds for my mother to try to cover, and even forged a check with a George Rickels name on it. And he sold her car, the one she bought with her teaching money. I will never forgive him that. She didn't tell me most of it. I had to find it out from other sources. Except about the car. She told me that.

When my father came back from Colorado, he got a job in Monticello working for Bill Folkers in some kind of sales again. My parents rented a house in Monticello in January 1943. Later my mother wrote: "When we went to Monticello I wanted our farm accounts kept separate, but he wouldn't hear of it. There was around $300 from the farm by that time, but when the bank statement came at the end of the month it was all gone and no account of his wages. I was just sick." I learned elsewhere that in the spring the sheriff had come after him for a gambling debt, but he had talked his boss into paying it for him against future wages.

This part isn't hard to piece together. He no doubt started hanging out in bars after work and got together with Edith, who was working in town and had a potful of troubles of her own. I'm sure Vaneta called this one right. My mother might have loved him, but she didn't trust him anymore. She was after him to have the money kept separate and she wouldn't sign any more notes. Edith thought he was witty and kind and the only one who understood her in her own mixed-up desertion case, where she couldn't gain custody of her little girl.

"I actually thought things were getting better. We didn't have any money, but he was working odd jobs for Len Campbell on top of his regular hours." She shook her head at her own naïveté. He was probably taking Edith home from Monticello—in my mother's car! "We talked of moving back on the farm the next year. He was especially tender and kind." I could have told her later that was a sure sign of an affair, but what did I know at twenty-one. "He said my happiness meant more to him than anything and if I wanted to move back on the farm we would, but he was getting along well with Bill Folkers, so we decided to wait awhile longer." She began to think things were turning around for them.

"Suddenly he was talking about a good job offer in Colorado. He didn't even ask me to come along, but I thought it was because he knew I wouldn't go again. And before I even knew what was happening, he had loaded everything in the car to move us to Grandma's house. He said he could make more money this way and we would still return to the farm the next year. I didn't believe him, but I was so taken by surprise I could barely object."

"Mom, didn't you even suspect there was someone else?" I found this hard to believe, as in my case I'd known for several weeks there was someone else, even halfway across the country.

"No. In fact those last weeks were some of the nicest ones we spent together. The last night he was very tender. In the morning he brought us to Grandma's and carried all the boxes upstairs. I think right then that I loved him more than ever. He kissed you children and told you to be good and mind Mommy, and then he put his arms around me. 'Goodbye, Kate,' he said. 'You'll hear from me in a week. Don't forget that, no matter what happens, I'll be loving you, always.' And he kissed me." By now I was crying hard, trying not to sob with noisy gulps, but she wasn't crying at all. She was just looking out that same window where she'd watched her brother walk up the driveway with the letter and felt the ice spread through her.

"You know, Barbara, your father did a lot of things that seem pretty unconscionable. And you'll probably hear about them some-day—if you care to know. I did feel bitterness—especially at first, when I was such an object of pity in the community. But when I say he was more than those stories will show, I'm not just a sentimental fool." She smiled at me and I tried to get my snuffling under control.

"I'm not a fool at all," she said quietly, turning to face me, "and neither are you, even if you are obviously going to make a life career out of being a student." She had argued for me to accept a teaching job instead of going to graduate school. I smiled, too. She didn't mean it and I knew it. She was proud of me. That was just her way of saying that I had a lot left in my life even if the guy had dumped me. She looked back out the window.

"That letter—the one Bob wrote to Len Campbell. What died in me was not the love for your father. It was the hope that he would someday come back. I understood then what I knew all along but didn't face. Bob had the same inner core of goodness all of us have—even a deeper core than many people, for it drove him relentlessly in ways that were hard to understand. But his mind could flip into separate grooves like a faulty phonograph needle. And when he wrote that letter, we really didn't exist in his mind."

I didn't know what to say. I was a kid, really, and I'd just failed in romance. Twenty-one is too young to talk to your mother.

"Life is much deeper than just loving men, Barbara." She gestured to the morning light. We had talked all night and the sunrise was beginning. "Look," she said. The sky was all scallops and almost iridescent feather edges of cloud layered against each other. She quoted:

> . . . *the Holy Ghost over the bent*
> *World broods with warm breast and with ah! bright wings.*

"You've been reading my poetry books again," I accused. She read every book I brought home with me from cover to cover. "I thought you didn't like this modern stuff."

"He's not modern. He died in 1889. Actually, I rather like the way he slants his words to rhyme."

"Hopkins was a Catholic," I teased. "And he was a Jesuit priest to boot."

"I don't care," she answered, not treating it as a joke. "Didn't you listen to Ella Clark in Sunday school?" Ella was my father's aunt, the one who taught my Sunday-school class for years and years—surely one of the loveliest women in the world. Mrs. W. B.

Clark, William Bert. "It's all part of God." My mother turned from the window and put her arms around me. I snuggled against her like a little girl.

Within four months from the day she finally opened her soul to me, my mother had a heart attack. I stood by the hospital bed and looked at the form with tubes and monitors that was my mother but not really my mother. I was terrified that she would die, and it suddenly seemed to me that my falling away from the church might be held against her. "Our father who art in heaven, our father who art in heaven, our father who art in heaven," I repeated softly over and over. But I didn't believe it. What a strange thing I'm saying, I thought with part of my mind. Faith of our *mothers*, living still.

But she died, too.

•   •   •

One more envelope completed the sequence of communications prior to my father's death in 1950. (Two letters were dated after his death. One was a short sad note from his mother, Kitsy, thanking my mother for her kind letter about the funeral, and the other was an answer from Bankers Life Company in Des Moines to an inquiry my mother had made regarding policy No. 1231106. The answer completed the futile cycle of her bewilderment at a father's failure to provide basic support for his offspring. It read, in part, as follows: "Policy No. 1231106 . . . became in default for non-payment of the premium due January 17, 1943. Upon default the policy . . . continued in force as extended insurance to January 6, 1949, when it expired without value. We are extremely sorry that Mr. Norris's insurance was not in force at the time of his death.")

The envelope that completed the sequence did not now contain a letter and there was no evidence that it had ever done so. The postmark was Encampment, Wyo., but the address on the envelope was Saratoga, so my father probably was still herding cattle at the One Bar Eleven Ranch. What it contained was a small white packet from Okinow's jewelers on Second Avenue in Cedar Rapids, Iowa. In this tidy little packet, which closed with a snap that by now had left a stain on the plastic casing, was a gold wedding ring. The simple band had six slight imprinted designs at regular intervals. He must have had big hands, for even with my knuckles enlarged with arthritis, the ring was loose on my middle finger and slid off my thumb.

What did my mother feel when that packet arrived in the mail? I can only surmise. She did not write much poetry, or if she did, she did not save it. Although I found lists of rhyming words and fragmented poetic images, all that remained in her handwriting that resembled a finished poem was this haunting song, which had gone through successive revisions:

> Call softly, swallow,
> circling wide above the blue-grass
> dipping down to touch the slough-grass
> darting off to where the willow
> drags her branches in the shallow
> water of the river.

> Call softly swallow.
> High above the purple thistle-stalk
> keens the lonely hunting hawk.
> When the new moon, thin and shallow,
> sinks into the foggy hollow,
> involuntarily, I shiver.

Apparently she had intended to end with a couplet. "Cry gently, swallow" was intact. But the last line was smudged with erasure marks and scribbles. One version read "My love has gone away." "Love" had been crossed out and under it was "heart." That also had a mark through it and "life" was beside it. Under all three words she had written: "My soul has gone away." But that was crossed out, too. She never recorded a decision as to how much his departure had taken from her.

(9)

The Fire of the People

[Hadfields Cave] was selected for excavation because it appeared
that it would contain a deep midden with a long cultural sequence.
In reality the midden was shallow and the intensive occupation
had taken place *only* between ca. A.D. 300 and 800.
—DAVID W. BENN, *Hadfields Cave:*
A Perspective on Late Woodland Culture in Northeastern Iowa.
Report No. 13, Office of the State Archaeologist,
University of Iowa, 1980

Vaneta and I were driving toward the Mississippi River
to the Effigy Mounds National Monument. She had been reluctant
to leave the house, because she might miss a reservation call for
the B&B and she needed business. The weather was not cooperating
either. "How far am I going to have to walk in the mud?" she
grumbled.

"You don't have to walk in the mud. They might have blacktop
paths by now. I was only there once as a kid right after the monument
opened to the public. With my mother and your dad. None of the
others wanted to walk then either." ("I don't want to see any old
heathen graves," my grandma had said.) "But I got to go along. All
we saw were the grassy mounds, but I think they have a visitors'
center now."

"You're a hard person to be around," Vaneta observed good-
naturedly. "It's not normal for a woman over fifty to gallop around
like you do. My hip is still sore from last night."

Last night after dinner we had walked from Sweet Memories to the cemetery. Many of the buildings that had been standing when we were children were gone. The old brick house, the Henrichs barn, the number five school. Not even a trace of the school remained. I had to guess distances to figure out where it had been. The building had stood just across the road where the gate allowed entry to the Ebenezer Sutherland place.

"What happened to all the trees?" The school building had been razed in my childhood, but for a long time the lot was defined by a ring of trees and the pump at the well.

"Bulldozed probably. They take water from the corn. Or maybe they were struck by lightning. If you don't keep replanting they don't last that long. It all goes back to prairie. Or slough," Vaneta complained. "See my lake?" We were walking up the hill where the Henrichs barn had been. She pointed south to the area that needed drainage tile so the tractors wouldn't get stuck again. Enough of the sunset was left to reflect in the shallow pond. I stopped.

"It's beautiful." Huge stacks of clouds curved in irregular shapes like limestone bluffs, golden as they caught the last sun. "Think what it must have been," I said, looking east to the fence line at the bottom of the hill where our land joined. "We should turn it back to prairie." I'd actually been researching this. She gave me a scathing look. I decided to make a joke of it.

"No, really," I continued, "we could raise buffalo and it'd be a draw for the B&B." Vaneta laughed. I'd been reading about the original tallgrass prairie and the wealth of game. "Vaneta, buffalo and elk once roamed here, *bear* even. I never thought of bear, but Maquoketa means 'bear' so there must have been quite a few." I'd just read an account of one of the last killed in the area in 1859, which involved a fracas between "Billy" Clark and George Sutherland arguing over the gun.

"You can keep the bear," said Vaneta. "I like seeing deer out my window, but I don't want to look out and see a bear. They might eat your chickens and pigs."

"You don't even have any chickens and pigs," I reminded her.

"Well, Grandpa did. The people who came did. You can't have

it both ways. The sixth day God created man. Dominion over nature. Read Genesis." That's when I had decided to come to the Effigy Mounds.

We crossed the Mississippi River at Dubuque to follow the eastern side in Wisconsin, before we recrossed at McGregor to reach the Effigy Mounds National Monument. I pulled the camper to the side of the road and we stared in awe. The expanse of water was startling, bearing out news commentators' earlier predictions that the excessive rainfall would produce record-breaking flood levels in 1993. The bottomlands were submerged, with only the tops of trees sticking out. Lower streets were lined with sandbags.

I felt guilty. Vaneta's back gives her problems, and I was making it worse. "You can stay in the camper," I offered. "I'll put up the table and you can read or write letters." Her mood immediately improved.

The parking lot at Effigy Mounds was virtually empty, because the flooding river threatened the approach road. The ranger wanted to stick to his tour schedule, so we decided to leave the visitors' center until later. Vaneta retired to the camper to write letters after she visited the first mound, which gave me the opportunity for a private tour. The familiar smell of the damp ferns resulted in a confusing mosaic of memories.

"Where are the Indians?" I asked as a child. I was disappointed. "They've been dead a long time here," my mother answered. "How long?" "Some of them thousands and thousands of years," said my mother. "Longer ago than Jesus?" I asked. He was always our touchstone for time. "Well, yes," she said, "I guess some of them have been dead longer than that."

The guide was a science teacher in a nearby school. His lecture was an entertaining blitz of the natural and native history of the area sprinkled with practiced statistics. I gave up trying to take notes and walked behind him, listening. He had summarized the seasonal occupation of the limestone caves by the Woodland people who returned from the tributary valleys of the Mississippi once a year to bury their dead in the mounds. "This was the spiritual core, right here," he said.

"Did they come from the Maquoketa River Valley?" I asked.

"Of course, the Maquoketa. One of the latest archaeological digs is at Hadfields Cave on the North Fork."

Ours was the South Fork. "The Mesquakies are part of the Woodland tradition, aren't they?" I didn't admit that I had just a few weeks ago learned the term Mesquakie. I never had heard it in the twenty-six years I lived in Iowa. Tama Indians, people had said.

"Yes, but they came later—actually from the Iroquois. But they're Woodland all right. That's why they came back from Kansas. Eighteen forty-three is when they were all moved out of Iowa. But the Mesquakies were pretty smart. They mostly came back during the Civil War, when the whites were busy fighting each other. They *bought* the land back, by the Iowa River, you know. To be in the woods. It's quite a story." I'd been reading it. Then the ranger turned his attention to plants.

I was a little girl again, following Uncle Jim in the timber. "Now this is nettles," said my uncle. "Note the leaf, because they sting. But you can make soup from it or baskets. Never eat the berries from the jack-in-the-pulpit. The Indians made medicine, but too much is poison." My head buzzed from the insects and the sticky heat that seemed to cling in a yellow glow on the undersides of the leaves.

We stopped by a limestone outcropping that walled the uphill side of the path. "Chert," said the ranger, pointing to a lighter colored layer. "It's what they used for projectile points in this area."

In the shanty with the anvil. An old cigar box held the arrowheads Uncle Jim had found. And on the wall hung old tools, coils of barbed wire, straps of harness, the blade from a plow, and the old tractor seat fixed like a chair. Through the dusty window sunlight caught on silver nails like candle flame. The shanty was a holy place.

The ranger knelt beside the mayapple plant. "What do you know about this?"

"That it only blooms if it has a double leaf." He looked at me with new respect.

I knelt beside the plant as Uncle Jim held the leaves apart. I cupped the yellow-green apple gently in my hand. It felt smooth and alive, like soft distended skin.

We had emerged at a large mound that was outlined clearly with a path. It was in the shape of a bear. We walked around it. "If this outline wasn't already here, we wouldn't mess with it today," the ranger said. Then he chuckled. "One curator came through and asked them if they were trying to make it look like a damn golf course." Now I remembered.

"This isn't a bear," I complained. "There's nothing to see." "It's sort of a bear," said my mother. "They made the mounds in the shapes of animals or birds because they believed they were part of nature." "I think it's not a bear," I said. I was purposely being stubborn. "I think next time you can stay home," my mother said crossly.

We emerged at the area called Fire-Point, high above the Mississippi. "This was a crematory site," the science teacher said. "They've done excavations here—carefully, although some sloppy ones were done earlier. The burial pits were lined with strips of red cedar bark." He pointed to trees clinging to the side of the bluff. "Some of those scrubby trees are actually several hundred years old. They're the oldest trees around. All the rest of the climax forest has been cut." He continued, pointing again at the mound. "Some of the nicest pottery pieces you'll see in the visitor center display came from this area—the Madison Ware with the cord-impressed patterns." The river spread beyond half-submerged islands. "Four miles across, even when it's not flooding," he said, sweeping his arm in an arc. The fog drifted below us over some of the islands, making the scene unusually pristine. "Keep watching and we'll see an eagle," he said.

I quickly scanned with the binoculars. "When did they come back?"

My mother stood with her back to the cliff, her face framed with leaves. Here or Eagle Point Park? "We've killed them all off," she said.

"Between the hunters and the DDT it's been a long haul. It got bad during the fifties. During the sixties and the seventies you never saw them. But the conservation groups got real aggressive and got DDT banned. That was the crucial factor."

Again I scanned the empty sky.

"I'll tell you another thing they ought to ban. Atrazine. They've been measuring the flow past Thebes, Illinois, during this flood. Twelve thousand pounds of atrazine a day are gushing past there. It's the most popular weed killer."

We sat on the front porch after supper. Uncle Jim slowly came up the tilted sidewalk, looking tired. "We're all going to get cancer from these chemicals. They make fun of me, Kate, but there's nothing to laugh about. I've put up the NO SPRAY sign twice and someone has taken it down again."

"Look! There's your eagle!" The ranger pointed over the curling fog.

And it was. I fastened my binoculars on the circling form, climbing higher and higher on the thermal. Fully mature with large plank wings. I wanted to tell my mother.

"They *are* back!"

"Yep," he said, "they are. And that's the only thing that will save us—that nature has incredible powers of regeneration." Three double-crested cormorants flew in a horizontal line across the channel. "For all the mess we've made, we're probably just some little scab on this ever-changing scene. And 450 million years from now, who knows? This limestone bluff will be back on the bottom of another sea. Dust to dust. Or in our case"—he smiled, because we could see that the rain had started again in blue slanted lines over the islands and would soon reach us as well—"mud to mud."

Vaneta had been writing letters, but she came with me to the visitors' center. The rain shower the ranger and I had watched come across the river had passed through and new pools gleamed on the blacktop. I went straight to the display case of pottery. *Madison Ware*, the label read. The pieces were thin-walled and finely decorated. "Fabric Impressed" was the archaeological classification for the decoration technique. Studying a reconstructed vessel, I was intrigued by the delicate pattern etched in the curved walls. A card explained the construction process.

A sleeve of complicated fabric composed of twined cords was woven into intricate combinations of triangles and knots. Then it was stretched over wet clay. The "impressed" pattern on the vessel gave an archaeologist a fascinating puzzle. From the external design one could deduce much about interaction with social groups as certain motifs recurred, even though each piece was highly individualistic. From the twisted materials of the threads, one could learn the unique dietary and cultivation habits of a particular band. I had an overwhelming urge to stroke the graceful vessel, but the display case kept me from indulging in the indiscretion. I glanced guiltily around, realizing I had put my hand on the glass. Hastily I wiped at the smudge with my sleeve.

We chose to return to Sweet Memories on the Iowa side of the Mississippi, initially following the river road that lined the floodplain below the bluffs. Traffic blocks were set up to prevent access to bottomland. Spur roads disappeared into the rising water. At each roadblock stood several cars and people who milled around with their hands in their pockets. "Be thankful all you have to do is replace some of your faulty drainage tile," I told Vaneta.

The road climbed higher on the bluff until we reached a shelf with a scenic overlook parking lot. A sign erected by the Iowa Department of Transportation confirmed my childhood lessons in the barnyard dust. THESE LIMESTONE STRATA ARE FORMED OF DEPOSITS OF MUDS THAT ACCUMULATED IN THE SHALLOW, TROPICAL SEAS THAT COVERED THIS AREA DURING ORDOVICIAN TIME.

I stood beside Vaneta. The river stretched to the east as far as we could see. Even in this brief pause between showers the moisture in the air was palpable. Fog curled in separate strands like currents both above and below us. We were small aquatic animals on a watery ledge—naked and vulnerable, without even the shells of brachiopods to fill with lime-rich mud and harden into interesting shapes. Layered grey clouds sagged with more rain.

•   •   •

In the beginning was the Land. And the piece of it from which the Scotch Grove Presbyterian Church was carved became mine when my grandmother died. After I betrayed my mother by losing her farm, I hated owning land in Iowa. The land remained part of the men who were already dead. My possession of it compromised me, gave them still some hold on me. If Paul Ernie hadn't handled the renting of it and sent me the money year after year, I would have ignored it entirely.

Even more cumbersome were the trees. My holdings in the timber were small, entangled in a web of common ownership of heirs of Gideon Hughes. When the first settlers came, the trees belonged to everyone. Even when John Newton Hughes was a boy in the 1870s, he rode his pony there to gather the cows from the community grazing grounds. By then, however, the land on which the trees stood had been divided with the formal filings of the 1850s, when the land office opened in Dubuque and the grants were bestowed by Millard Fillmore, President of the United States of America.

Only my Uncle Jim understood the Hughes divisions of the timber, for he knew each tree personally. So he was for all of us the keeper of the trees. Although it was not virgin timber, among the second growth stood many giants. The big black walnuts were so valuable that clandestine operations were organized to fell and remove them at night. After I left Iowa, checks would occasionally appear in the mail for my share of the sale of a tree or two. Uncle Jim reluctantly cut the largest walnut trees to keep others from stealing them and he divided the money among the heirs. Each time I received a check the enclosed note said: "This is the last there will be of them in your lifetime. Use the money wisely."

So I used the money from the land and the trees in the most un-Gideon Hughes way I could, which was to spend it. On travel. I wanted my sons to see that their world was more than the world of the men who were already dead. For I had been taught by my mother and Ella Clark of the equal preciousness of all the Children of the World, red and yellow, black and white. And I wanted to give my sons the same lesson in my own way. When my husband and I argued about spending money (he did not care about getting rich but wanted to pay for everything, even cars, with cash), I would say angrily, Your name is James *Hughes* Trusky and he would retort, And yours is Barbara *Norris* Scot.

When I finally went back to Scotch Grove in 1983 and got the trunk with my mother's letters, I sat on the porch steps, which were broken then, and I talked with my Uncle Jim. He was worried about the trees. We had just returned from one last time together in the timber. I had still walked behind him like a child, through the sultry summer light to the Maquoketa River. Why don't we make it into a park, I suggested, for he could have spoken for all the heirs, but he didn't want anyone to pick the wildflowers or the mushrooms. Well, how about some sort of reserve, then, and he wanted to, but when I made all the phone calls from Oregon, got a man to come and look at the woods with him, and drew up the papers, he was too Hughes to sign.

I knew I should go back again and try to organize the heirs, but I had found other trees in Oregon to splinter the sun in green-gold shafts, other rivers to slide in silver slabs under shadowed bridges. So after he died no keeper remained for the trees.

.　　.　　.

I couldn't convince Vaneta to come with me to the Mesquakie settlement. One day away from the phone was all she could handle. "I'm having enough trouble with the Department of Natural Resources," she said. "I don't have time to fight the Indian wars, too. Especially not if you're going to let them win." So I went alone.

The information I'd learned about the Mesquakies had been entirely from books. The best was the autobiography of a native woman, transcribed in both a syllabic rendition of Mesquakie and in English in 1918 for the Smithsonian Institution. The introduction stated that the study of this woman's training and social interactions had allowed unique and important insights into the cultural core of the Mesquakies, absolutely an essential record for a social group threatened with extinction.

The old woman had been asked to portray her childhood. She did so in charming and open detail, so open that the transcriber had been forced to delete some passages as "too naïve and frank for European taste." She described her training in sewing and gardening. I was enchanted by her description of dolls ("I made little wickiups for the dolls to live in") and the strict coaching in morality so similar to my own ("You will be thought of as naught if you are immoral. The ones who are moral are those whom men want to live with. And they will only make sport of the immoral ones").

I had hoped to speak with a Mesquakie woman at the settlement, but they all seemed to be busy at their computers or other thoroughly modern tasks, so I followed the young man to whom I had been assigned into an office. Jonathan Buffalo, with his black, black hair, looked so authentically "native" that as I was being introduced, I became acutely aware that I must look just as authentically "European," with all the concomitant associations that could hold for him. I immediately confessed my childhood ignorance of the term Mesquakie.

"People know it now." Jonathan Buffalo smiled wryly. "Ask anyone. They'll say, 'The ones with the casino?' There's been grumbling about 'giving' the Indians all that money." My first question revealed further ignorance. I inquired somewhat hesitantly whether I could ask him some questions about previously published material which dealt with the religion of the Mesquakies.

"No," he replied. He was polite, soft-spoken, but firm. "You can't. We do not discuss our traditional religion with those who are not believers." He would not, he assured me, discuss traditional religion even with other Mesquakies who were not believers. He himself was not a Christian, although some among the Mesquakies were. "I told my son, who asked what I believed, that I don't expect to go to heaven or hell. I expect to be with my ancestors."

I had a sudden disquieting image. Children around the table in the upstairs balcony of the Scotch Grove Presbyterian Church. We were making Christmas cards. The Sunbeam Mission Band. We were sending Christmas presents to the Navajos in Arizona. We wanted them to observe Christmas. This was the wrong time to dwell on that. I plunged ahead.

Would he share with me history as it would be taught to a Mesquakie child . . . that is, the history of the Mesquakies? He smiled a little. "I should have to speak Mesquakie."

I smiled back. "That is your first language, then?"

"Yes," he answered firmly. "Many native groups lost their languages entirely, but we have never stopped using ours. When I go to other gatherings people say to me, 'You must be from Iowa,' because of my accent when I speak English."

I had read in the minutes of the Sunbeam Mission Band that Miss Skea, the Presbyterian missionary in 1890, solicited money and prayers. The Tama Indians were resisting the white man's version of education. The Sunbeam Mission Band pledged help, closing their meeting with "Bringing in the Sheaves," a song with an agricultural metaphor for harvesting souls. "As I don't understand Mesquakie, would you tell me the history in English?" I asked. So he did.

His was a grim history lesson, quietly delivered. I knew much of it, having done my homework before I came, but his simple, short account moved me. He traced the Mesquakies as they came south from the Iroquois lands in the 1600s to settle in villages along the Wolf River, the area of reddish soil that gave them the name Mesquakie, or "red-earth people." Initial peaceful contact with the French in 1666 ended in a massacre near Starved Rock, Illinois, in 1730, where 1,200 Mesquakies died. The settlements in Iowa at the very end of the woodland were disrupted when the pressure for land increased. In 1842 the treaty was prepared, lumping the Sauk with the Mesquakies, which gave the natives three years to move to Kansas.

"We are Woodland people," said Jonathan Buffalo. Smallpox and alcohol supplied by the agents took a heavy toll of the five hundred Mesquakies who finally made it to Kansas. "So we began to drift back from the prairie to the woods." Actually, some had never left, he told me. "God made the road for us so we could come back." In 1856 the state of Iowa made it legal for the tribe to remain. In 1857 the Mesquakies repurchased, with money from the sale of ponies, the first eighty acres of woodland along the Iowa River, which became part of the settlement. "That part has been under water all summer this year," he observed. "It's a good thing they bought more."

Not that life was easy for them, even when they returned. "No big game remained. The last time the Mesquakie hunted elk in

Iowa was in 1866, but none were found. Of course we couldn't live like we used to live without the game. The men tried to get work with the railroad and keep their traditional ways in the homes."

The departure from traditional ways moved slowly until 1939. But with the Second World War, when "every eligible man was sent off to fight," change accelerated. His mother went to make bullets in a war plant in Waterloo, Iowa. Her job was to inspect bullets for rust. In 1945, when everybody came back, "our worldview was much bigger."

Was that bad? "It just *was*," Jonathan Buffalo answered matter-of-factly. "Now those war stories are part of our tribal history. Mesquakies were part of the occupation forces to arrive at Hiroshima. Mesquakies participated in the liberation of the concentration camps. As a tribal member I've seen those camps in my mind because of the stories." Again he emphasized his pride at retaining their language. "But we're still Mesquakies. Within our tribe we still speak Mesquakie."

The Korean War, the Vietnam War, and even Desert Storm. "Now we have more cars, televisions, and VCRs." Also a casino, I reminded him. "And a casino." He sighed. I asked him how he felt about the casino.

He leaned back in his chair. "If I were an artist I would draw a cartoon with two panels—a comparison of time zones. On one panel I would put people in the dress of the 1600s and have a trader who came to the villages with an Indian scout. His scout would say, 'My white man's beads are better than the other white man's beads.' On the other panel I would put a casino outfit with their Indian scout. When the people began to consider a casino for revenue, the casino men began to appear—twenty-two different outfits. The scout for the casino men in the cartoon would say, 'My white man's casino is better than the other white man's casino.' "
I laughed aloud and he smiled genuinely at me.

"Our problem for hundreds of years has been how much of the outside do we let in. The white man always shows his goods." Could they preserve their traditions now, in the face of the video onslaught, MTV, computer networks? I asked. "I hope so," he answered. He paused. "Think of it like a circle. The number of Mesquakies has fluctuated widely before. But always a core remains traditional. Only about three hundred survived the French. Less than that survived Kansas. It's like a fire. Even when the fire dies down there's always that little heartbeat." He looked at me seriously, one parent to another. "I hope my family will be part of it." I nodded.

I thought I had been dismissed, but he turned back and said, "Our fire has died down before. As long as that little center is still red, all God has to do is to blow on our coals and the fire starts up again." He smiled before he left, sharing one line. "In our traditional religion," he said, "we call it the 'fire of the people.' "

Sweet Memories was a two-hour drive away, for I was west of Cedar Rapids on the road I had taken when I first came back to the family reunion. The rain had started again. I'd had good teachers in my mother and my Uncle Jim, but the issue of Native Americans had always been addressed in the past tense. We had all been part of the Sunbeam Mission Band mentality—that children's adjunct to the Ladies Missionary Society which had been founded in the old brick house at the Ebenezer Sutherland place in 1879, the minutes recorded in a tattered book whose cover had a picture of children holding a flag with the inscription *Our Country for Christ*—and no romanticism on my part could make it otherwise now.

I felt tired and a bit depressed. The encounter with Jonathan Buffalo was informative and had ended on a positive note, but I had wanted to talk with a woman. Reading the Mesquakie woman's biography, I had felt a kinship—I was more comfortable sharing some tie through common tasks than feeling vague unproductive guilt over forced relocations and slaughtered elk. After all, I thought defensively, I wasn't born at that time, either.

Ahead of me, through the blur of the windshield wipers, was a small white sign. LUZERNE—4 MILES, it read. I pulled to the side of the road. Should I go back to the cemetery, now that I knew more and felt at least some personal connection with the man who had been my father? The rain didn't encourage me. And it was getting dark.

I just sat there for a moment. I'd always felt a special outrage because my father had forced a mortgage on my mother's land. Land was sacred in our family. "Always hang on to your land. Once it's gone, it's gone. But as long as you have your land you can live," my grandma had said. My mother had been given her farm by her father, who bought it during the Depression from a bankrupt Livingston of the same family who had come in the oxcarts. The list of recorded owners seemed ridiculously short. I worked backward. Norris . . . Hughes . . . Livingston. Then who? Jonathan Buffalo's people? They themselves had come in the 1600s from the north. Before them? A period of "rapid culture change" making specifics hard to define, complained the archaeologist in a report I'd been reading about people here in the period between A.D. 300 and 800.

I saw successive streams of people spreading over the land like the temporary rivulets produced this summer by constant rain: linear ribbons of bands returning to the Effigy Mounds with their dead for yearly ceremonies, Mesquakies winding down through Wisconsin past the Red Earth, the Scots in their wooden carts plodding down the Red River Trail, Clarks coming in successive waves from Pennsylvania, the family of John Hughes alighting from the steamer in Illinois, later crossing the frozen Mississippi, driving the cattle beside them.

Rain bounced off the windshield so fiercely I thought it was hail. I pictured the paper bundle of the title abstract I still held for the Ebenezer Sutherland place in the shine of the headlights. In this deluge it would dissolve in a few minutes, blue cardboard cover and all. My mind blurred like the liquid windshield in front of me; it dissolved like the image of the title abstract. I leaned my forehead against the steering wheel, feeling an unexpected wave of relief. *The land was never ours to lose.* No matter that I had argued that fact intellectually for years—only then did I feel it emotionally.

The darkening Iowa landscape was doing its best to return to the shallow warm-water seas of 450 million years past. Twisting the steering wheel, I pulled the camper back on the highway. I wasn't going to stand in a cemetery in this downpour, but I momentarily felt a certain sinful camaraderie with my father, anyway. We had both betrayed my mother with the farm. But even Gideon Hughes had never owned the land.

• • •

"Are you going to the cave *alone?*" the nice woman asked when I had sought permission to enter the land. I had decided to explore Hadfields Cave, the site of the archaeological dig on the North Fork of the Maquoketa River that the ranger at Effigy Mounds had mentioned. The cave was less than fifteen miles northeast of Scotch Grove, near the historic Catholic settlement of Temple Hill. No one I knew had ever been there.

"Yes, I am." I almost added something that would make no sense to her. Uncle Jim is dead.

"I wouldn't go alone," she cautioned.

"Rattlesnakes?"

"Snakes . . . or you could fall." I felt her genuine concern. "I wouldn't go alone," she repeated.

I followed the woman's directions, turning left into the woods that lined the riverbank. Crossing a creek, I balanced on the larger stones. The North Maquoketa flowed at the bottom of the lane. Turkey vultures circled above the trees on the opposite bank, the way they did at Dales Ford. Maybe they were the same birds, I thought, knowing they ranged far for carrion. I was less than ten miles from the south fork and my childhood haunts. At the town of Maquoketa, twenty miles to the southeast, the two strands of river joined. Underfoot the grassy path felt spongy from last night's rain.

I had spent the morning at the state archaeologist's office in Iowa City reading about Hadfields Cave. Had Uncle Jim known about it? Maybe not. The report hadn't even been published until 1980. I did not want to think of my long absence and silence after Grandma's death in 1968. Why hadn't I at least written him letters? He didn't die until 1988. What would I have said in a letter? We didn't have conversations, I just followed him and he taught. "I'm going to the timber, Kate," he always said. "Do you think she would like to come along?" I had troubles of my own during some of that time, I thought defensively. And I hadn't wanted to answer questions about my brother. But guilt hung over me as I walked.

Uncle Jim surely would have been interested in the archaeological report I'd read that morning. My mother would have been interested, too. But I wasn't going to Hadfields Cave because of them. I was going for the same reasons I had galloped my horse so furiously toward the woods whenever I was engulfed by lonely questions. To my mother the land had meant self-sufficiency and security, a way of life integrated with God. But her myths were not mine. I needed to find my own integration with the land, with the past, with the *place* of my childhood. And whenever I went to the Iowa woods, I went with the ghost of Uncle Jim. Maybe, I thought with a stab of surprise, the same questions about the land we called home had haunted him, pushing him back in time, sending him to the river and the bluffs.

The archaeologist, who had expected to find evidence of a couple of thousand years of occupation, was disappointed that the midden in Hadfields Cave yielded only five hundred years of seasonal use, from approximately A.D. 300 to 800. Five hundred years was barely enough to establish distinct cultural boundaries, especially at a time "when culture change in eastern Iowa was fairly rapid and distinct." But he had to make do with what was found in floral and faunal remains, tools, and ceramic shards.

The ceramic shards, the largest share of which qualified as Madison Ware pottery similar to the vessels I had seen at Effigy Mounds, were extremely valuable in cultural interpretation. Cord-impressed patterns on the fragments decisively proved, according to the archaeologist, that a "coterminous" relationship existed between seasonal inhabitants of Hadfields Cave and other woodland groups within the Effigy Mounds Tradition. Impressions on the fragments, which came from the fabric sleeve stretched over the wet clay, revealed that the people of the Maquoketa collected Indian hemp. Slippery elm, basswood, nettle, and cedar bark were used for cordage, not only for fabric pottery sleeves, but for construction of sacks in which to transport processed corn and sunflowers from summer agricultural villages. This winter-reserve food supply was supplemented with large quantities of nuts—hickory, butternut, walnut —and a plentiful supply of meat, some dried and stored, and other from fresh kills when weather permitted.

So these natives had spent much of the bone-chilling Iowa winter at 55 degrees constant cave temperature. Standing inside the commodious opening, where swallow nests rounded in little cups, I fumbled in my pack for my flashlight. My hand did not connect with the familiar shape. I had an annoying image of it on the camper seat where I had left it when I repacked my pack. Now what was I going to do? It was too late in the day to retrieve it and return to the cave. At some inconvenience I could come back again tomorrow. Inviting coolness emanated from the darkness. Did rattlesnakes come in caves to escape the heat? I didn't remember being told that. It wasn't that hot. In fact, it was late in the day. Snakes would be more likely to seek the sun, I told myself.

Turning from the light of the opening, I let my eyes become accustomed to the black interior. Actually, it wasn't black at all, more a soft grey. The cave mouth was high in the limestone wall of the river's intersecting gully, which held and reflected slanting late-afternoon sunshine so that light slid along the blackened roof of the cave. Three contiguous rooms separated by shallow arches, the report had said. I stood in the first room. Suspended beads of light hung on the ends of small stalactites. I stared for as long as I could fix my gaze, but no bead fell.

Moving through a wide arch to the next room, I was surprised how much I could actually see. Deep blackness to my side must mean the room extended left. Placing each foot tentatively before I moved, I went deeper into the cave. The slant of light allowed me to continue through another arch into the third room. On the side of the arch, more beads sparkled. Touching one gently, I confirmed that each was a water droplet, clinging to a vertical slab. How long did they hold before they fell? Weeks? Years? Or did they turn to stone? I wanted to ask Uncle Jim. Time slowed, held in tiny, shining globes.

The ceiling in the third room was higher, or at least disappeared in blackness. I stood fully upright. I could barely see. The cave seemed to end in front of me with a wall holding the last weak light, but black holes gaped to both the right and left. Side galleries, perhaps. Tomorrow I would return with a light, I promised myself. I must have been approximately 150 feet inside the cave, but distance, like time, was disconnected. Turning around, I faced the light source, blue-grey like fog on moonlight nights in the creek pasture.

Returning through the arch into the second room, I suddenly and distinctly saw a silhouette of a woman on the left side of the passage. I stopped. The image was definitely female, seen from the side, with a curved line of breast, and the head bent over the lap. The figure seemed that of a native, someone engaged in some sort of work, or perhaps tending a child. Was I imagining something from the display I had seen in the Natural History Museum in Iowa City?

I glanced toward the cave opening, which was still partially obscured by the first arch. Perhaps light was catching on a protrusion which cast a shadow. I stepped toward that which appeared to be a woman. How odd. The rock wall was several feet behind the shape. It was almost as if the shape were a cardboard cutout with space behind it. The thought flickered through my mind that this was some sort of trick.

I extended my hand. Nothing met my touch but black air. Then the light shifted and the shape was gone.

Feeling a sense of loss, I squatted on my heels. Had I given up some chance for communication with the past because my mind had not accepted the image as real? Why had I not considered that possibility when I now gave Mabel's bells and ghosts in the mirror some credence as real manifestations tied to place? Was I trapped in my ancestry, unable to connect with the pre-European past? I felt a disturbing sense of alienation—as if my intellectual mindset had kept me from participating in a deeper mystery. I stood again and touched the rough limestone of the wall. It gave no clue to the existence of the woman's form I had observed.

The air felt sultry and oppressive as I emerged from the cave, the slanted lines of sunshine gone. I should get out of the woods before dark, I told myself, trying not to slip in my haste on the narrow muddy trail that descended the side of the gully. When a startled wild turkey flushed and flew across the wash in clattering, clumsy flight, I sat down on the steep incline, trying to smile at my breathlessness. I began to jog-trot toward the camper, my pack thumping solidly on my back.

The forgotten flashlight lay on the front seat where I had left it. As I drove back to Sweet Memories, I thought of the Mesquakie woman's autobiography. Not, I reminded myself, that the Mesquakies had ever lived in Hadfields Cave, as the signs of occupation predated their arrival by eight centuries. But at least they had come from the same woodland tradition, had utilized the same plants for food, and had practiced a similar mud-flat agriculture, growing corn, squash, and sunflowers.

I had felt a closeness when the Mesquakie woman described the little hoe she had been given to learn gardening skills. I'd had a little hoe of my own. I wanted to feel that same closeness with the shadow I had seen in the cave. Yet I hadn't even accepted this woman's shape as real. Maybe I'd just had too much of ghosts—family and otherwise—lately, I decided unhappily. Each one had involved a mentally exhausting unraveling of the past to figure out my own connections. That could account for my reluctance to accept a new one. But I felt a sense of loss. I was almost half a century from the child for whom the blue-bonneted woman in the mirror had smiled.

When I returned to Hadfields Cave the next day, armed with two flashlights in case of accidental mishap, I thought again of Uncle Jim as I walked along the river. Had he ever seen anything in all his forays in the woods, like the woman in the cave, that might not fit comfortably in his Presbyterian elder's consciousness? If he had, he hadn't told me, or Vaneta either, even when he talked about the bells. But it suddenly seemed quite likely, I thought with interest. He'd been so out of step with the agricultural race toward new technology and chemicals, so much more interested in wildflowers and weeds than in whether the corn was in the crib before the snow. I imagined him striding swiftly in front of me. *Swiss, swiss, swiss, swiss.* His stiff overalls made a sound like dry cornhusks. A rosy-breasted grosbeak hopped from a bush to a higher tree. *Teechur,*

teechur, teechur, teechur, called the slim ovenbird from the bluff side of the path.

Even with the flashlight the cave was impressive and mysterious. The limestone wall behind the place where the woman had sat offered no clues to the shape formation. But just a little farther back into the cave, the rock opened to a side chamber. With the flashlight I could actually look in. A small, dry alcove ended with a flat shelf of rock. Of course. A perfect storage place for clay jars, cedar-bark sacks of corn, and bags of nuts. It even smelled like the fruit cellar at Sweet Memories. I felt the same continuity with the women of the cave that I had sensed with my own female ancestors the night I sat in the cellar looking at Vaneta's fruit jars. My feeling of alienation lessened.

I toured the rest of the cave, surprised at how much living space it had with all the side chambers. Plenty of room for the small bands of the archaeologist's estimate—nine or ten people to a family grouping. At the far end of the third room, a sloping ramp, coated white with mineral deposit, rippled upward. I could not resist climbing it to see if it extended to a larger room. It didn't, but a small circular chamber held an amazing stalagmite on its slanted floor, a short, blunt pillar, almost pure white, right in the center of the room. The domed ceiling gave the feel of a baptistry, the simple central font done in Carrara marble. I almost fell as I slid down to the third-room floor.

Sunlight still hung in the V of the little canyon below me when I emerged from the cave. I had no sense of time, although it was again late afternoon. My watch sat on a nightstand at Sweet Memories. I paused on the shelf in front of the cave to put away the flashlight and take out my binoculars. My shoelace flopped loosely, and I knelt to tie it, accidentally bumping the pack.

The binoculars, which I had set on my pack, leapt sideways and bounced down the talus slope. Involuntarily I, too, leapt sideways, trying to catch them mid-air, losing my balance to tumble down the steep, slippery incline. As I somersaulted, I saw the binoculars come to rest before I did, halfway down the side of the gully. I lay still for a moment where I had landed, surprised at the sudden sequence of dislocated images, but unhurt because of the foliage and soft ground. I sat up. In an effort to regain my footing, I reached toward a small rock outcropping for assistance.

The snake coiled in a metallic, patterned braid. The rattles stood straight up and the sound whined in my ears. My arm was suspended above the mouth as the head reared back. I could see the snake's eyes, wild with light. My whole body jerked down the slope as Uncle Jim pulled my other arm. "Never, never do that again." And I didn't.

I pulled back my arm and stood up slowly, using a fallen limb to balance as I looked at the dry flat rock. Two slim shapes slid into the undergrowth on the uphill side of the outcropping. Harmless blue racers. I hadn't been in danger this time at all. But the little shelf was a perfect place for snakes to catch the late-afternoon warmth. A timber rattler might well have been there. I sat down again with my back against the golden rock.

I was shaking. *So I did have a father.* Uncle Jim had tried to keep me safe. He taught me to pursue the lonely questions. Through him I had learned of nature and time. And I never even wrote to him after I left home. When my mother was dead and my grandmother was dead, I moved away, as far away as I could, and I didn't look back for a long time.

Guilty anguish sliced through me. In one swift moment I had gone from child deprived to prodigal who had squandered an inheritance not even understood. I *did* have a father. *And I had let my father's trees be felled.*

I put my head down on my arms. My shaking turned to genuine sobs. I had been looking for a man who threw the stick for Spot in the reading-book picture, the Dick and Jane father.

But how could I have known then? I was just a little girl.

And he didn't even call me by my name.

•   •   •

Eloise set me up for the phone call from Uncle Howard. I'd told her I was coming to return some books, so she had obviously called

Montana and told my father's youngest brother what time I would be at her house. She knew I was a little embarrassed to call him myself. But I'm glad she told him to call, because I heard the story of Bill Grogan's goat.

I was sitting in the front room talking to Eloise's husband, Edwin, about no-till agriculture when the call came. Edwin was showing me a booklet entitled *Fields of Tomorrow—Making the Transition to No-Till*. Its text was an interesting blend of advertisement and education, aimed at corn and soybean producers. The history of agriculture included in the booklet skipped at least three thousand years of plant cultivation in the area and started with the Europeans.

"No-till? If that's what the fields of tomorrow will be, we're coming full circle," I said. "That's the way the natives did it."

"No kidding," said Edwin. "Well, they knew something we didn't."

I agreed. "Except they didn't use the chemicals this company is trying to sell you."

"Well, you gotta have something that keeps down the weeds," Edwin said.

"Where *do* all those weeds come from, Edwin?" asked Eloise, who had just come in from the kitchen. "We never used to have so many weeds."

"The big machines," said Edwin. "Why, we used to cut out all the thistles by hand, but now they just get scattered through the whole field with one long sweep. It's an endless cycle," he sighed. "You just get one under control and something else takes over, so we need a new chemical for it. They say now that some of those seeds stay dormant for hundreds of years." He sat back in his chair. "Back to the Garden, I say. It all started with Adam and Eve. It's their fault. Thorns and thistles." That's when the phone rang.

"It's your Uncle Howard," Eloise said, coming back from the kitchen, "and he'd like to talk with you." I had a gripping sensation in my stomach. I went in the kitchen and picked up the phone.

"Hello . . . Howard," I said almost timidly, trying not to sound like a little girl. He put me immediately at ease. He said I should come to visit him in Montana. He'd heard good things about me from his cousin Eloise and he wanted to see if they were true. I laughed. But after a little small talk, I asked him some questions. And he tried honestly to answer.

"Robert was my hero, Barbara," Howard said of my father. "Of course, he was twelve years older than I was, and I worshipped the ground he walked on. My father was always yelling at him. And I hated my father because he was always mad at Robert."

"Why?" I asked.

"I never knew. I suppose I was too young to tell. Do you know about the difficult birth—the misshapen head?" I did. "I think my mother always wondered if that had anything to do with the way he couldn't seem to get straight with anything. She said he could never stick with anything longer than six months—always had to be off on something new." I didn't answer. I didn't know what to say to that.

"I know my mother wrote him a letter when he left Kate. She read it to me. 'You have broken all the laws of God and man.' I was only eighteen. But I'll never forget it."

I told him I'd heard she wouldn't let my father in the house after he left us.

"Well, no," Howard said. "He could come, but he wasn't allowed to bring Edith."

I suddenly felt extremely sorry for Edith. And her three daughters. "Can you tell me something nice, Howard?" I asked. "Something you remember from when you were a little kid?"

"Easy," he said. He had an infectious laugh. I couldn't imagine I had been nervous about talking with him. "On rainy days he would take me fishing."

"He *did!*" That sounded impossible. I had a picture of my brother at Dales Ford with the little silver fish. "*A fish, a fish, I caught a fish!*"

"Yes, and we would dig up worms together." He paused, then added, "He built me a little wagon."

There had been a photo album lost in a fire at my brother's house. *Home with Grandma*, the caption on the first picture had read. Two babies bundled up in heavy coats were sitting in a wagon. "Go on," I said, but my voice sounded funny.

"Gosh, Barbara!" (He honestly said gosh. They were such good people, really. One of the few things I remember about my Grandma Norris is that she said they never did fieldwork on Sunday because that was the least they could do to show respect for the Lord.) "I almost don't want to tell you this, because I feel like I got some of the love you should have had."

"That's okay, Howard."

"Well, the best memory of all that I have," Howard said, "is about Bill Grogan's goat!"

"Goat?"

"Yes, Bill Grogan's goat." His laughter was musical like Eloise's. "I must have been an awfully little boy. Robert would take me with him to milk the cow in the evening. He would pick me up and set me in a little depression in the cement foundation that was curved like a chair so I wouldn't get kicked if the cow stamped her foot. Then he would lean his forehead against the cow while he was milking her and sing 'Bill Grogan's Goat.' "

"Sing it," I commanded. I'd never heard it.

"What?"

"The song. Sing it. How did it go?"

Howard hummed a little on the phone. "Bill Grogan's Goat," he sang on a descending scale. He's quite musical and can still play the piano even though he's blind. He sang a song about a goat that ate three red shirts. The farmer was so mad he tied him to the railroad track. The goat coughed up the shirts and flagged down the train. And each verse was interspersed with a refrain of "Bill Grogan's goat." I was laughing so hard at Howard's rendition, I was almost crying.

"Robert would sing this song for me every night and I would sit in that little depression and kick my feet against the cement and laugh and laugh and laugh. When he'd get through, I'd beg him to sing it again and he would. I'll never forget it."

"Thank you, Uncle Howard," I said. We talked for a little while longer and I promised to try to come to see him in Montana sometime soon. I went back in the living room with Eloise. Edwin had gone outside to talk to the renter who was there with a gigantic tractor.

"Now, you're not mad at me, are you?" she said.

"Of course not." I hugged her. "It was wonderful. You were right." I knelt on the floor to sort out the books I'd returned. Eloise momentarily disappeared. When she returned, she had a little box in her hand.

"Do you remember my mother?" she asked.

Blanche Clark Sutherland. Frank and Blanche Sutherland sat on the south side of the church in the fifth pew. Under the light like the upside-down wedding cake. The light from the yellow glass glowed in the summer around her white hair as the minister talked on and on. Frank did not have very much hair. His head did not glow. The glow meant Blanche was an angel and that underneath the dress with the flowers were little wings. Blanche was not the same as when the beans in the heavy cloth were blanched in the boiling water before the fruit jars were filled. This Blanche was an angel, and if I closed my eyes just a little bit, the glow behind her head had rainbow colors. My mother put her hand on my knee to stop the swinging of my feet.

"Of course, I remember your mother," I answered. I could see her dishing up potato salad at the potluck suppers upstairs in the balcony before the church was raised and a basement was put underneath.

"I'd like to give you this," she said, holding out the small velvet box. I could tell she was just a bit embarrassed. "It was my mother's engagement ring and I'd like you to have it because you knew her and because you're part of the family." *She was right, I thought. I was.* I had never believed it before. It was a tiny, bright diamond with a thin, delicate band. I put it on my little finger. Eloise didn't have any children. "And you're part of the Scotch Grove Church," she added.

"Well, now . . ." she said, "there's not much for me to come back here for anymore. All the old names are gone, the old families. I'm the last Clark here and the last Sutherland. The Sinclairs are all gone, the Livingstons. The McKeans only come back to be buried. I still own the land, but why I keep it, I don't know. We're most of the time in Arizona. And I send money every month to the church, but I don't like to speak up much when we're not here to deal with the problems they have. Which," she sighed, "are many. They're definitely, like all the small churches, facing a financial crisis. And the farmers don't have any money anymore."

I slid the ring back and forth across the knuckle of my little finger. I knew I didn't have to say anything then. I've always loved Eloise. And she was giving me a little ring that bound a lot of things together. "Do you think it will continue, Eloise?" I asked.

"The church? I don't know. The community? It's all so different now. We thought of it as having a central core, the church, you know. Of course, in the old days it was really the heart, and things spread out from there—why, people who didn't belong to the church came to the dinners—it was a social center, you know. Now everything's so fluid."

"Maybe it always was," I said, stooping to find a little pamphlet in the pile I had returned. It was the souvenir booklet put out for a Thanksgiving Day celebration in 1911. That was when the reincorporated church with its new building, dedicated in 1861, had celebrated an official "Jubilee," even though the original founding was twenty years earlier. "Check the records," I said. "People poured through here as if it were a funnel, always headed for new land. The session was always writing letters of dismissal—complete with details of past sins." Eloise laughed. I continued, opening the booklet: "I was just amazed at the letters quoted here from members who had moved elsewhere—to Wyoming, Montana, Idaho, Missouri, Kansas, Nebraska, Indiana, Florida, even Oregon."

"Oh, I know," Eloise agreed.

"Here," I said, finding a typical example. "This one must be related to you—probably me, too. Her name is Ida Clark Sutherland and she writes from Tarkio, Missouri. 'I assure you that it would give me the greatest pleasure to be with you all in the old church on Thanksgiving Day . . . Fifty years have passed since our church became a real factor in the lives of so many—the church still stands! Only eternity can recall all it has stood for . . .' Honestly, Eloise, they think fifty years is eternity. I'm older than that! They all refer to the 'dear old church.' They had no sense of history. How could they think fifty years made something old? I can still run marathons." I felt a stab of conscience. I was talking to an elder. "If I'd get back in serious training," I added to be truthful.

"Well, I guess in the life of each of us it is an eternity." She smiled. We started out the door together. "It's longer than your father had, anyway." She was still a little worried about the Clarks' honor. "I hope you feel a little better about your dad, Barbara."

"I do," I said, and hugged her. I told her Howard's story of Bill Grogan's goat.

She laughed. "Well now . . . I can imagine that," she said. "He was so considerate about little things."

"And such a turkey about big ones." I sighed. But I wanted to allay her fears. "He gave a lot of love, Eloise. That's the most important part." We parted fondly and I thanked her for the ring. I didn't try to explain how much it really meant to me.

At the end of the long lane was an old cemetery. I stopped and got out of the camper. This was where the Wayne Presbyterian Church, the so-called Four-Horn church, had been. The Scotch Grove Presbyterian Church session records described the Wayne Church's advent in the 1860s in rather mournful tones. The new church momentarily decimated the Scotch Grove ranks when their own permanent building was under construction.

The cemetery was quite small. The church had flourished only for about fifty years compared with *our* church, which was still operating after 150 years, I thought with pride. Then I laughed. I sounded like Ida Clark Sutherland, whom I'd just quoted to Eloise. What *had* I learned, anyway? I sat down, my back against a grey tombstone with indecipherable names. It didn't feel very solid, so I leaned forward, hugging my knees. I had to think a minute.

I pictured the Scotch Grove Presbyterian Church and its community in my mind. From 1837: elders in beards and black suits; women in white or flowered dresses carrying mounds of potato salad; children with sweaty hands clutching countless nickels; weathered farmers with stiff collars rubbing sunburned necks; black hearses in a seemingly endless procession making the short journey from the church to the cemetery; shifting light in the sanctuary through the changing seasons of my childhood.

I had learned the beauty of our brief uniqueness, I decided fondly. Even if we were no more than a little tidepool, caught momentarily in the cup of the prairie between limestone ridges of recurring seas, we were still part of the eternal searching for the spiritual core.

Extremely tall grass lined the fencerow of the "Four-Horn" cemetery fence. I looked at it with sudden recognition, as I had just seen a display in Iowa City of natural prairie. Was this it? The big bluestem? The grass that had covered the entire area when the Europeans came? I'd read that small patches were often intact in the oldest cemeteries. I got up to inspect it. It looked like the display. Certainly some of the big bluestem would have been left when the church was flourishing. John Newton Hughes, recording Scotch Grove life in the 1880s, spoke of areas of unplowed prairie and even of prairie chickens' mournful booming on their traditional mating leks.

Suddenly I wished my father were buried here, at the end of Eloise's lane, for she had cared enough for him to defend his positive qualities even forty years after he had died. And this church was where William Clark, Junior, absolved of his anti-nuptial fornication, had come with regained honor before he went off to his own early death. I picked one strand of tall bluish grass with a three-pronged top. I should be more respectful of long-dead Calvinists, I decided. This church, in spite of closure after only twenty years, might still be preserving important genetic stock.

Reunion

All lose, whole find
—E. E. CUMMINGS, XVI, *One Times One*

"I wish I could get people as interested in the future of this church as you are in its past," Paul Ernie said wistfully when I returned the church records to him. I sat down on the screened porch for a cup of coffee. He showed me a chart he made for the session that illustrated the membership fluctuations throughout history. The church faced serious financial difficulties now, with only thirty-five families.

"Well, see, it's always gone up and down. Sometimes way down," I said consolingly, reviewing his chart. "I was surprised myself at the records. The elders were always worrying about whether the church would fold." But the possibility of closure was real and we both knew it. I would be sad if that happened, too, even if I didn't live here anymore. We talked for a while of general community and church news. The weather was presenting a threat to several farming operations. The congregation was looking for a new minister, which was always a trial. Then we turned to talk of families.

"What do you hear from Sherry?" I asked carefully. Sherry, Paul Ernie's daughter, was seven years my junior and I'd always loved her. I'd been her hero in her childhood. I could picture a little brown-haired girl running down the lane, her hair in braids in emulation of me. Reaching down, I grabbed her outstretched hand and swung her behind me on the horse.

Paul Ernie shared her most recent activities. She had become a missionary and was currently engaged in anti-abortion counseling in the South. I wouldn't be her hero anymore.

As we walked out to the camper, Paul Ernie resumed his worries about the Scotch Grove Presbyterian Church. "So few young people are interested now. And people are moving away from the farms. Who's going to carry on the traditions for the next generation in the church?"

"I just met someone else with the same worries." I told him about Jonathan Buffalo. " 'As long as that little center is still red, all God has to do is blow on our coals and the fire starts up again,' " I quoted.

Paul Ernie grinned. He liked that. "Well, in that case, I should pray for a big wind." He laughed. "But I better not. In Iowa that would probably turn into a tornado."

I decided not to return immediately to Sweet Memories. In a few days I would be going back to Oregon, and I felt vaguely uneasy, as if I had unfinished business. This journey had started as a search to understand my mother, and even though I felt a resolution, I wasn't quite where I wanted to be. Maybe I just needed time for things to jell, I decided. I had absentmindedly taken the highway to Monticello. I went north past the high school. What did the teachers say now about evolution? I had taught there in 1964, when I came back to take care of Grandma before I was married. Evolution wasn't taught then, as theory or fact. Soon I reached the small town of Cascade.

Turning on Highway 136, I was delighted by a long row of bluebird houses on fence posts. I didn't see any bluebirds, but they must be coming back. Their disappearance had been a preoccupation of my mother's. I turned on the gravel road toward the Eby's Mill Bridge.

The sign said NO PARKING ON THE BRIDGE. I left my camper at the north end of the flat cement structure that had been built my last year in high school. Parallel to the new bridge about an eighth of a mile upstream, the old bridge railings curved in a graceful arch. I was unsure of the access. I probably shouldn't go through the old Eby farm on the south bank, as it appeared occupied. So I followed a lane north of the river. I eventually came to the old bridge, although I had to climb the last few hundred yards through brambles and poison ivy. Obviously no road needed to go to it, as most of the floorboards were missing. The river churned closer under the spans than I remembered. The flood stage of the water probably accounted for the difference.

Until 1968, when I moved from Iowa to Oregon, I had made a yearly pilgrimage to the bridge. Each year I had walked the arc of the railing where I once followed Uncle Jim. But I had never again seen the whirlpool. I had, in fact, avoided looking down at all, using my peripheral vision to assure that I would not stumble on the protruding bolts. Now I pulled myself up on the bridge floor, the frame, really, as so many of the boards were gone. And I sat there watching the river.

But I was not thinking of Uncle Jim. I was thinking of Sherry and the brief conversation I'd had with Paul Ernie earlier in the day. His reference to his daughter's anti-abortion counseling had started old reels spinning in my head, and my stories were getting all mixed up with the people I had met in the church records— like Josephine Johnson.

Josephine Johnson, together with her two married sisters, had joined the Scotch Grove Presbyterian Church in 1864 with a letter of transfer from the Wayne "Four-Horn" Presbyterian Church. But by April of the next year the elders had heard rumors "affecting the chastity and moral character" of Josephine. A research committee's conclusion, presented in July, stated that the rumors—that Josephine had procured an abortion the year prior to her admittance to the Scotch Grove Church—were well founded. Thus, the way for a church trial was prepared. It was scheduled for August 17 at 1 p.m.

The minutes record a saga of months of public humiliation for Josephine, as letters flurried back and forth between Scotch Grove and Mercer County, Pennsylvania, where she had fled, summoning her home for trial. Finally, she was tried in absentia during an extended process that even included the elders of her previous parish. The ecclesiastical law involved became so complicated that the case had to be referred to the presbytery in Dubuque.

I could well imagine the spectacle of a solemn-faced elder reading the minutes of the trial proceedings aloud to the entire congregation, intoning the conviction of guilt for the crimes of fornication and abortion, and announcing the sentence of suspension. But even more graphic was the human tragedy conveyed by the wording of the initial citation. "That you Josephine Johnson . . . in concert with Richard Perrine in Scotch Grove Iowa and vicinity, actually attempted during the month of April 1864 and finally succeed[ed] in criminally procuring abortion in your own person about the close of that month."

When I first read that section of the session minutes, I physically winced in pain. "Actually attempted . . . and finally succeeded." How many times did it take and what did they have to do? And who was Richard Perrine? The sexual partner? A concerned relative? Some sympathetic young man who loved her and wanted to save Josephine from a life of social disgrace? A Dr. McQuire of Anamosa was listed as a witness against her, as was Ebenezer Sutherland.

Sitting on the bridge piling, I thought of Josephine Johnson and again felt the physical pain for her that had flooded through me at my first reading. The doctor had testified against her. He may have been the one who revealed the secret. If they'd had to notify a doctor, something must have gone terribly wrong. She surely had almost died. And I had almost died. In Cheyenne, Wyoming. I could not possibly go through with the abortion. And he wanted me to. He knew he wasn't going to stay in the marriage, because he didn't love me anymore. I had failed, just like my mother had failed, and my husband would leave me, too. I had swallowed the aspirin, one after another . . . *Oh, Mom, I'm so sorry . . . It's such a shame, such a shame.*

I had been in a good situation compared to many women who were pregnant when they didn't want to be. I was still married, I had a good education—land to fall back on. And no one would ever have had to know I had an abortion. Poor Josephine Johnson.

Had she told her sisters? Surely not her mother. *I can't bear any more shame, Barbie.*

Where do you go when there is no one to go home to?

I knew we shouldn't have another baby when he wanted out of the marriage. He knew it, too, and was trying to make a responsible decision about the future. I couldn't see that at the time. I could see only that the love hadn't lasted. Even that night, retching again and again, I knew the main issue was not whether to have the abortion. I had wanted to die because I wanted him to love me and he didn't. When I flushed the toilet, the pills lined into long white swirls.

I stared down at the brown river. It surged in a chocolate race, carrying branches and sticks in its heavy flow. Looking across the water, I could easily picture the old mill. Nighthawks had begun to swoop across the river, collecting insects. I needed to go back to Sweet Memories.

A path led from the far side of the bridge through the farmyard of the old Eby place. Even if I had to apologize for trespassing, that would certainly be an easier way to get to the car than crawling back through the poison ivy. I could make a complete circle back to the car. A welt was already forming on one arm. But the remaining floorboards were decidedly unsafe. That left the railing. I could walk the curved metal span. Why not? I'd done it twenty times before. I stood up.

But as I stood, one foot slid sideways from the beam I had been straddling and I came crashing awkwardly back into a sitting position. For a brief flash I was looking full into the swirling water and seemed already to be falling. I felt myself spinning and hung on tightly, closing my eyes. The sound of the water rushing under the bridge, which I had not focused on before, went from a throaty whisper to a roar. Surely the water level had suddenly risen and the old bridge would be swept downstream.

The water sounded like the train that came across the field behind Clark's on the way to Scotch Grove. Young trees ordinarily out of reach of the river leaned helplessly into the relentless current. The pilings shuddered visibly as the water roared across the deck of the bridge. Then, with a loud crack, the metal ripped and the piling leaned, trying to hold it. Snap! The noise crashed against limestone bluffs and the bridge broke loose.

No. I opened my eyes. That was in 1951. Then we had stood halfway down the hill on the road that led down to Dales Ford, watching with the neighbors when the bridge gave way. This was 1993. The nighthawks swooped as before. The roar subsided. The river, though full, had not changed level. The sound must have been in my own ears. Late sun slanted in long, filtered rays through the trees to the west. Enough of this foolishness, I said to myself. I climbed down from the bridge, battling my way back through the poison ivy to the lane. Sweaty and still shaking a little, I sat in the camper.

I thought again of the first time I had walked the bridge railing. I saw the white limbs, twirling, twirling. I heard the tenderness of my grandmother's voice. My uncle called my name gently . . . I did not remember any other time in my childhood he addressed me by name. How desperately we want love, I thought, and how drastic the action when it is withheld or withdrawn. Even my own gentle mother had recognized the danger. "I never thought I'd tell you this, Barbara, but there was one awful night when all I could think was that we were both too miserable to live." Ten years later, I stood alone in the bedroom when my own baby cried and cried. I felt the same desperation, with the same threat for us both.

I started the engine. Scores of swallows flew back and forth in the copper light.

•   •   •

On a final trip to the State Historical Society in Iowa City, I returned to the manuscript collection of photographs of my grandmother's brother, the Reverend G. Rickels. I remembered meeting this man, Lenore's father, only once before his death in 1948. "Oh, John," my grandmother had said mournfully, stroking his head as he sat in the wicker rocking chair when he had stopped briefly to see her on a trip back to Scotch Grove, "you're getting so bald." "I can't help it, Deanee," he replied solemnly. Gerdjanssen Rickels had occupied an emblematic position in my consciousness for the last twenty-one years.

An image of my grandmother's fingers shriveling at the washboard while her brother pursued classical Greek at the seminary became a symbol I held in my mind when I tried to redefine my life during my divorce. Enough deference had been given to men in my family, I thought resentfully. Not only financial desperation but defiance drove me to sell my portion of the Livingston farm which my mother had rescued by renting the land and saving every penny to service the debt. The strands of women's servitude and the sanctity of the farm had plied in my mind. And somewhere at the center of my resentment stood G. Rickels, because my grandmother had quit school at twelve to help send him to college. So I was surprised at my positive emotional reaction to his pictures the first time I reviewed the photograph collection.

As a composite the 143 photographs conveyed a representative but intimate sample of late-nineteenth- and early-twentieth-century life in the rural Midwest. Many were artistically beautiful, both those of portraiture and those of nature. Surely photography could have been a vocation rather than avocation with this country pastor. Several pictures were of the Maquoketa River limestone bluffs. The Reverend G. Rickels seemed to have lived in a perpetual state of longing for the untended beauty of the wooded hollows and the wildflowers of his childhood. He returned to them from the prairie parsonage by Atkins (near Luzerne, where my father was buried) every chance he could wring from a busy parson's schedule. His photographs reflected the tenderness of his passion for nature. I circulated among the remaining Rickels relatives I knew, looking for all available copies of his work.

At the Historical Society I put on the white gloves routinely issued with photographic collections and carefully re-examined all the photos of the rocks and hollows with their wide sandy bottoms. I recognized some of the locations precisely, although areas pictured were more overgrown during my childhood than in the early twentieth century, when the pictures were taken. One depicted a bluff-lined sandy meadow filled with wildflowers. I was sure I knew this very spot. I formulated a plan for the late-afternoon sunshine when the incessant cloud cover of this unusual summer had at least momentarily withdrawn from the sky.

Rather than return to Sweet Memories, I continued north, but before I topped the hill where the road branched to Millie Kuper's and Dales Ford, I turned west on the Rocky Ridge road. If I had not been guided by both ancestral memory and childhood experiences, I'm not sure I would have found the beginning of Sand Hollow. Trees and underbrush had obscured the entry. I parked the car at the side of the road and changed from my sandals to my running shoes. Before I crossed the fence, the thought of trespass suddenly loomed. Should I be asking someone for entry? That idea had never troubled me as an adolescent. But there was no one to ask.

Immediately my shirt snagged in the barbed wire, leaving a triangular tear. Brush and nettles reached for my clothes. When the incline leveled, pools of water from the recent rains cupped behind boulders. I felt a surge of exhilaration at having confirmed my location by the sandy bottom of the ditch. The undersides of the leaves on the slope above me were almost translucent, tinged with yellow, as if the light shone from below. Wings fluttered, a flushed covey of something. Quail, perhaps?

The pale gold sand hemmed by green brush proved the easiest place to walk. Animals obviously thought so, too. Deer hooves, raccoon hands, and the pawprints of either a fox or a coyote marked the wash. Surely no wolves. Until the day of her death my grandmother dreamed of wolves, whimpering in her sleep.

Following deer tracks, I climbed over a fence of rusty wire. I could see deep impressions where the deer jumped and then landed. Blue jays screamed in the trees, and again I heard quail-like cluckings. Gravel patches were potential treasure hordes of fossils or coral. I picked up a creamy chip. Chert, I thought. Was that a worked flake? I fingered the serrated surface. Probably not, I decided, and put it back. I remembered how soon pockets bulged. The tangled brush became less insistent and more flowers bloomed in the grass. Then the bluffs began.

First on the left side. Scrub cedars hung from the cracks, like the ones I had seen at Fire Point on the Mississippi. The terrain opened and became more familiar, more what I remembered from my youth. I knelt again, looking for fossils. This time I found a little hunk of coral. Putting it in my pocket, I sifted through other gravel. A perfect little shell with only a little extra limestone residue appeared. I stuffed it, too, in my pocket. Uncle Jim would be pleased. Standing up, I caught my breath in surprise. A deer stood ahead of me—a buck with a full rack. He looked back, clear-eyed and unalarmed. Then he bounded forward in slow motion beyond a curve in the hollow. I climbed over a downed log and emerged into a meadow.

The grass was alive with color—daisy fleabane, Queen Anne's lace, early goldenrod, fireweed, yarrow, and the starburst flowers of the burdock weed that would be so pesky later in the year. This meadow surely was the place my grandmother had picked the wildflowers, the meadow of G. Rickels's photograph. Maybe he hadn't wanted to be a minister, I thought, but an artist with his camera. Did he envy his younger siblings the freedom of their life in the woods while he studied his volumes of classical Greek? This was a new thought for me.

The buck stood ahead of me in the tall grass. He turned his head sideways, quite unafraid. Through my binoculars I became acutely aware of an enlarged bumblebee on the startling darkness of the furry center of the black-eyed Susans. Again, the buck bounded in the magical slow motion, then disappeared between the trees on the left sloping side of the hollow. The limestone bluff on the right side of the hollow broke abruptly from the grass, rising at least thirty feet from the meadow. In the center of the sandy wash a druid-like rock, four or five feet high, humped with a scrubby cedar on one side.

The rain-packed sand made easy walking, and soon I caught the light on the river through the trees. I did not go there first. At the end of the hollow on my right side a chimney bluff between two towers, with a saddle effect, rose from the curved embankment. That was the saddle where the rattlesnake had coiled and Uncle Jim had caught my arm so I would not reach into striking range. I was standing far below it now. A curved ring of limestone extended from the chimney, and cupped in the wall was a small cave where I had once taken shelter during a thunderstorm. I climbed the remarkably steep and slippery slope, which was covered with ferns and old leaves from previous seasons. The thin threads of a spiderweb caught my face, clung to my hair and eyelashes.

I sat down on the rocky shelf. This little shelter was not big enough for seasonal occupation like Hadfields Cave. I looped my binoculars around my neck, not wanting to repeat my acrobatic performance from the ledge at the other site. Below, the flat sandy bottom of the gully arched against a deep grey slash of clay that protruded from the bank. The archaeological dig at Hadfields Cave yielded over two thousand pieces of forty-six clay containers. Not one vessel was intact. For several minutes I sat, absentmindedly sifting the dry ashes on the cave floor through my fingers, thinking about my mother and the note that had driven my quest.

I sat back on my heels, consciously formulating a metaphor in my mind. As surely as a vessel of Hadfields Cave, my mother reflected the intertwined strands that had molded her. The religion of the Scots, the mythology of the farm, the dignity of the women's service had impressed on the vessel a tight, complicated pattern. For my mother, as for the Madison Ware, the walls were fine and thin. When the blow came, it spread throughout the vase in fractured lines. *To move would have meant to shatter into jagged shards. And so my mother remained still.*

The picture that formed in my mind was not of utilitarian pottery at all, but of the blue vase on the mantel with the lightning lines, the one we had dusted so carefully.

So for the others, as well, I thought, my mind spinning out the metaphor to include the rest. Uncle Jim, the son. The father, the son, and the holy farm. My father equally caught, no doubt, in the myth of family and farm. Trying to play out the role expected of him, only to fail repetitively, feeling such pain he took his own life. Gideon Hughes, it occurred to me with a start, whom I had thought so domineering, controlled by his own cord-impressed patterns. The eldest son of landless immigrants, did he live out their dream, emulating the gentry, whom they had admired? And Gerdjanssen Rickels. Did his early show of intellectual promise cage him forever in a prairie parsonage? Why had I thought life was so much easier for the men?

Shaking the dust from my fingers, I stood up, looking over the mouth of the hollow to the river. I was feeling rather kindly toward them all. And happy. Wasn't this it? What I had been seeking? Even though I knew each one was vastly more individually complicated than I'd portrayed, I'd fit them all into my metaphor so I could untangle my own cords and recombine with more eternal strands. I smiled. I even raised my hands triumphantly.

To tell the truth, I was a bit tired of taking them all so seriously. And I was glad I was soon returning to Oregon. Then I did a totally spontaneous thing. Cupping my hands around my mouth, I yodeled across the gully.

"Yo—a—lay—tee—o."

The sound bounced back from the bluff on the other side, the echo more haunting and tuneful than my original. How lovely. I was never very good at yodeling. I had thought it too much of a timber roogian thing to practice when I was a child and was actually rather embarrassed by Uncle Jim. But the echo, like memory, had glossed over the imperfections. I did it again.

"Yo—dle—o—a—lay—tee—o. Yo—dle—o—a—lay—tee—o. Yo—dle—o—a—lay—tee—o."

The bluff sang back the answer, musically and clear: "a—lay—tee—o."

And I did it all yet again, because Uncle Jim could go on forever. *Honour thy father and thy mother.* But when he finally left, Grandma would be sitting in the chair by the window, rocking with her slippered feet, and she would smile because I was a good girl. And my mother would smile because she had taught me well.

And I was a good girl, even if I wasn't a Presbyterian.

Deliberately sliding down the slippery hillside in a standing glissade, I emerged, breathless, on the grassy bank of the gully. The late-afternoon sun turned the flowing river to a shifting golden mirror. A huge maple leaned far over the water. Sitting down on the tree roots, I closed my eyes halfway against the glare.

My heart was thumping wildly. Maybe Vaneta was right—maybe

it was unnatural for someone my age to gallop around the way I did. I should think of that. Perhaps I should slow down. My mother was only fifty-eight when she died. I leaned back against the tree trunk.

No, I decided. I'd rather run till I died. Or climb till I fell off a mountain. The leaves of the maple flickered, encasing me in a net of reflected light. My heart slowed to a lighter, steadier beat. Such a selfish thought, anyway, to want to live forever. I nodded sleepily against the tree.

And such a long way down the sandy hollow home.

.   .   .

Vaneta was not ready to hear about my epiphany. She could tell I'd been in the woods. "Hold still," she said, "and don't come in until I sweep you off." She brought the broom out on the back deck, where I had taken off my muddy shoes.

"What kind of infestation do you think I have?"

"Ticks. I don't want any ticks in here. Lean over." She picked through my hair. It felt rather nice, actually. I nuzzled against her like a dog and she laughed. I was suddenly very tired. "Now, where have you been?" she asked as we went inside and assumed our familiar spot at her kitchen table.

I started telling her about Sand Hollow, but it was too soon. "You'll have to come there with me," I ended lamely. "I'd forgotten how much beauty is around here. I tend to think mostly of the cornfields when I'm gone."

"I'll do my walking in a mall," she said firmly. "I get plenty of exercise and no ticks. Did you hear about the new minister?"

"No, did they hire one?"

"Not exactly, but we have a student from the seminary at Dubuque."

"Well?" Something wasn't quite right.

Vaneta gave a little laugh. "It's a woman."

"A woman!" I was truly astounded. "A *woman!* Well, *hooray* for the Scotch Grove Presbyterian Church!"

"I don't know," said Vaneta doubtfully. "I'll have to get used to this. I know this seems old-fashioned to you, but when I think of God, I think of a man."

"Vaneta," I scolded, "welcome to the twentieth century." Then I realized something was wrong. Her eyes were too bright and her smile was a little forced. "Are you all right? Did something bad happen?"

"Yes." Her mouth twisted a little. I waited for her to tell me. "My husband's company declared bankruptcy. Needless to say, this throws a kink into our retirement plans."

"Oh no." I didn't know quite what that meant. "Can he get another job?" He was a chemist with years of experience.

"He's already trying. But think of it. He's sixty. Even at fifty his résumé would go to the bottom of the pile." I knew she was right. Too many of my business friends had landed in the same situation.

Artificial encouragement seemed out of place. "What happens now?"

She looked out the plate-glass doors at the long twilight. "Oh, we'll live," she said with a bitter edge in her voice. "We have the farm. But it just seems so unfair. He's put over thirty years in the company. Now the corporation is bankrupt. All the big guys will somehow come out with their million-dollar homes, but the middle management like my husband end up without the kind of comforts they'd counted on for retirement. What a screwed-up system."

And she was right. We sat by the glass door with the lights off for a long time, talking and watching the last light. Vaneta and I don't pretend to each other. She talked about selling her remaining timber and her options with renewing tile, even though she knew I would disagree. It certainly wasn't the time to talk with her about the plan I'd been working on to return my own part of the land to prairie. I didn't have the money to buy her out—not even to buy the cut-over timber land she wanted to sell. Finally, she stood up to turn on the tea water. "Let's talk about something else," she sighed. "You're leaving and I haven't had half enough time with you. Tell me again about Sand Hollow."

So I did. This time I captured more of the magic of what I had felt. She was quite interested, especially in the image of the vase and the fact that I finally understood and respected my mother's choice. "Now that makes me feel better," she said. "I always had the feeling Aunt Kate wasted so much potential in her life, but when I think of it that way, it seems altogether different."

"Good," I replied. We smiled at each other. We both had loved my mother.

"Barb," Vaneta said.

"What?" I answered. We had our familiar routine.

"One more thing."

"*Anything*, Vaneta," I replied, and we laughed.

"About your brother."

Anything but that, I thought. "What about my brother?" Vaneta had loved my brother, too.

"Don't you think Aunt Kate would want you to try to find Bob?" Vaneta could cut right to the nerve.

"Probably." For a second I felt an old flash of resentment at my mother's self-sacrificing attitude toward men. "I *could* find him," I added defensively.

"You could?" Vaneta hadn't known this.

"Yes. And he knows where I am." I especially avoided thinking about this. "For a long time I didn't know where he was. And sometimes I still don't. But his ex-wife and I are in touch—good friends, actually. She would help me. She's usually been able to locate him."

"Why don't you, then?"

I sighed. Vaneta was definitely not going to let me off the hook. We were still sitting in semidarkness. The twilight had all faded, but moonlight had taken over. The house and garage made big black shadows, but the cornfield reflected white light.

"Think how it was for him, Vaneta," I began. "This house might be 'sweet memories' for you, because your sorrows were up the road in your father's house. But this place was definitely bittersweet at best for the rest of us. None of the money was ours and we knew it. We didn't belong here.

"It must have been especially hard on my brother. It was all so complicated and confused. Bob was the son. But he was the wrong one. He was the son of the father who wasn't here, and the sons who were supposed to be here died." Vaneta knew what I meant with that one. She was a daughter who had lived. She nodded.

"I used to wonder why no one could make the switch. Here was my brother, a little boy without a father, and here was your father, a farmer without the son he so longed for—why couldn't he just train my brother in farming?"

"Because he didn't know how . . . and besides, this land would not pass to Bob."

"So what? Other land would." But Vaneta was right. "This was a strange and quiet place," I began. But I couldn't elaborate. I had a sudden, sad picture in my mind of the cords that impressed the pattern for my brother knotted and hardened into the clay itself. It was the land, I thought tiredly—the land which for him forever had remained the Land. His ex-wife told me he spoke of it that way still. Even as children we had known the money wasn't ours, but we lived on my grandfather's land. And we felt it.

We felt the wind blow over the land when we took our picnic to the big tree that stood on the fence line east of the house toward Paul Ernie's farm, the tree with the branches so big we could spread the cloth on the second limb. We felt the rain water the land as we ran back through the pasture where we had been building a dam in the creek, the rain that was laced with lightning lines. We felt the snow cover the land as we slid across the black ice on the barnyard puddles that scrolled with swirled patterns before the solid whiteness came. He had always talked about the land as if we owned it. Doesn't he know? I thought each time he spoke that way. Doesn't he know it isn't really ours?

Thank *God* I had not been the son.

Vaneta looked at me steadily. "Have you tried to help him?" With difficulty I pulled my focus to the conversation of the moment.

"Vaneta," I said with a touch of exasperation, "just because his biological composition is a little more traceable to me than to other human beings doesn't mean he owes me any explanations. He has a right not to be found, if he chooses." My voice was shaking. "Even my father doesn't owe me any explanations." I meant it. Standing up, I put the dishes in the sink. "I'm exhausted," I said. "I didn't mean to get so wound up. You're the one who has had a hard day.

I just read and went for a walk in the woods. And I *didn't* get any ticks," I reminded her. She smiled.

The moonlight was disturbingly bright from the stairway landing. I absolutely longed for the horse to be there so I could slip down the steps, fly through the pasture toward the blue fog—galloping, galloping, letting the haunting, conflicting currents of sadness in the house flow away from me. I leaned my elbows on the windowsill.

When our mother died my brother trembled, but he did not cry.

No, life was not easier for the men.

I sat down on the floor of the bedroom and sorted out my things. I had just switched off the lamp when Vaneta came up the stairs accompanied by a musical clinking of little cups. She stood in the doorway. "Room service," she said softly, in case I was asleep. I switched on the light.

"I thought for a minute it was Mabel's bells coming up the steps." We both laughed. I had never heard the bells. "Do you treat all your guests this way?" I asked, looking at the fresh pot of tea and cookies.

"Right," she said. "All ten of them I've had for the summer." The B&B wasn't going to bail her out of the financial crisis at this rate. Scotch Grove wasn't on the way to anywhere—which was a shame, as she was such a great cook. We mulled over the possibilities for improving business. But we'd been through them before. Vaneta was just sorry that she'd made me feel guilty about my brother. And she had. When I finished my tea, she switched off the light. "Now roll over," she commanded, "and I'll rub your feet and tell you a story."

"My feet?"

"Yes, that's what I always did for my kids when they were little. Now, come on, you're the younger cousin here. Do as I say."

I laughed. "We're both over half a century old. And you're the one who has had the tough day." But I rolled over on my stomach. Her light strokes on my feet made me want to cry.

"Now for the story," she mused dreamily. "This story shall be about snow. Snow in Iowa. It swirls and swirls in the prairie wind, curling around the railing of the porch, making drifts in front of the garage door." She was silent for a minute. Both our minds were full of pictures. "Do you remember how we would take our sleds to the top of the little hill that formed the approach to the second story of the barn?"

"Of course." Her soft touch was hypnotizing me.

"So now you will pretend that we are together on that old red sled with the runners that curved up high in the front." Yes. The red sled. It had belonged to our parents—her father and my mother. They had used it as children and so had we used it, bringing it down from Grandma's attic at the first snow. "Now I have pulled the sled with you on it down the driveway across the road and all the way up the hill because I am such a good cousin and you're kind of a cute little squirt yourself, even if you are still sucking your thumb at a ridiculously old age." How did she remember that?

"And now we are perched at the top of the hill ready to make the one good sled run in this whole flat prairie. Are you ready?"

I was. We were together, with Vaneta in the back and I, a little girl, in the front with my knees drawn under my chin. And the sled leaned crazily just before it started down the hill. I held my bottom lip between my teeth because I was so excited and a bit scared.

"Now you hold tight, because I am going to push with my foot!" And then we-were-flying-down-the-little hill and I was holding tight to Vaneta's knee because right at the bottom where the hill joined the driveway was a jump—BUMP—and then we *leeeeeaned* just so to make the sled turn and if we did it just right and both leaned forward at the end bobbing, the sled would go all the way to the barnyard gate coming . . . slowly . . . to . . . a . . . stop and pushing the wire net of the gate forward.

Is this what is meant by family? For who else would have known that sequence?

Except a boy with bright blue eyes and a cowlick in the front of his black hair. A little boy who resembled the childhood pictures of his father.

(top) Rickels siblings in the woods by the Maquoketa River; (bottom left) Sister Lena and husband; (right) Mother Gesche Rickels

(opposite, top left) Gideon Hughes; (top right) Dena Rickels Hughes;
(bottom) Hughes children, 1915: left to right: Besse, Katie, Emmy, Jim;
(above) Jim Hughes, 1965

Kathleen Hughes Norris

Robert George Norris

(above) The Scotch Grove Presbyterian Church, incorporated *1841*. Present
building constructed *1861*; *(below)* Sweet Memories Bed and Breakfast.
Formerly home of Gideon Hughes family, constructed *1904*

(above) *Kathleen Norris and Barbara, 1945;*
(below) *Vaneta Hughes and Barbara, 1946*

(above) Kathleen Norris, Bobbie and Barbara, 1944;
(below) The red sled, Bobbie and Barbara, 1944

Epilogue

In the season of 1886–87 near our own home, a farmer had cut
and shocked and left in the field some forty to sixty acres of corn.
When the snow was deep and feed was scarce, the prairie chickens
found this fine field of rich food as if it had been left especially for
them. The flock when winter had come in earnest increased daily
until it was estimated that more than fifty thousand birds made the
daily pilgrimage. It was an inspiring sight on some of those hazy
winter days, when the hand of the clock had just passed four and
there was a feeling that night was not far away, to see company
after company sail in from the four corners of the earth, but mostly
from the east and south, until the sky was almost black with their
presence and the rustling of their wings was similar to an approaching storm.

—JOHN NEWTON HUGHES,
describing his Scotch Grove childhood in *Iowa Sketches*

I knew I should be driving if I had any intention of
making it all the way to Oregon by Saturday night. But I sat for a
few minutes in my camper after I had returned some books to the
library in Monticello. Something wanted doing and I wasn't quite
sure what it was. The sun brooded in yellow smudged clouds that
probably would result in yet another torrential downpour by
evening.

Finally, I started the engine. Still without a conscious plan, I
began driving. I headed east on the highway toward Sweet Memories
again instead of northwest toward Oregon. I did not go all the way
to Scotch Grove. I turned left on the road that passed the hill where
my grandmother had once gone to Rocky Ridge School. A surprising
amount of scrub cedar had taken over the ridge. This was the road

of the old Ahrnken place with the spring, the road past Sand Hollow. Now I knew I was returning to Dales Ford.

I noted that the ruts of the road were even deeper than they had been the last time I came. At the place where I could see the sandbar on the other side of the river next to the rusty pilings, I paused. No turkey vultures circled in the hazy sky. Turning right, I followed the grassy lane along the river. I stopped by a cedar tree. How old was it? Probably not too old, considering that the ranger at Effigy Mounds had said the virgin stands were all gone. Carefully, I pulled off several strips of bark.

The meadow opened on my right. A movement along the edge of the trees caught my eye. Wild turkeys. They were big, slim birds with rusty tails. They knew they were being watched and moved silently into the cover of the trees.

The tall grass freckled with color. Wood lilies, black-eyed Susans, and Queen Anne's lace. The ubiquitous wild roses had started going to seed. Putting my binoculars and the cedar bark in my pack to free both hands, I began to gather flowers. I picked selectively so as not to strip any area, choosing only common blossoms that were in abundance. When I had an armful, I turned back the way I had come. A maidenhair fern with its dark ribs quivered in the wind under the large cedar. I knelt, set the flowers down carefully, and selected a few fronds from the back of the stand.

I put the flowers and the cedar bark on the front seat beside me. Leaving the timber, I drove past the Sinclair house, where I had sat on the quern stones during my piano lesson, past my land in which small ponds had resurfaced. I pulled into the slanted driveway that led into the cemetery. *The day that she was buried it was twelve degrees below zero.*

First I took the strips of cedar bark and laid them on Uncle Jim's grave. Then I went to my mother's tombstone at the north end of all the Hugheses. Placing the bundle of flowers in front of her stone, I sat on it and looked around. The water from last night's thunderstorm had washed in a stream through the lower part of the cemetery, out into the field. I smiled, imagining myself saying to Vaneta, "Are you sure you want my cemetery plot? What if you get buried there and the Department of Natural Resources wants to reclaim it as a wetland?"

Then I began to talk to my mother. I didn't talk aloud. I sat there and looked to the west at the land I still owned, the land from which this little cemetery and church plot had been carved from the first claim of Ebenezer Sutherland, the land on which buffalo and elk had grazed. First I told her that I did understand now, that staying there had been more than loving my father, more than even loyalty to the farming way of life. *To move would have meant to shatter into jagged shards. And so my mother remained still.*

I told my mother about the wild turkeys at Dales Ford. I described the eagles I had seen circling above the Mississippi at Fire Point. And I talked about the doe and fawn who had bounded across the field close to the house in which we had both lived as children. The windbreak of pines on the west fence of the cemetery made a sound that as a child I had imagined must be the sound of the sea, a low, tuneful moaning. The setting sun illuminated the standing puddles in the field and it was easy to imagine the slough had returned, that the vast network of drainage tile had never existed, and that in the autumn, canvasbacks, redheads, and giant Canada geese would linger in the shallow golden ponds as John Newton Hughes had described. I knew then what I wanted to do. This time I spoke aloud, because I was not really talking to her, although I framed the words that way. I was talking to myself.

"I'm not fooling myself that you'd understand what I'm doing, or maybe even agree with me completely. You fought to save your farm for us. And I'm grateful for that. But land isn't my livelihood, so I can give it back. I'm going to try to restore it as tallgrass prairie—close the tile and let the slough return. It'll take some time—and money, too."

I stopped for a moment. I'd researched enough to know this was a complicated, costly business unlikely to succeed unless I could incorporate more land into the project. Did I really want to tackle something that might be nothing more than a symbolic, naïve gesture—an idealistic statement? What was corn but another tall grass, anyway? Natives had been raising it for thousands of years before the Europeans ever came. The ranger at Effigy Mounds was right. Mud to mud.

But just as working hard to make the farms had seemed right to my ancestors, working hard to try to restore some of the natural balance seemed right to me now. I spoke aloud again. "I've got plenty of time, now that I know what I want to do. I'm not the only one—it's beginning to happen in lots of places. You'd be amazed at the wildlife that's coming back. At least I know you'd like the idea of the natural life returning."

A cardinal with its pointed crest, sitting low on a pine limb, was silhouetted against the sun. *Whit, whit, cheer, cheeer, cheeerr.* Of all of the birds, my mother loved the common cardinal the most. Some of the flowers had already wilted. I felt a little sad. I did not want to think of shriveled stalks on her grave. So I knelt down and took all of them, wood lilies, black-eyed Susans, Queen Anne's lace, and even the maidenhair fern, and I gently fragmented them into little pieces. When I was done I had a substantial pyramid of color. Taking handfuls at a time, I scattered the shredded flowers around and over her grave. Then I wiped my hands on my jeans.

I looked again to the west. In the one dead tree near the north end of the windbreak was a black-and-white bird. Across the tail a white streak caught the fading light. Eastern kingbird. Suddenly I felt an acute sense of loss, and the thirty years since her death melted. I wanted so desperately to ask her if kingbirds had been common in my childhood or if they, like the eagles, had returned. Abruptly I picked up my pack and the binoculars. I loved her then even more than I had loved her as a child. I was sorry to cry. My eyes were already tired and I would have to drive all night.

Family Tree

Maps

Ackowledgments

Additional Sources

RICKELS   HUGHES

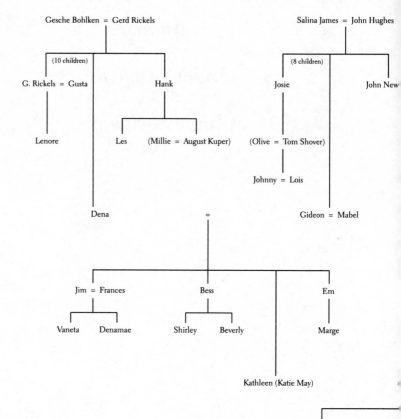

Gesche Bohlken = Gerd Rickels   Salina James = John Hughes

        (10 children)   (8 children)

G. Rickels = Gusta   Hank   Josie   John New

    Lenore   Les   (Millie = August Kuper)   (Olive = Tom Shover)

                                                        Johnny = Lois

            Dena   =   Gideon = Mabel

    Jim = Frances   Bess   Em

Vaneta   Denamae   Shirley   Beverly   Marge

                       Kathleen (Katie May)

                                        Barbara

CLARK   NORRIS

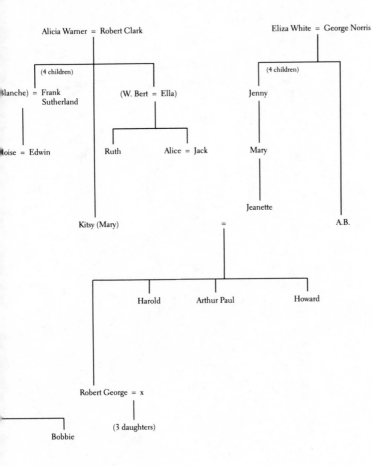

Alicia Warner = Robert Clark   Eliza White = George Norris

(4 children)   (4 children)

Blanche) = Frank   Jenny
             Sutherland

(W. Bert = Ella)

Moise = Edwin

                 Ruth   Alice = Jack   Mary

                                                      Jeanette

Kitsy (Mary)   =   A.B.

          Harold   Arthur Paul   Howard

Robert George = x

                 (3 daughters)
Bobbie

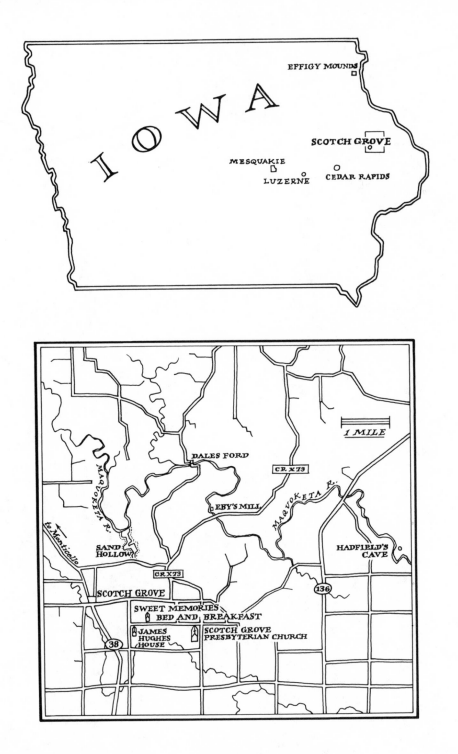

Acknowledgments

The process of converting experience to anecdote required that three trips of discovery be condensed into one summer and that a few episodes in this story be retold in altered sequence. Only when I integrated my experiences, research, and tears into an artistic whole did I understand the true distance of my internal journey. I changed very few names of people and none of places. I do want to clarify in regard to my ex-husband that the narrative of this story covers an early disruptive period in both his life and mine and does not incorporate the significant ongoing contributions he later made to the education and development of his sons.

The dialogues recorded in *Prairie Reunion* are based on actual exchanges, and some are practically verbatim. Only one, the interview with Jonathan Buffalo at the Mesquakie settlement, was conducted formally. Many relatives and citizens of the community contributed to this story by sharing their memories. Credit for particular information which became part of the story after conversations or letters is due the following: Les Balster, Emma Hughes Feddeler, Ruth Clark Grom, Frede Hanken, Edwin Helgens, Eloise Sutherland Helgens, Karen Hendersen, August Kuper, Millie Rickels Kuper, Alice Clark Naylor, Howard Norris, Evelyn Paulsen, Paul Ernest Paulsen, Beverly Pigott, Lester Rickels, Lenore Rickels Salvaneschi, and Lois Shover. Special love and thanks go to my dearest cousin, Vaneta Hughes Luce. She gave freely of her time and resources as I gathered information. We shared both laughter and tears in the formation of this story.

I wish to acknowledge several personal and professional friends for their contributions to the process of writing this book. My husband Jim Trusky provided the financial and emotional base that made it possible for me to write. A grant from Literary Arts, Inc., of Portland, Oregon, also supplied financial assistance. The rest of my immediate family, Taig and Lon Murphy, Maxine Trusky, Dick and Bert Trusky, supplied unflagging love and interest in the project. My friend and running partner Elly Branch listened to endless ruminations, as did Bob Tidwell with his cogent comments. Jan Engels-Smith, Martha Cannon, Roberta Cohen, Judy Woodward, Elizabeth Wartluft, and Sarah Demers provided ongoing interest and support. Editors from CALYX Books, Cheryl McLean and Margarita Donnelly, encouraged me in the development of my ideas and search for a publisher, while Mickie Reaman supplied professional editorial advice. My friend Linda Forbes provided valuable comments for final changes.

Lynn Balster Liontos, compatriot from Scotch Grove, Iowa, carefully edited and wisely suggested revisions. Her comments provided psychological insights, which helped me understand my experience. Ray Sherwood, patient and astute in his guidance from draft to draft, sharpened my focus and tightened my prose. Charles Cannon, my former professor at Coe College, gave me confidence and professional assistance, never betraying any doubt that I could turn personal pain, tangled memories, and jumbled research into a more universal story. My most constant and compelling beacon in this writing has been my soul sister, Marilyn McDonald. My companion from the very inception of *Prairie Reunion*, she read each draft with insight and sensitivity, and believed in me so thoroughly that I could not fail.

The quiet insistence of my friend and literary agent, Jean MacDonald, that I needed to show more of myself at last convinced me that to tell one's own story is not arrogance. It is instead evidence of an understanding that the more ordinary one's experience is, the more that experience reflects the essence of the human condition. So I was able to share more of my pain and offer, at last, a fairly complete manuscript to editor Jonathan Galassi. He skillfully orchestrated diverse parts to more harmonious melody and gave fuller resonance to my humble song.

Additional Sources

I have expanded on family and community memories through extensive consultation of records from the Jones County Courthouse and area newspapers, *The Monticello Express* and *The Anamosa Eureka*. *The Jones County Historical Review* provided local history. I specifically utilized articles from the Iowa Historical Society by Lenore (Rickels) Salvaneschi, "Harvest-Time," *The Palimpsest*, November–December 1984, and Bruce Mahan, "The Scotch Grove Trail," *The Palimpsest*, November 1923, as well as *The Rickels Photograph Collection* from the Manuscript Collections. Information from the following publications of the Office of the Iowa State Archaeologist is informally incorporated into the narrative: R. Clark Mallam, *The Iowa Effigy Mound Manifestation: An Interpretive Model*, Report 9, 1976, and David W. Benn, *Hadfields Cave: A Perspective on Late Woodland Culture in Northeastern Iowa*, Report 13, 1980. The Mesquakie woman's account was transcribed by Truman Michelson as "The Autobiography of a Fox Indian Woman" and presented in *The 40th Annual Report of the Bureau of Ethnology* to the Secretary of the Smithsonian Institution in 1925. Old editions of *The History of Jones County*, published by the Western Historical Company in Chicago in 1879 and the S. J. Clarke Publishing Company in 1910, furnished entertaining and conflicting stories.

I am especially indebted to the following sources of information in addition to my mother's box of letters. Marjorie Feddeler Phillips spent several years sorting out Hughes and Rickels family genealogical records, and the availability of her compilations saved countless hours of research for me. My great-uncle John Newton Hughes's memoir, *Iowa Sketches*, edited and privately published in 1992 by Michele Shover Flynn, furnished a unique community history from a family point of view. Additionally, I am grateful to the assistance of women in the Jones County Courthouse and the Anamosa Genealogical Society, which helped locate records. Ray Sherwood and Mary Cannon also assisted with legal research. Lenore Rickels Salvaneschi was an invaluable source of family history and photographs, as was Eloise Sutherland Helgens.

The entirety of the remaining original records of the Scotch Grove Presbyterian Church provided concrete testimony of social attitudes and events. Although I had access to the original records as a member of the congregation, I benefited additionally from obtaining a typed copy of some of them which had been compiled and privately published by David B. Taylor in 1991 and filed with the Anamosa Genealogical Society.